Interculturalism, Education and Inclusion

Jagdish S. Gundara is Professor of Education and Head
of the International Centre for Intercultural Studies,
Institute of Education, University of London. He is
President of the International Association for
Intercultural Education.

Interculturalism, Education and Inclusion

by

Jagdish S. Gundara

P·C·P

Paul Chapman
Publishing Ltd

Dedication

*For everyone who has contributed to the
work of the International Centre for
Intercultural Studies.*

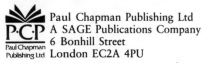

Paul Chapman Publishing Ltd
A SAGE Publications Company
6 Bonhill Street
London EC2A 4PU

SAGE Publications Inc
2455 Teller Road
Thousand Oaks, California 91320

SAGE Publications India Pvt Ltd
32 M-Block Market
Greater Kailash – I
New Delhi 110 048

British Library Cataloguing in Publication data
A catalogue record for this book is available from the British Library

ISBN 0 7619 6622 6
ISBN 0 7619 6623 4 (pbk)

Library of Congress catalog card number available

Typeset by Anneset, Typesetters, Weston-super-Mare
Printed and bound by Athenaeum Press, Gateshead

Contents

Preface

This book has been written at a time of great changes not just in Britain and in Europe generally but also internationally.

A strand that cuts across these changes is the issue of intercultural or intergroup relations. This is particularly the case where societal diversities and relations between groups are becoming more complex. This complexity ranges from groups working out strategies to make cohesive and stable communities, to others where there are social, political and economic problems which lead to tensions and fragmentation of communities.

There are also major changes taking place at the level of the state and this book discusses the issues relevant to education. Hence in Britain there are dual processes happening, with devolution on the one hand and greater unification at the level of the European Union on the other. This will change Britain into a new type of state which will have to work out strategies, mechanisms and institutions to deal with multi-jurisdictions. While Commonwealth countries like Canada, India and Nigeria have a longer tradition of the federal systems which have to deal with societal diversity, in Britain the state is only just beginning to deal with them. In Britain, at the present time, there is widespread discussion in educational circles about citizenship education. There is the issue of what children know about citizenship and where they learn about its values. However, such issues in Britain are in direct contrast to those in many poorer countries of the world where over 125 million children do not even receive basic education. This high level of exclusion from basic education is an indication not only of grave inequalities but also of the deterioration of intercultural and intergroup relations. The discussions about turning exclusion into inclusion in Britain are qualitatively different from the international issues of inclusive policies needed for basic education. Such policies are necessary to establish a basis for stability in socially diverse polities at local, national and international levels.

The work deals with questions of exclusion being turned into inclusion by examining in a critical manner issues like institutional policies, affirmative action or positive discrimination. Social and public policies to ensure greater levels of equality are needed to avoid the emergence of a new barbarism which can arise from ethnic and cultural conflict. There are only a few countries which are immune from conflicts arising out of narrow nationalism with its potential of destabilising polities.

The work deals discursively with the question of how education can help in the task of developing cohesive civil societies by turning notions of singular identities into those of multiple ones, and by developing a shared and common value system and public culture. In many complex societies processes like economic globalisation are erasing autonomous and distinctive economies, cultures and ways of life. There are discussions about how education systems begin to deal with these difficult and sometimes contradictory and divergent demands. Schools and educational systems have an important role to play in helping to create peaceableness and stability in socially diverse but unequal and divided communities. The failure of local institutions to develop inclusiveness has the potential of exacerbating local conflict as well as violence. Hence, those who live in such localities can become more distant and violent unless mutual adaption and co-existence through a learning process can be facilitated.

Intercultural education has the complex function of developing dynamic local cultures which lead to confederal links with other localities and identities. These tasks require not only the democratisation of institutions like schools but also the development of democratic civic cultures so that the human rights of all citizens are protected. One of the problems discussed is how to deal with dominant and hegemonic views of education.

With the development of devolution and centralisation within Europe there is a need to take a fresh look at what is considered to be legitimate knowledge within the education system. Unlike much of the literature in this field from across the Atlantic, this book engages constructively with the issue of the curriculum. The histories, literatures and cultures of peoples who have either been subordinated or dominated cannot be ignored from dominant western or European perspectives. In fact, socially diverse or multicultural communities already provide us with complexly structured pasts and presents which are leading to plural futures. This book is a contribution to the process of developing critical and analytical perspectives in intercultural education. It unpicks the substantive issues of anti-racism as distinct from the rhetoric of anti-racism. The more intractable issues of institutional racism have obvious implications for dealing with the way in which organisations ought to develop ethos, practices and policies which enhance the rights of all who are members of an organisation. The persistent problem of the highly disproportionate rate of exclusion of black young people from school is an important aspect of the failure of school policies to develop an inclusive ethos.

Such high levels of school exclusions also raise major issues for lifelong learning. This is partly because many young people require opportunities for second chance learning as well as the need to acquire skills which lead to gaining employment. Hence, the book outlines the role of both formal and informal education which is critical to the improvement of educational outcomes and of life chances. This does require joined-up policies because educational policies on their own cannot lead to the transformation of relationships.

Intercultural education as such is not a discrete area of study which is appended to the process of mainstream education. It is part and parcel of the educational process. In fact, the assumption here is that educators need to create a culture of intercultural education to be effective.

This book is a result of work in the intercultural field for over thirty years.

It began with reflections on teaching in London schools, further and continuing and community education.

During the 1970s the Inner London Education Authority decided to take an initiative to provide greater equity in education to all London children. These policies were put into effect by Peter Newsam, then Education Officer, and an Inspectorate for Multi-ethnic Education headed by Bev Woodroffe.

The Institute of Education at the University of London, the largest teacher education institution in the country, also decided to contribute to the education of teachers by setting up a Centre for Multicultural Education in 1979. The Centre was set up to cut across the departmental and disciplinary structures of the Institute. It worked horizontally across it with a Co-ordinating Committee and with senior chairpeople and joint Centre and departmental staff appointments. This work has played an important role in the way in which the field has developed and informed the current piece of writing.

At the national level the Centre is a unique institutional mechanism, far in advance of any other higher education institution. Its express purpose was to ensure that issues of multiculturalism and anti-racism were integrally part of this large complex institution organised into departments. As an interdisciplinary entity, the Centre pursued work in various areas. I was concerned with two issues: politics in education and the legacy of past research in the field. However, once the Conservative government came into power in 1979 intercultural and anti-racist policies went into reverse, culminating in the 1988 Education Act. Meanwhile, however, the Centre for Multicultural Education was establishing links internationally – with British agencies working overseas, and far closer links with individuals and institutions working in the member states of the European Union. It was in recognition of this broader European interest and changing needs that it eventually changed its name from the Centre for Multicultural Education, with implied focus on education of different groups, to the International Centre for Intercultural Studies, working in education between groups with an implied international focus. This change was approved by the various committees of the Institute of Education and had the support of the Director, Professor Peter Mortimore. These institutional issues inform much of the discussions that follow especially because of the importance of changes in terminology and concepts.

In 1984 a number of educators from Europe attended a conference held at the Institute of Education on the theme of an international curriculum within the European school system. At this conference an International Association of Intercultural Education (IAIE) was founded in which the International Centre for Intercultural Education played a major role. Over the years the Association and the Centre have collaborated to establish a network of institutional links which have worked on various projects, and sponsored seminars and conferences. The IAIE has also established a journal *Intercultural Education* which publishes work in this field from across the world. This book is informed by much of the work undertaken in conferences, seminars and the journal of the Association to which the author has contributed.

The Centre has further links with other institutions and universities in the EU through the Erasmus and Socrates Programmes. Moreover, the EU and the Council of Europe have commissioned the Centre to undertake projects and research into intercultural issues. As a result the field has become better defined in at least some pedagogic circles. However, much needs to be done to refine it further, and to persuade the universities to recognise it institutionally.

This book results from work undertaken at the International Centre for Intercultural Studies, Institute of Education, University of London. In the twenty years I have worked at the Centre I have learnt a tremendous amount from my colleagues, students, Visiting and Teacher Fellows. My debt is to everyone who has collaborated with it and worked with me.

I would like to thank the successive Directors of the Institute, Sir William Taylor, Professor Denis Lawton, Sir Peter Newsam and Professor Peter Mortimore for their support. Professor Mortimore chaired the Co-ordinating Committee of the Centre and as Director has always provided guidance and assistance. In personal and institutional terms, the Centre is largely the brain-child of Professor Basil Bernstein and the Working Party and the Steering Committee he chaired.

It would be invidious to single out any from the numerous colleagues and friends from whom I have learnt so much. I am singularly privileged to have colleagues who are friends, friends who are family and family who have become friends. All of them have supported me in innumerable ways. The Institute of Education has over the years been an extremely stimulating institution and all those who have worked on issues of intercultural education have been pioneers in many aspects of the work in this field. Amongst the researchers, Phil Cohen and Roger Hewitt have done extremely important work. The late Keith Kimberley was a steadfast worker and colleague. There are enormous debts to Crispin Jones who has shared in this experience for the best part of two decades. I would also like to acknowledge the help and support of Robert Ferguson, Robert Cowen and John Van Santen.

I am not, in general terms, supportive of writing from an autobiographical frame but was urged by my colleagues in the Urban Education Group to write this book using my own learning experiences. If the book is successful in doing this it is to their credit but if it fails it is not their responsibility. I would like to thank Christopher Fyfe for his sustained support in the preparation of the manuscript.

In addition Alice Henfield has provided assistance and encouragement beyond her duties at the Centre. Sarah has supported this enterprise at a personal level. To all of them I owe a deep debt of gratitude.

Jagdish S. Gundara

Introduction: An Intercultural Apprenticeship

GROWING UP IN KENYA

My home was Kenya. I was born of Indian parents and spent my first eighteen impressionable years in an atmosphere replete with contradictions. My father, a Sikh, was a forester at Ngong. Ngong lay on the outskirts of Nairobi, neighbouring the elite and exclusively European residential area of Karen. At first my father's position as a government officer seemed to me to have a certain glow of authority and respect.

However, it became clear that, although he was a dedicated forester with a passion for flora and fauna, under the colonial system he would receive little recognition of his dedication or advancement of his career. This prompted the belief that ambition was a fruit devoid of sweetness and that I would be allotted a similar position in a closed social and political world based on racialism. The concept of a proud but independent, egalitarian Sikh nurtured through the stories of the Gurus, told passionately by my mother, thrived only in the dusk of my imagination.

We were an isolated Indian family living in the forest. We could not go and worship in the Sikh temple in Nairobi. Because of this cultural isolation I did not receive the support of other members of the Indian community – a community that, with the partition of the Indian sub-continent in 1947, became known as 'Asian'.

We spoke Punjabi. My father knew English but would not normally speak it at home. I naturally turned to African children who were my neighbours and we spent much time playing together. I picked up their languages – Kikuyu and Swahili – and I learnt the secrets of the forest from them. We grew up together as an integral part of the forest and of each other. This was a broad group of older and younger children. My brother, sister and I shared many common interests with our African friends surrounded as we were by the overwhelming sounds and aromatic smells of the woods at Ngong.

1

European children too were attracted to the forest environment, and to the plant nursery and dam, to play. We would play with them, and learn their games and how to horseride.

But there was one aspect of our home which marred my childhood. In a stratified Kenyan society, our thatched house in the forest seemed to reduce our status, which I felt was further eroded by the lack of electricity in the house. The power-lines, which stood barely four hundred yards away from our home, supplied electricity to the neighbouring European residential area. I was embarrassed by our house, and refrained from mentioning to my city friends that we used paraffin or gas lamps. My subsequent association with city children made the issue seem important.

Upbringing at home played a complex role in my learning processes. Our family was basically a nuclear unit which was reinforced because of our geographical location. However, a constant stream of people drifted in and out of the home. My father tended to be strict, loving, authoritarian and prone to exercising discipline, including an occasional thump. But the complex elements of relationships within the family considerably dampened my teenage anger and rebelliousness towards my father. This dual adult authority and affection mutually and continually reinforced the superior status of parents and other adults, and relegated peer group relations to a secondary position and importance. One grew up in an environment of moral values and decisions made by adults.

I subsequently subscribed to Arnold Wesker's remark that 'men are mere rebels, women are the true revolutionaries', because I felt that in our household my mother was the essential person who loved while she instructed, who placated wild emotions and saved against the rainy day. On reflection, however, I feel that there was a balance of paternal and maternal functions in our household which aided my training and acted as a backdrop to it. The rest of us seem to have relegated these skills, and those dealing with creativity and other physical rhythms of life, to a more secondary place.

Schooling

Before I went to school learning was done together with others spontaneously. I was not instructed *why* certain things in the forest had to be learnt. Somehow much of what my parents taught seemed to be valid. It was the school-oriented teacher-learning that was agonising, because the information imparted had no immediate relevance.

Parental authority was not the only agent fragmenting my peer group relations. As an Asian, I was not permitted to attend a school in my neighbourhood because it was an African school, although all my friends attended this school. I was also debarred from going to a European school which was only one mile from my home – I was compelled to go ten miles into Nairobi to attend an Asian school. I travelled to the city and operated alone, outside of the milieu to which I belonged and understood. In my new environment relationships were based on the personalities of individuals, and I became very shy, insecure and depressed, having to cultivate such relationships.

I travelled by bus into the centre of Nairobi and from there to my school in an Asian neighbourhood. I recall enviously watching the African and European children travel in an opposite direction to their respective schools nearer their and my home. However, I continued to treasure my deep relationships with the children with whom I spent so much of my real life outside the artificial construction of an equally artificial school. The Asian pupils attending my urban school had hobbies and interests that did not necessarily coincide with my own, although we were supposed to share common cultural and linguistic norms. However, this was not necessarily a rationally planned policy.

In school I had to learn English and Urdu. My mother tongue was Punjabi, but there was no opportunity to learn this formally. Of my two new languages Urdu proved the most difficult. Unlike Punjabi and English, it is written from right to left. This made hand and eye co-ordination extremely difficult, and was problematic since the teachers did not understand this aspect of teaching language. The result of such haphazard teaching of language is that I cannot read or write Urdu well – and nor do I write my own mother tongue to this day. This is in marked contrast to my parents' generation who were fluent in Punjabi, Urdu and Farsi (Persian). This dubious advantage of being sent to an 'Asian' school relatively late, for cultural and linguistic reasons, became particularly suspect when we were instructed to speak in English throughout the school day. It was, in fact, a crude division of children on the basis of racism.

From the first day, going to school proved to be a painful experience. My father, a driver and Ngure Maina – my favourite 'uncle' – and I were driven by lorry to this neo-classical, whitewashed, red-tiled-roof structure. To induce me to stay I was given sweets (as was the teacher) and a hundred-shilling note, and Ngure Maina, a Kikuyu who worked with my father till his retirement from the Kenyan Government, was requested to stay in the school compound to provide moral support.

This was an interesting paradox. I was a cross-culturally attuned child, and only stayed in this Asian school because I felt secure that Ngure Maina, my trusted 'uncle', would not forsake me. It is possible that had Ngure not acted as the important link between my rural home and this urban Asian school, I would not have adapted to the school environment supposedly created for the benefit of Asian children such as myself.

My first teacher was a rather severe Indian matron who was, however, kind to me. City children nevertheless taunted me as a 'hick', pinched me, and played games to which I was unaccustomed. I had to unlearn some of my earlier skills and learn new ones. I continued to be withdrawn and never quite mastered playing marbles which was the passionate occupation of my school contemporaries.

After school, my classmates walked to their homes in groups while Ngure and I had to make our way back home to the forest. We must have appeared a strange pair to the city children as we transcended the peer group camaraderie. For them there was continuity in their social and school life; for me it was a fractured experience.

My discomfort at school was not made any easier by being constantly late because I lived so far away. The bicycle trip from Ngong was three miles to the nearest bus stop, then a five mile ride to the centre of Nairobi, followed by another bus trip to the school. Buses were invariably late, but the class teachers did not appreciate the reasons for my tardiness. I was treated like any other urban child although in my experiences I was a very different person. My teachers often punished me in front of the class, an experience I found humiliating. This impacted on my academic performance and interest.

At least subconsciously, I rejected this sort of racially segregated schooling. I deeply resented the fact that I could not go to school with the children amongst whom I lived. While it was the urban children, because of their group solidarity, who felt that I was an oddity, I secretly rebelled against their narrow city-interests. I was averse to children who displayed little rebelliousness and slavishly emulated roles ascribed to them.

I could not identify myself with one single group of children, but tended to hover between those who excelled at academic work, others who were good athletes and a group of rebels who rejected school altogether. These three groups were not part of the mainstream of school life since they defied mediocrity and were sometimes mutually exclusive.

In retrospect I felt that no one group had the monopoly of the learning experience, and only by relating to these diverse groups would I be able to re-establish some capacity to learn which I had originally brought to school. The mainstream, it seemed to my rebellious friends, had accepted their marginal role in society and the narrow norms laid down for them without question. To preserve this precarious balance at school I had to keep my parents as far away from there as I could.

Contacts between parents and school at the primary level were extremely limited. There were no parent–teacher get-togethers. Many children only managed to get educated by sheer dint of personal effort. In my own case, the home–school distance in geographical terms made school remote for my parents.

As a forester, my father dressed very simply in khaki shirt and trousers. Along with a thatched house, khaki clothes did not signal social importance in stratified Kenya. Once I started attending school in the city I became increasingly aware of subtleties of social status, based on the clothes one wore, the type of houses and parts of the town in which one lived.

My parents and our home in the forest became a secret haunt. They were protected from the narrow and mediocre status that I felt we, as Asians, had to endure. In as much as I respected and admired my father, I wanted to protect him from this social milieu which I did not particularly accept. I was having such a difficult time developing my own techniques of synthesising diverse and sometimes contradictory strands which I felt my father would not understand, that I preferred him to stay away from school altogether. On the occasions when my father did visit school on a prize-giving day, especially if I had won a prize, I remember pressing him to dress up in a suit and tie.

The lack of contact between my family and the school was not due to their lack of interest in my education. It is asserted that sometimes children fare badly in school because their parents lack contact with the school. My parents had such implicit faith in the ability of the teachers to perform their professional duty that they felt they had no right to interfere. My parents always ensured that we did our homework and attempted to help when they could. When they could not help, they secured tutors.

During the middle years of my primary school we attended for half-a-day because the classrooms were used for a second shift in the afternoon. This practice was abandoned, however, when more new schools were built, and during my last year in primary school we were transferred to one such modern structure. I did not particularly like this nondescript building, particularly because we now had to attend school for morning and afternoon sessions. I had preferred the one session in the mornings because it enabled me to return home in the afternoons and spend time with my friends in the forest.

There, my initial attempt to reconcile my friendships with my African and European peer groups which stemmed from common interests were reinforced with the rather nefarious activity of smoking. I became the prime instigator of an underground smoking club in the anteroom of my study. We papered the windows of our hideout to discourage intruders. It was furnished with slatted plywood boxes stolen from the nursery where they were used for growing seedlings and plants. We turned them into seats that also concealed the various brands of cigarettes that made their way into the den.

Two very clear issues emerged. Firstly, although I was the one who took the risk of providing these premises and of bringing together these African and European children, I perceived their disdain towards me. After all, was I not one of them – did we not share the forest and many other interesting things together? I was the one who became the intruder in my own den. I did not quite fit into their respective worlds. This became a painful experience because I was wrenched from my peer group friends by their indifference to me. This indifference was, of course, part and parcel of the racially segmented life officially sanctioned in Kenya.

The second element was that my father discovered the smoking den and was so incensed that he dealt me a sharp slap across the face. When he realised that he had hit me too hard he placed his arm around my shoulders while we walked under the acrocarpus and chestnut trees. He attempted to explain to me why smoking was a bad habit, but he did not refer to the religious sanctions (Sikhs should not smoke) during his discourse. The head of the family had thus asserted his authority and protective role, and this integrative aspect of the Asian family system made it extremely difficult for me to break away from what was a cohesive and functional unit.

Another aspect of living in colonial Kenya affected my social learning. Going on holidays was impracticable and therefore non-existent during my early youth. Asians were not allowed into hotels, and had few of their own, an indication of this community's regrettable inability to cater for its needs. So broadening one's vision through travel was therefore limited. A substitute was to be permitted to stay at the homes of various friends overnight or for a weekend. In this way one was able to escape periodically from home and, at the same time, to value its worth.

I managed to pass my public primary-school examination at the end of my first seven years of schooling and was sent to an academic secondary school which appeared quite grand.

Political Awareness and Renegotiation of Identity

Kenya was in political ferment and turmoil during the 1950s, and everyone was inevitably aware of it. It caused me many emotional problems because it raised issues of identity and of belonging. This provoked a fair amount of thought and was not directly related to academic and classroom learning.

The first four years in my secondary school were extremely difficult. But, once I had passed the Cambridge School Certificate Examination and was accepted to complete my Cambridge Higher School Certificate, school became more acceptable. When I had completed sixth form successfully, the officious aspect of schooling, for some strange reason, seemed to have evaporated, and I was left with a rosy-tinted image of what had been agonisingly difficult years of learning and growing up. I particularly remember, after accepting a prize at the last prize-giving day, fondly walking away from my secondary school with its avenue of purple jacaranda flowers which carpeted the long driveway.

But I became increasingly aware of the pressures of living in a racially and socially stratified society. I continued to live in the rural African world, and more marginally with my European friends. These friendships were increasingly undermined because I attended an Asian school in the city, and had begun to develop a complex set of relationships at my school. My complex response to my 'Asianness' both at home and at school created conflicts. The strenuous pressures of the secondary school cut a swathe through my ability to integrate and function effectively in both worlds.

One affliction of this era that impeded my academic pursuits was a disdain of my apparent 'Asianness' as defined by the colonial elite. Since I operated in an inequitable society and could not shed the colour of my skin, I felt I ought at least to change my name. I thought perhaps that if I Anglicised my nickname it would assist me in assimilating, and some of my problems would disappear. At the same time I was ashamed of contemplating such an idea.

Many years later in North America, when I realised that other people were similarly preoccupied, my private shame at my youthful attempts to break out of the confines of mediocrity from outside abated. From my point of view at that time, I thought that I might be able to relate better with my European and African friends, from whom I was becoming increasingly alienated. Perhaps identification with the dominant group was the easiest answer, whilst, in effect, I instinctively identified with the Africans. Since the issues were essentially political in the context of complex Kenyan society they created a fair number of dilemmas which could not be easily resolved.

It would probably be true to say that Asian schools performed relatively well. Education was seen as the only avenue that would lead out of the trap of the complex middle position of the Asian minority in Kenya. While I admired the academically bright students, I could not systematically apply myself to formal learning and therefore did not spend much time in their company.

Another group of friends with whom I associated rejected both the dominating elite and the adults from amongst our own community. They despised their parents and teachers because they had accepted appallingly abject political and social conditions. Many of these friends were senior to me and were used as role models, not only to establish my identity but also to challenge authority and the accepted norms.

Their rebellion took the form of enhancing physical stamina, or asserting premature manhood by staying out late and drinking. A small group of boys played truant from school to drink beer and play snooker. Others became good cyclists, scouts or hockey players. Apart from an occasional act of bravado like driving a car fast without parental permission, I preferred the more congenial pastimes of sitting in coffee-houses or watching films during school time on Saturdays. Resistance to schooling but respect for education was somehow natural: I still cannot discern how the mind was able to distinguish between the two.

A third group of people with whom I associated were either adults or were senior to me, and had either qualified in their field of specialisation or had returned from abroad and rejected the mediocre Anglicisation of our parents' generation. I found this group fascinating because they had returned from the metropolis and were critical of it. While this was a new and thrilling experience in many ways, it also generated insecurity because one felt out of one's depth.

My feelings about European domination and oppression on the one hand and the mediocrity and pettiness of the Asian community on the other were lent credibility by a friend and relative of my parents' generation. I respected him because I considered him to be my intellectual mentor. Mr N. S. Mangat Q.C. was a leading criminal lawyer in East Africa and the president of the East African National Indian Congress during 1954 and 1956 when I was in secondary school.

During the first year of his presidency he criticised the Europeans for their arrogance and presumption of superiority. This clarified some of my earlier dilemmas and the errors of my ways, and I began to realise why we, as Asians, were placed in such a tenuous position. In 1956, however, on a similar occasion, he took the opportunity to criticise the Asians for their narrow-mindedness, pettiness and lack of vision. This too struck a note which put my feelings in perspective and I felt more relaxed about issues that had hitherto perplexed me. Needless to say Mr Mangat was not re-elected to the presidency of this august organisation after his second scathing speech on the Asian community. He was obviously a person with a vision and a sense of pride appropriate to the grander values of life, and was able to attack the weaknesses of the community.

Exposure of this nature at home had made me politically conscious and compelled me to look critically at my teachers and the school system. On the whole Asian teachers taught us but an English Oxford graduate taught English literature. This teacher took an instant dislike to me and he referred to me as a 'lesser Caucasian', being himself blond, blue-eyed and arrogant in the extreme. I did not know what this meant and in an attempt to protect me from such an insult my parents papered over the incident.

However, when I did realise the implications it prompted an extremely complex response. I began to read avidly, partly because of the fear that I might not do well in English literature. My avid reading was reinforced by the fact that the teacher persisted in treating me invidiously and openly taunted me that I would fail in my final Higher School Certificate examination. As it turned out, I was the only pupil who obtained a distinction in literature. That this teacher never congratulated me was no surprise. I was, however, exhilarated by my results and my headmaster and other teachers became extremely friendly.

The discovery that the teaching profession included teachers who were racist and insensitive remains one of the unforgivable experiences of my school life. My negative experience with the literature teacher provoked another personal response. I had been brought up in a cross-cultural framework despite the sectarian and racial divisions cutting right across Kenyan society. But I was turned by this teacher to think in terms with which I basically disagreed. I became an inverted snob after his rebuke, in order to protect my sensibility and inner person.

It was only many years after, when I saw the Gandhara sculptures in the Boston Museum of Fine Art, that I established a realistic sense of personal identity. This civilisation, which existed from the first to the fourth century AD, was a syncretism of Graeco-Roman and Indian cultures in North West India. The realisation that ancestrally I belonged to a complex and ancient culture – a knowledge hitherto denied – gave me confidence and an ability to function as a composite person. The inverted snobbery and somewhat false pride in being a Punjabi did not then need assertion.

I became conscious of the general problem of how dominant cultures wiped out the histories and identities of dominated groups. The predicament of the African-Americans came into prominence in the 1960s and I gave some thought to their problems as one group which had been forced to lose their African identity. I felt that the dominant American society had done a disservice not only to the native Americans and the African-Americans, but also to themselves in denying a real possibility of becoming genuinely American. They had, it seems to me, in fact imposed a fragment of a certain period of Europe on North American society and were destined to remain a Euro-centred paranoiac community which had imposed itself on but not allowed itself to take root in this new, varied and fertile landscape. Problems of my own personal identity paled into insignificance in comparison.

Thinking and research on political issues associated with these conditions demand original multidisciplinary work by social scientists. This is perhaps one of the major challenges of the twenty-first century, particularly as the national minorities all over the world have a new consciousness. My attempt to explain the results of being labelled inferior by my teacher's remarks has been to demonstrate the long and tedious process of examining issues of personal and cultural identity. The school in Kenya should have avoided judging certain groups as culturally or racially inferior. The ideal task the school had to perform should have been to demonstrate the differences between people without labelling them as 'better' or 'worse'.

My literature teacher in particular and the school in general had succeeded in reinforcing differentiation on a false basis rather than on a basis of equality. The school added to problems of identity and therefore failed to educate us with open, humane and sensitive values. As a result of this educational incident, I turned against the elitism in English academe which I felt I could not count on to solve the grave issues that I perceived and which haunted the country in which I was brought up.

Didactic Learning at School

Asian teachers trained in British colonial India or Kenya taught us, but mainly on the basis of a British-centred curriculum and through books stressing the role of Britain in civilising the world. For the life of me, I could not understand why I was not allowed to attend an English school if the purpose of my education was to be taught an English-based curriculum. When I was sent to an Asian school and taught by Asian teachers, I might have expected that the content of the education would also be Asian. However, the colonial school served imperial interests.

I now feel that teaching an Anglo-centred curriculum, using Asian teachers who only understood it in second-hand terms, was unfair on the teachers and the pupils. After all, these teachers had no close experience of England to perform a first-rate teaching job of imparting knowledge about England and English values. But when they taught us subjects like Urdu language they recited the verses from Urdu poetry with such verve that momentarily the far away and long forgotten Indian sub-continent became real. If any real aspect of it was taught in the school it was through language teaching. It was the preservation of this aspect of Asian society which allowed Asian culture and poetry to thrive in Kenya. My generation did not adhere to the values of the temple, so it was mainly the linguistic aspect taught at school which ensured contact with the variety of the sub-continent.

Another aspect of being taught by Asian teachers was that the teachers reinforced paternal authority at home, in the context of the school. On the whole these teachers, as members of a dominated community, were exceedingly committed to their work. Many were in the profession because they experienced a genuine need to help children from this community to overcome the hurdles placed by the dominant community.

My own responses to the stern and disciplinarian teachers only changed later, after some reflection. The harsh responses of teachers towards those of us who were difficult, lazy or none too keen to learn were easy to understand. These teachers felt that we, as youths, did not see the barriers to our advancement in a prejudiced society. When we refused to accept rules laid down by them they felt obliged to point out to us the error of our ways. In some senses it was our fault that we did not understand the urgency of our situation, prompting our teachers to resort to corporal punishment. Some teachers felt that the school was the only institution that could positively change our lives, and they saw us missing this opportunity.

Relations between our teachers and us were formal at one level but informal at another. At the informal level they could relate closely to us because, as members of the oppressed community, we were in the same boat. A few teachers were either radical or nationalistic, and attempted to correct the imbalance of the curriculum and the books, particularly in history lessons. However, the Inspectorate of the Education Department rendered such teachers powerless. Teachers who accepted the mores and norms of the English dominated department were rewarded by promotion to senior posts.

The first Asian inspector in this department was an Anglicised headmaster who also happened to be an extremely good teacher of Shakespeare. On the other hand, a teacher who was nationalistic, and wore *khadi* (traditional Indian cotton suits) and taught Gujerati language, remained at the lower-scale post, despite his ability. He was given 'low-ability' classes which, in professional terms, must have made him feel a 'second-rate' teacher.

The same was true of an Urdu and physical education Sikh teacher, who was very popular with the students. He had a strong sense of Punjabi values and was a good teacher of Urdu and Punjabi. He did not attempt to operate in the mainstream of the English-dominated Education Department. He was not only ignored in the line of promotion but was also transferred to another less 'prestigious' school. The treatment of such teachers demonstrated to me that the struggle for a newer and different, but fairer, society was long and arduous.

Teaching in school was, in general, formal and based on a syllabus with the sole aim of eliciting good examination results. My initial introduction to English language in the class was through teaching by rote. Literature was taught on a similar basis with set textbooks. Story telling at home, apart from those stories with religious connotations, was non-existent. Since Punjabi literature and poetry was, and continues to be, heretical and progressive, it is a matter of concern that its oral traditions in Kenya were so easily suppressed. This type of delegitimizing of life and knowledge also silences the voice of women on their experiences of life and living.

Both at home and school, there was little opportunity for expanding learning through stories and general literature. Although my father was unable to assist in formulating a sensible pattern of reading, he was, however, successful in encouraging an interest in books. He made it a practice on Saturdays to take us as children to a reasonably good bookshop in Nairobi while he visited his head office. This gave us an opportunity to browse and choose books. This self-selection of books in literature has left large gaps in my reading. For instance, whereas I had read Steinbeck's *The Log in the Sea of Cortez* I have yet to read *The Wind in the Willows*. Similarly my familiarity with African and Indian literature is very superficial.

My interests were therefore directed by what and how we were taught. Our teachers used traditional methods mainly to impart facts and schools. Various teachers taught us specialised subjects and the students had to organise and structure materials to make them comprehensive. One of the drawbacks of being taught by traditional methods was that teachers applauded only the work of good students. Those who were not identified as achievers were either criticised or ignored. Many of us sat at the back of the class so as not to attract the teacher's attention. Creativity in writing that somehow related to one's own experiences was not encouraged and therefore did not emerge for a number of children.

There was no systematic teaching of specialised subjects within an integrated framework. There was no flexibility in the teaching system, no team-teaching or guidance to younger teachers from those more responsible and experienced. For instance, no connections existed between subjects like geography and history, or the various sciences and specialisms in mathematics. There appeared to be no synthesis between these various subjects, and I tended to focus on those subjects which I liked or found easy.

I was also dissatisfied with the way history was taught which perpetually reinforced the positive values of the dominant group and the negative features of India and Africa. For instance, the 'Indian Mutiny' was taught not to demonstrate its nationalistic aspirations but to exemplify the disloyalty and untrustworthiness of the Indians. Africans and Asians were presented adversely without asserting each other's positive contributions in historical terms. Additionally, the British in Kenya had a totally misplaced conception of who they were. This misconception of their own history, and their role in it, was profound and based on erasing that of other peoples.

This system of education rejected any subjective values of students. Perceptions of certain subject matters, even within the limitations in which they were taught, could possibly have been explored from different perspectives. All the arts subjects, it seemed to me, could be enriched by diverse interpretations. My English literature teacher illustrated that my interpretation was unacceptable by denying my subjective values and rejecting interpretations which did not conform to his dominant values. Was it possible, for instance, that literature was considered by this teacher to be near the core of his own culture, and since he felt threatened in this different country, he imposed his interpretation even more vigorously?

Whatever, it denied us as students a genuine opportunity to interact and learn positive features about him and each other. We were fortunate at least to have some teachers who did understand our background and to some extent upheld it as valid. But they could do this only marginally because the whole schooling system was formal and oriented to English public examinations in which they did not want us to fail.

I had brought to school a fairly wide and associative linguistic network which, if it had been systematically tackled, might have furthered my cognitive processes. I was able to develop categories and analyse issues which became useful in the learning of social sciences, in terms of developing abstract frameworks. I had, however, to wrestle with my mother tongue, Punjabi, with Urdu, another sub-continent language, and English. Since these were neither systematically taught nor learnt, there were limitations to my ability to categorise abstract thought.

At university level I found it difficult to cope with linguistic analytical philosophy because I found the concepts too erudite or abstract. As we were categorised in general terms between technical and academic schools, and streamed according to our examination performances, I did not become accustomed to the formal testing and examination situation and consequently did not perform well. In the formal classroom I learnt slowly because I was afraid of making mistakes and therefore tended to avoid subjects like mathematics which I could not deal with competently.

Going to school in the city gave me experience of the man-made city environment in addition to the rural environment of a temperate forest. We combined in our psyche the vertical planes of the trees in the forest and the horizontal planes of the grassland and open spaces. In addition I spent some of my time in the rectangular environment of the city. The combination of these two aspects of learning possibly developed perceptual and inference habits which varied from those of the other children I knew in and out of school. If the school had encouraged a systematic fusion of the visual perspectives then I might have not only developed an appreciation of various arts, but also contributed to them. As it is, I attempted to accomplish this through a process of self-education.

Living in Kenya, I had, for instance, an interest in the non-perspective African art. I continue to have an interest in the works of various angular and rectangular artists like Albers, Mondrian and the Bauhaus school. Is this a result of the imprint the city made on me? I also appreciate the two-dimensional art of the Impressionists and the Post-Impressionists, which entails seeing depth in the intentions of the artist's work of a 'softer' nature. Is this facility of appreciating or operating in both the two- and the three-dimensional worlds a result of operating in both the rural and the rectangular man-made city environment at an early age? Furthermore, is the ability to appreciate – but not to be able to draw – a result of the impractical and non-pictorial aspects of education? It is possible that if the schools had channelled our perceptual experiences in some systematic manner, students like me would have been able to relate African, Asian and Western art and literature. This process, however, never took place, and it was left to the individual to synchronise these various aspects of life in whatever manner one could.

These varied concerns and interests did not lead to an excellence in academic terms in school. When it came to embarking on higher education and acquiring A-levels in England, I worried because I had seen many older friends return from England without having completed their education or securing a qualification. Since my father was a civil servant, and there were four of us to be educated, I felt reluctant to accept any remittance from him to continue my education abroad. I, therefore, re-applied to my old school to complete my Cambridge Higher School Certificate.

This turned out to be an excellent decision because as a fifth and sixth form student I received special attention. I was not one of the many downtrodden and forgotten in the lower forms and streams of the school. It was also the first time that boys and girls in our school had studied together. This was a thrilling new experience. Only two of us studied the arts and we had tutors who taught history, geography and economics. Both of us were under pressure to work and produce results because a great deal of attention had been devoted to us. There was no escape to a bench at the back of the class. For the first time we began to enjoy our work in school since we could discuss it with our teachers. Even the history of Anglo-Saxon Britain seemed to come alive, remote though it was from contemporary Africa.

NORTH AMERICA

Once I had completed my Higher School Certificate examinations I was again faced with the dilemma of whether or not to study in England for my higher education. The high failure rate of friends who had gone to study in England, my family's inability to finance such a risky proposition, and the experience of my literature teacher who was English, led me to decide against further education in England.

I, therefore, took a job with a horticultural firm which I really enjoyed. My brother-in-law, a qualified barrister, also worked as the manager of this firm and jokingly remarks: 'It has been downhill ever since'.

I was eventually awarded a scholarship to study in America. The American experience was an eye-opener, particularly since it was a total break from Kenya. As a scholarship student I felt secure in the feeling that I was not risking my parents' meagre savings on this venture. The liberal professors reciprocated in my new intellectual and political awakening, and I was free of the English domination felt in Kenya. Nevertheless after three years in the United States I left the country because I feared that I might become Americanised by default.

The American experience was very productive in academic terms, but also in having to cope independently by trying to find work. It was the first time that the cocoon of the family, the forest home, had been left behind. There was therefore no support or network, and one had to create one's own network of friends and individuals inside and outside the college.

Since I was a scholarship student, I needed to work during the school term as well as in the summer. Finding work outside college was not all that easy and provided me with major insights into the complexity of American society and of the exclusions within it. I learnt, for instance, about the extremely brutal form of racism towards the African-Americans. This acted as an antidote to the romanticisation of the United States, which many other students from abroad tended to.

Stints of research work in offices in the United Nations and at Columbia University provided an inkling into the way in which people lived, thought and worked. Friends would take one home, and one had a glimpse and some understanding of the warmth, friendliness and openness of America generally.

There was, however, also the other face of America. For those of us from overseas the Kennedy 'Golden Era' was not necessarily the progressive period it has been portrayed. The super-power politics and America's role in suppressing progressive forces tainted it. The Cuban Missile Crisis in the early 1960s and then the Vietnam War raised complex questions at an international level for a foreign student from a small country. The racism that was so prevalent within American society became very evident. This made it less easy to identify with the country. Hence, ultimately, I had to decide whether to stay on in the United States, with all the advantages that, despite everything, it offered, or to move.

My decision was to leave and study in Canada. Quebec was in a dynamic phase, having rebelled against the Catholic hegemony and the autocratic Duplessis regime. A progressive Quebec was a welcome change from the hegemony of the Anglo-Saxon-dominated, commercially dominant superpower. I chose to study at McGill University in Montreal because it seemed to be an interesting city. Also the French and English conflict in Canada was an example of dominant and subordinate group relations in the process of change.

There were certain assumptions about the teaching of the social sciences in the United States which were legitimised in the Canadian context, a factor I found depressing. The assertion that the social sciences could formulate 'value free' theoretical constraints, and that the mainstream of North American social sciences was based on these, was unacceptable for me. These pseudo-scientific norms which incorporated within their framework the rationale of North American society in no way could have been assumed to be 'value free'.

Meaningful learning in my case did not begin or end within the formal institutional framework. Learning started informally and socially at a very early age and continues outside this framework. Learning in this social milieu is complex and sometimes contradictory. For instance, how and why did I, having been brought up in a racially segregated school and social system, come out of it thinking differently? It can only be because of a learning process that went on in and out of the institutional framework and operated not only at a personal level but also at various levels of consciousness.

EXPERIENCING BRITAIN

A Historical Approach

The complexity of North America left me enchanted as well as disenchanted and would have meant a complete engagement and involvement; therefore I decided to complete my formal education in Britain.

North American social science in the 1960s was preoccupied by ideas of modernisation and development. Aspects of this type of social science were of obvious interest to those who were interested in using concepts like social change and status discrepancy, or analytical concepts like class, or quantitative methods of study. The one tradition that was not strongly represented there was the historical tradition, as exemplified by the French *Annales* model with its *longue durée* approach. Those who came from a non-American background, and especially those from the 'modernising' and 'developing' ex-colonial states, found this remiss. So we were not very excited at using input/output models and systems theory. Though we could not know it, the social sciences were then riding on the crest of an understated triumphalism. This is an issue we will explore in Chapter 9.

I therefore moved to Scotland, to the University of Edinburgh. It seemed familiar ground since Scotland stood in a similar relation to England as did Canada to the United States or English Canadians to the French Canadians. Here was an opportunity to bring together the diverse strands of social science and law, and to examine them in detail in a proper historical framework.

I felt I had to come to grips with how, as an Asian from East Africa, I had ended up where I was. I determined to investigate in my doctoral thesis how historically the British Imperial project had caught the Asian community in East Africa in a double bind – they were legally British, yet they remained outsiders. The longer I stayed in Britain, the more I saw the relevance of this theme to the status and treatment of Asians, indeed of all the marginalised communities, in this country today.

The assertion of British nationality, and at the same time the denial of it, has been particularly painful to the British Asian community. What I came to perceive, as I studied for my thesis, was that this situation had not suddenly arisen in the post-colonial era, but has been and is firmly rooted in the nineteenth century – something that previous studies had not adequately analysed or examined. It became clear, for instance, that the vulnerability of the Asian community in Uganda in the 1970s was a consequence of a long process of pre-colonial and colonial history when they were alienated from the local East African societies.

In the nineteenth century Britain used the concept of extraterritoriality to keep Asians under control. Today, when Britain no longer has pretensions to exercising extraterritorial powers, it is used to disclaim responsibility for them. For example, as a result of the 1968 Immigration Act, the British government has refused to accept Asian citizens to give an example:

The British Consul cannot interest himself officially in the case . . . because not having 'landed' in Germany, they are not formally within his 'parish'. The consul said, 'They are in the extraterritorial position, so I have not been to see them. But I would not go anyway, unless I was asked to, or if someone was ill.'

(O'Brien n.d.: 10)

The concept of extraterritoriality has come full circle. Yet both Britain and the Asians will find it difficult, if not impossible, to shed their nationality which was asserted and acquired through such a long, painful and tedious process. A dominant power might impose its will over a powerless minority, but the historical process, its Nemesis, will not allow it to shirk its obligations so easily.

I also came to realise the inadequacy of previous studies. These academic discourses had constructed an image of the East African Asian community within the narrow focus of their own disciplines and had tended to fragment its history. There was therefore a need to re-interpret (or re-construct) its past in a more holistic manner. This could be undertaken by trying to re-interpret its present position by analysing its past, focusing on disciplines like economic history, law (extraterritorial jurisdiction), and social and political analysis.

These were the issues raised for me by the East African Asians at the PhD level. Subsequently I was to take them up again to analyse the notion of how Europe constructs itself, and in particular how knowledge about Europe is constructed, and how outsiders and the 'other' are portrayed as not being civilised.

Experiencing London

Research for my dissertation had to be done in London where the archival materials were based. Yet again because there was no grant to carry out research, and no scholarship, study for the doctorate became more of a challenge. One had to find jobs, preferably part-time, and preferably in education. But the exclusions that I had felt in North America were compounded even further. The first problem was that foreign qualifications were not accepted or acceptable. Secondly, there was the issue of exclusion, racism, even in circles that were 'progressive'.

After interminably large numbers of applications, I was eventually able to get part-time jobs in London secondary schools, further education, adult education and then in community education. This provided me with a broad insight into the various levels of the education system. A main preoccupation was the ways in which the poorer and the black Britons did badly. It became clear that only a major shift of thinking, and of personnel and resources, could change the educational outcomes and learning capacities of the marginalised groups.

Rural England: The Village

Prolonged living in the city led to yearnings for the quiet and solitude of forest and rural life in Kenya. Over the years since the late 1960s I have had an opportunity to spend time in a friend's cottage in a Bedfordshire village.

The local landscape has changed as storms and Dutch Elm disease have knocked down trees, and the hedges have disappeared over the years because of changed farming methods. Changes in my own life brought about another set of associations with the place.

The village has changed since I first knew it in 1969, changes caused by the migration of young people, and increased traffic of vehicles and aircraft. The old farm workers have retired or died, the tenant farmer has retired and a new one has taken his place. As this old community disappears new faces, not only from the farming profession, appear. The Manor House is no longer a manor but an office for some business enterprise. The current blend of local residents and 'outside' interests makes for an uneasy mixture of old and new, tradition and its absence.

There are also social changes as generations move on and others move in. A lawyer takes over a derelict cottage and transforms it. He is open and friendly because we share experiences of the city and the countryside. A couple who stayed in the cottage in the intervening period and then moved up the road connect with me as a previous occupier of the cottage. So I have stories to tell about the place. Another family, who have now moved away from the village, turn up for tea unexpectedly. My presence is reassuring. Hence, those who belonged and then moved away to other parts of England are now getting a sense of reassurance from someone who was previously a non-belonger. So have I now become a belonger? And if so, what is it I belong to?

The notion of belonging to a place, a locality or a community, is a complex construction. One's own understanding of it may be valuable for, and be valued by, oneself. But it also has other layers consisting of gaps in understanding, and of rejecting and being rejected, which detract from its being a straightforward relationship. An urban person rejecting certain things in rural areas, and the rural communities rejecting the urban person or other outsider, add to the complexity of the situation. Yet shared feeling of belonging in cities and rural areas is borne out in the ways in which images of green and pleasant countrysides, with their villages and towns, are seen in essence as being part of the English national identity.

This imagery is evoked in films and literature, particularly in the pervasive cult of 'English heritage'. National Front politicians also use it. Enoch Powell's reference to an 'alien wedge' can only be seen as an intrusion into notions of Englishness which lead to a confrontation with the English yeomen. But as the uncertainties in the polity grow as a result of devolution, and the rural economy is decimated, the conurbations encroach and the rural becomes a haven for the upper middle classes, patriots and refuge seekers. The construction of this safe ruralism by those who are themselves thoroughly urban harks back to the purities and certainties of the past. The values of being English, like those of the German Volk, emanate from what is perceived as the close connection between blood and soil. Inevitably it must exclude 'the other'.

In Kenya the English sought to impose an imagined fragment of what they interpreted as their own rural life on the Kenyan countryside and to belong to it (just as it belonged to them). It was a haven where 'the other' was excluded. In England I found it was much the same. 'The other' tended to feel excluded in the English village. It was as if the overseas colonial relationship (a relationship which also prevailed in the countries of British settlement, Australia, New Zealand, South Africa) had been brought home as an internal colonial relationship. The English village too resonated as a haven constructed in an imagined, class-based and allegedly manorial mould.

As Alex Potts suggests, writing about nationalist ideology in the interwar period:

> A theory of racial identity was transferred to the inanimate landscape, a kind of reification in which the people still living and working in the countryside were assimilated, not just pictorially and aesthetically, but also ideologically to the landscape.
>
> (Potts 1989: 166)

As he sees it, the construction of this excluding and exclusive rurality detracts from the development of a viable and inclusive polity. This would see 'England as an epicentre of dynamic change rather than England as a refuge from the more violent and thrusting tendencies of the modern world' (ibid. 172). Instead, the trauma of the post-imperial, post-colonial period has led to a retreat into what are conceived as being rural 'organic communities' representing an ideal of wholeness, in itself an excluding concept. Hence, the rural domain is re-colonised to regain what the English mind thinks has vanished.

Hartmann presents this trend in a political context:

> Unfortunately, simplification and demagogic exploration make the appeal to the (lost) land and landed virtues, to native soil, *pays*, *patrie*, *Heimat*, *Heimatland*, a dangerous weapon of the revolutionary (i.e. counter revolutionary) Right.
>
> (Hartmann 1997: 184)

Belonging in England

While I think of the village and the rural area as an entity, the present village inhabitants look at me as a stranger, a non-belonging, non-comprehending intruder. Yet, I think back to how 'they' intruded into the contexts to which I virtually belonged, resulting in my being here in the first place. In their imaginations, that past which constitutes my past, and the past of imperialism and colonialism – and, did they but realise it, the colonial model that is replicated in the village – is absent. To make the new rooted in the rural, they need to create links with the stability and continuity of a presumed, coherent past. I represent an uncomfortable feature that disturbs such a posture.

Their posture derives from constructing a past to make the present more accepting of them, based on selective historical knowledge. In the rural context of England the country's past escapades, which relate to its complex imperial history, lose any immediacy or relevance. The pristine, innocent nature of the imagined countryside, disassociated with outside elements, makes it seem unrelated to the nation's complex entanglements. Hence, I am seen as someone who is an outsider and does not belong, precisely because my presence activates uncomfortable, best forgotten, constructions about a person who looks different. Many others would like to erase the memories of past dominations in faraway lands because they necessitate complex associations with 'the other'.

To establish cognition of me as a part of the village requires the villagers seeing neither themselves nor, more importantly, me fitting into stereotype categories. But then one realises that the discourses prevailing over the village for many life spans have not challenged the stereotype of 'the other'. The imperial and colonial past remains as a legacy based on the terms of an English-centred understanding. Yet suppose that I were to be recognised by the genuine locals, not to be seen or treated as 'The Same', but as an 'autonomous person who belongs' in the village. The question would then be whether such recognition detracts from their own sense of belonging and their notions of Englishness? Does an autonomous acceptance of 'the other' dilute that Englishness? Here too a very complex issue opens up because the question assumes that there is a singular, identifiable, notion of Englishness. Are there – even within the lives and lifetimes of this village – very distinct and multilayered identities? Can, for instance, the old English, or even the new English, become South Africans? Are those who are already there already South Africans?

This is an important issue. In Malaysia the Muslim Malay constructs himself as the Bhumaputra (son of the soil) while the Orang Asli linger on the margins unacknowledged. This, however, is just one example of long settled and so-called indigenous communities where privileging one's belongingness may lead to the ethnic cleansing of 'the other'. Are these certainties and purities of the past substantively correct – or are these imagined communities, purposively constructed, and based on narrowly imagined pasts? Does it provide them with greater certainty in a present which is seen as uncertain?

I am reminded of my father who, on his retirement from forestry and conservation in Kenya, returned to India to retire on an orchard he had planted. As a Sikh Punjabi, did he go to the Punjab to retire, and die among his Punjabi-speaking Sikh people? He did not, he retired in the small state of Rampur which was a heterogeneous community with Muslims, Sikhs and Hindus. What understandings did he have of himself, and of what constitutes a society?

There seems to be a danger of constructing a singular identity in England, as in other parts of the world. There are, however, people who can claim that they are distinct enough to be firmly located as pure communities. If there are fears in England of the English identity being swamped by a few million immigrants, there is something fundamentally wrong with constructing a notion of Englishness that is locatable, timeless and perhaps quaintly archaic. In fact, the vibrancy of Englishness has a greater chance of being dynamic if it is seen as being multilayered, vivacious and interactive. To turn oneself into a tweed-clad squire does not make the village more indigenous and English. Interactivity has perhaps more possibility of developing inclusive and rooted understandings of being English. Are there possibilities of developing dynamic values which enhance the belongingness of all within the village?

As the diversity in British society, initially based on the Scottish, Welsh, Irish and English nationhoods, is now enhanced by those who came from other countries, a new different paradigm is operationalised. As the colonies have disappeared, and the autonomous ex-colonial represents new realities, their contribution to the British polity is of a very complex nature. It represents, for instance, liberation and freedom from colonialism – for both the coloniser and the colonised.

The young black British of the new generation which is predominantly socialised in Britain are now losing the memory (or if born here never had the memory) of their country of origin and are perhaps more of the society where they have been socialised. They have complex – positive, negative and indifferent – readings of this polity. They cannot be converted back to subservient coolies, slaves or plantation workers, nor become squires – sahibs in brown skin.

But is there only one logical consequence of this – that the more British and comfortable a black feels in Britain, the more uncomfortable and out of place a white Briton becomes?

Perhaps the uncertainties presented by such a map of different British nationalities, of the complex reading of the past and present of the new British communities, represent the reasons for not understanding them in open terms. To develop an understanding requires a more rational mind, based on a more rational system. Yet, these islands have had an insecure elite which has not had the courage and openness to deal with these urgent and intractable matters. It has ignored the positive dimensions of such a challenge and, through a sleight of hand, the deep social changes and inequalities are reconstituted as belongingness to the market place.

The rural, shaken by the urban, and the sudden thrust of the market, cannot come to terms with the paradoxes. Perhaps because the dilemmas currently faced are so great, it is difficult to accept such an enormous amount of change in consciousness. The village sees itself disappearing, the change speeded up not only by the current elites, and manifested by the new owners of the Manor House, but by the disappearance of the village shop, school and parish priest. An institutional void has been created where comprehensible changes could have been understood and stabilities re-created.

Alternatively, is it possible that increasingly marginalised villagers can understand the process as a result of which another set of people – the black British, perhaps many of the Scottish, Welsh and Irish nationalities – are likewise marginalised? Is that a matter of politics and/or education?

While they may have become marginalised, their consciousness and notions of autonomy are not totally erased. The slaves, the indentured and the unemployed did not all lose a sense of who, where and what they were. A more constructive rather than a reactive stance remains a possibility. Strident attempts to devoice and silence cannot be synonymous with total voicelessness. Total voicelessness would entail an assumption by the state of total submission of all, and the silencing of all resistance and rebellion.

The lack of voice also entails lack of visibility. It is the feeling I have had of being seen, but ignored and dismissed. By ignoring and dismissing my present my past is erased. Not only do I become voiceless but invisible.

Were the villager and I to get together and weave a more authentic tapestry of our complex present, it might resonate with the more vibrant dimensions of both our pasts, to reactivate the values and histories of the locality and the community. Juxtaposing local pasts with those of 'the other' does not of necessity invalidate either, or make them lose their meaning. It may provide new meanings which have, because of the interactive present, possibilities of a more relevant and meaningful future.

To make 'the other' local is not to lose the local – it is to take off the tinted glasses and have slightly clearer lenses to see who and where one is at present. This mutual recognition does not have the negative connotations of 'being assimilated'. It is a much more substantive engagement to develop a newer language of which both are part, to broaden the horizons of the local by empowering it, and by setting out a new agenda of what are the historical memories of those involved in this process. To stretch the imagination and accept that not only is the multicultural present based on the playing of a complex multicultural past within us, but that we are by definition part of a multicultural future.

But where is this multicultural future to be defined? Today the country seems even more specifically an England than it did, but an England that needs definition. The exclusivities and racisms may continue, or even become sharpened, but the underlying rationale and substantive ground is shifting. With devolution, and democratic divorces and muted mutual antipathies between the English, Welsh and Scots, the English must now find new ways of replacing the previous exclusivities of the English nation. But this will mean re-thinking how to re-create a more mature and broader sense of nationhood which looks beyond the St George's flag.

The changing new English nation must learn to derive political legitimacy not from the received wisdom of the dominant nation, but from popular and democratic sovereignty. And here the role of education in consolidating a democratic English state cannot be overestimated. The new political integration has to build on inclusive understandings to establish a political integration which is based on a citizenship which includes religious, cultural and ethnic bonds. It must also mean that the English working class and the English poor do not get left out. Otherwise 'the long night of the crisis of English national identity' (Rattansi 2000: 26) will only breed a culture of resentment and anger.

Local custom, practices and ways of life are one dimension in which community functions. They are subject to legal norms which are operative in society. In democratic and constitutional states the issue of legal belongingness also pertains to rights of citizens which do not define issues for rural or urban communities or areas separately. The combination of levels of belongingness also presents challenges to the education system to develop local and relevant curricula and teaching that is inclusive and fosters social peace and cohesion and is governed by constitutional principles at the national level, which pertain to all those who live in localities and society.

FURTHER READING

Loita Nehru (1989) *Origins of the Gandharan Style: A Study of Contributory Influences*, Delhi: Oxford University Press.

Madeleine Hallade (1968) *The Gandhara Style and the Evolution of Buddhist Art*, London: Thames and Hudson.

Dharam Ghai (ed) (1965) *Portrait of a Minority: Asians in East Africa*, Nairobi: Oxford University Press.

Gabriel A. Almond and James S. Coleman (1960) *The Politics of the Developing Areas*, Princeton: Princeton University Press.

David Steel (1969) *No Entry: The Background and Implications of the Commonwealth Immigrants Act, 1968*, London: Hurst & Co.

Jagdish S. Gundara (1993) British Extraterritorial Jurisdiction, Imperial Enterprise and Indians in Nineteenth Century Zanzibar, in Israel, Milton and Wagle, N. K. *Ethnicity, Identity, Migration: The South Asian Context*, Toronto: Centre for South Asian Studies.

1

Multicultural Britain

STATE AND SOCIETY

In this chapter I present multiculturalism differently from how it is commonly presented. I argue that British society has historically always been multicultural, and show how the descriptive and taxonomic features of societal diversity are persistently camouflaged by the hegemonic state. Nevertheless, devolution within Britain to the Scottish and Welsh nations and the constitutional arrangements in Northern Ireland are now visible as strong markers of the fundamental historical features of the multiculturality of British society.

The immigrant presence merely highlights aspects of the historical diversity and has itself a historical dimension. So, despite attempts during the contemporary period to 'otherise' Blacks and Asians and construct them as aliens, they remain an integral part of Britain's diverse society. The Black and Asian communities have now become rooted, and are demonstrating, women as well as men, their own complex patterns of rooting — patterns which include resistance to racism and marginalisation. The young Black generations born and socialised in Britain are creating their own syncretic and multiple cultures, politicised cultures that give them a measure of autonomy, and are contributions to national culture, making British society more complex and vibrant, despite the lack of official recognition.

Multiculturalism, therefore, has not weakened but strengthened the cultural life of Britain. The issues it raises are not issues of political correctness, but of recognising that the inherent divisions within Britain enrich national culture and should not be marginalised.

A Multicultural Approach

If we are going to use the terms 'multicultural', 'multiracial', 'multiethnic' we must begin by deconstructing the nature and relationship of the cultures of the British Isles and the concept of the British nation/nationality. The very use of the terms Briton, Britain, British is liable to raise confusion, since to many English people English/British, England/Britain are synonymous – something many Scots, Welsh, Asian and other British nationals find misleading.

Moreover the customary ascription of the label 'ethnic' to some, but not all, of these differing groups not only problematises those so labelled but implies that the recipient majority are themselves not 'ethnic'. 'Ethnicity', however, is something shared by all humans.

Like the other European societies, British society has been, and continues to be, historically diverse – diverse in terms of language, religion, territoriality, class and 'race'. In linguistic terms, Britain has a very long history of a variety of languages and dialects. The Celtic, Icelandic, German, French and Flemish languages provide a basis of language development in Britain. Although English is the official language of Britain, the Gaelic and Welsh languages are still used. The contemporary use of African, Asian and Caribbean languages merely enhances the already existing multilingual nature of British society. In religious terms Britain has had a long experience of a multifaith past, as evidenced by the pagan, Roman Catholic, Anglican, Presbyterian, Methodist, Baptist, Congregationalist, Fundamentalist and Jewish faiths. The contemporary presence of Muslims, Sikhs, Hindus and Rastafarians simply extends this diversity. Scotland and Wales are now recognised as nations within the British nation. Regional loyalties (Yorkshire and Lancashire) are further evidence of the territorially based diversities within Britain. Similarly class divisions are part and parcel of the fabric of Britain. The social hierarchies and issues of domination and subordination are not new phenomena.

Racism and xenophobia in Britain have had numerous manifestations, as evidenced in the treatment of Jews, Celts and Roma (under their pejorative name of Gypsies). The colonial and imperial past has led to the presence of people from the ex-colonies in the British Isles, and because they are seen to be visibly different in terms of colour they are exposed to the racism they were subjected to in the colonies.

The Hegemonic State

Most, if not all, nation states are differentiated polyethnic states using a variety of mechanisms to maintain their social and economic differentiation, usually presented with an accompanying rhetoric emphasising social cohesion. Such stratification has operationalising criteria attached to it in addition to those of class/status and gender, because of the way the modern nation state is structurally and ideologically constructed. It is not surprising that the modern state is based on a fallacious ideal-typical model of a small-scale society. This is because the modern unitary nation state disguises its predatory origins by attempting to demonstrate a hegemonic unity in terms of its citizens' allegiances and affiliations.

Such a unity is, in fact, a codification of the dominant groups' social and economic arrangements, a legitimation of an unequal set of socio-economic arrangements. Thus the model that has emerged through this process asserts that access to membership of the nation requires (1) the capacity to operate within certain linguistic parameters and (2) acceptance of notions of a common history, religion and other socio-cultural factors.

Failing to operate within these parameters, or unwillingness to
makes the individuals likely to be regarded as outsiders by the n
more pejoratively, as 'alien'. Within this model, members of a nation state should
share one or more of the following characteristics – a common language, history
and economic arrangements, a common set of cultural practices and aesthetic
preferences, and if religion is present, a religion accepted, if not believed in, by all.

Groups that fail to meet these criteria are seen as 'the other' or 'alien' to the
nation. By definition they lack cohesive capacity or positive identity and are seen
as a divisive element within the nation. Consequently they tend to be located at
the periphery of the nation, not accepted, but tolerated, to a degree that depends
on the economic and socio-political needs of the dominant groups. These groups
see themselves as the legitimately constituted nation, and use the 'others' as a
means of maintaining this ideological fiction. Thus many ethnic and racial
minorities are positioned at the periphery of the nation in cultural, political and
economic, as well as spatial, terms.

A Plural Britain

One has only to walk through the streets of London to be reminded of the contribution made to all aspects of its life by immigrant communities, still manifested in architecture and street names. The history of the Jama Masjid mosque
at the corner of Fournier Street and Brick Lane, Spitalfields, illustrates dramatically the successive communities who have made their homes there. It
started life in 1744 as a Huguenot Church; fifty years later it was a Wesleyan
Chapel. Then in 1898 it became the Spitalfields Great Synagogue until 1975
when it was sold to the East End Bengali community as a mosque.

Given this long history of immigration it is no surprise to find that dominant
group hegemony is not a contemporary construction, activated at the end of
World War II when large-scale immigration from the Caribbean and Asia began.
Its pedigree takes it back to the early development of the British nation.

The nation state in Britain has not only had to mask the pluralism in British
society based on language, religion, social class and territorially based nationalities. It has also had to confront the divisive threats which emerged from capitalist industrialisation. As the nineteenth century advanced, the ruling class
which controlled the state, and recognised the importance of the state in preserving its own interests, felt that if capitalism were to survive, action had to
be taken to mitigate some of the harsher features of the new industrial system.
The fear of disruption of the state by trade unions and workers' movements led
to the rise of state-directed 'positive' liberalism, and to the decline of laissez-
faire or 'negative' liberalism.

Simultaneously the rise of nationalism in Britain and in Europe demanded
that subordinated groups be moulded by means of economic and educational
policies into a seemingly coherent whole. The notion that these nation states
were homogeneous and cohesive rested on falsely constructed imaginations of
national identities. The 'nation building' of the nineteenth century excluded fun-

damental questions of diversity – interests of class, language, religion and those of territorially based national minorities – and camouflaged them within the framework of the unitary nation.

'Nation building' bred its cultures of resistance among those who felt their identity threatened, cultures of resistance which, instead of replicating the stereotypical notions of 'ethnicity', created their own new dimensions. Paul Gilroy has documented the present-day cultural, particularly the musical, features of the Black culture of resistance in this country, features to which we shall return (Gilroy 1987). It has its equivalent in the Celtic response to English authority in the nineteenth century where the new 'Celtic culture' had little to do with its ancient counterpart but was a culture of resistance in response to a situation which may well be described as colonial.

The Celts had to face sharing with the other colonised peoples the label 'inadequate' or 'barbarians' – and their internalisation of this message made them easier to govern. Subordinated cultures were suppressed in Wales as in India. Political, economic and cultural dependence created by the dominant power had adverse effects on most aspects of life. Vast numbers were compelled to migrate from the Celtic regions.

But if the unification of the British Isles represented a loss of Celtic sovereignty, the Celts were incorporated into what, with their participation, now became a 'British' Empire, part of an advanced European society, and benefited from the development of the industrial state, as well as the overseas Empire. Not only did these Scottish or Welsh national groups benefit from trade, and employment (civil and military), but imperialism served indirectly to expiate some of the inferiority associated with peripheral social origins. From being disadvantaged groups within Britain, they were able to leave their victim status to become part of a conquering group themselves. Hence, the Celtic regions of the British sovereign state contributed to oppress the Black Britons of the empire at the receiving end of imperial exploitation. For their part the English persistently went on using the terms English/British and England/Britain interchangeably, as if still writing off the non-English as 'outsiders'.

Nevertheless, even after the devolution of 1999, the Welsh and Scots are still felt to be a part of a British society from which the immigrants from the former empire are excluded. In a historical framework the cultural traditions of those who were previously part of Britain's imperial colonies differed from those who were national minorities within the British state. The imperial colonial empire broke up with the pressure of nationalism. As a result, these communities brought to the British body politic a distinct historical experience and memory. They experienced not only the notions of the cultural superiority of the dominant group, but also the coercive apparatus which held imperial structures together. Yet, having observed their culture being treated as an inferior phenomenon in the imperial context, they saw it subsequently validated with the rise of the new national identities when imperial rule broke down.

If, as it is increasingly realised today, the Third World countries should ques-

tion their own processes of national unification to ensure that they do not construct national entities and identities based on the dominance of particular
groups, then these same type of questions ought to be directed at Britain and
the other states of Europe. When people see their traditions, religious beliefs
and social arrangements change or crumble, it is important for them to try and
isolate where such changes may be coming from. They may feel that the movement of other peoples of non-European origins may be the cause of the crises
in their societies. Yet the real reasons lie within the body politic – the corporate onslaught on society by continuous innovations which the states are not
able to understand, ascertain, absorb or challenge because of the need to preserve the stability of vested interests.

It is not the rule but the exception (if indeed there are any exceptions) for
nations to emerge united as one people on the basis of religion, language and
race. While one group may have dominated the core of many societies, others
have become peripheralised. And though many metropolitan societies possess
constitutionally safeguarded, politically democratic, frameworks, there may
nevertheless be fundamental denials of economic, social, linguistic, religious and
legal rights. Peripheral groups which are minorities in numerical terms do not
have the wherewithal to bring about a reallocation of political-economic power
in their favour. Hence they can remain un- or under-represented in the political
economy of the nation.

A dominant-subordinate situation may lead to the assimilation of a subordinated group. And if the relations are more or less based on equality there may
be interaction between them and, through the process of diffusion, the development of a new syncretic culture. But though in Britain, even between England
and Scotland and Wales, there is a legal British nationality, in terms of the
citizenry, society remains segmentedly plural.

The development of mediating groups within the various peripheries may at
first slow down the process of providing greater equality and justice, but may
in its wake lead to a more assertive leadership, calling for greater equality and
justice, even secession. Indeed such peripheralised communities may come to feel
themselves besieged, and develop their own urban culture of resistance.
Subsequent actions would depend on the political understanding of the leadership. There may also be differing responses from the different peripheral groups
themselves, given their different situations – as between minorities in the territorial periphery, and those peripheralised within the cities or rural areas of the
nation's core. The interactions in schools, churches, temples, workplaces and
clubs are bound to determine the manner in which the struggles are determined,
and the way in which they are either collectivised or conducted separately.
Minorities in predominantly minority areas may see their struggle separately
from those in majority areas. And Muslims and other religious groups may articulate a religious identity to distinguish themselves from an oppressive and un-
responsive core.

The dominant and subordinate hegemonic relationships require a broader analytical framework and formulation to include the subordinated nationalities in Britain. Plainly it will not do to present core and periphery as antithetical structures. The apparently solid British core is itself diverse and contains fragments revealing a Britain that is not 'nationally integrated' but is a plural society. This any serious intercultural approach must realise. Thus, when it is asserted that over recent decades, 'our society has become multicultural' (Department of Education and Science 1977, 1981), the question that needs to be asked is, 'What was it before'?

'Excluded' Britons

The fundamental issue is whether a nation state is so structured that it denies citizenship rights and justice to its citizens. So long as there are large groups of people in Britain who are considered to be minorities and feel that, despite the democratic framework, they are disenfranchised, one must question the stability of the British state. Women, first and foremost, who constitute at least half the population and are in no sense a minority, are amongst them. So are large numbers of working class and, increasingly, unemployed people.

With devolution, the identity of the Scots and Welsh has now been politically recognised by the British state. But there are still linguistic and religious minorities who feel that their interests are ignored. These and other alienated or disenfranchised groups are in a position to form alliances to represent their common interests. The growth and development of such alliances and common interests could create powerful forces which could lead to destabilisation of the state.

Moreover, as well as those who feel excluded, there are individuals who withdraw, or are withdrawn, from society. These include the alienated victims of technological innovation or family break-up, those unable to comprehend the workings of the social system, those who 'opt out' and live in communes and lead alternative life styles, those driven by lack of housing and welfare provision to live in the streets, all those driven down by poverty into an underclass where they exist on the margins of society.

We must not assume that because the political institutions are stable, and backed by effective law enforcement, withdrawal from or challenge to the established order should be seen as marginal, as representing only a minority. Here we see gender and class differences which, added together, cannot be considered to be those of a minority, and large numbers of people and groups who feel that the state is denying them entitlements.

This pervasive discrimination against the poor, against women, against those speaking languages different from the dominant language, and against those marginalised on grounds of race or religion, denies their diminished 'assets', their cultural capital, the possibility of competing on fair and equal grounds to attain not only an equality of opportunity, but also an equality of outcomes. Multiple disadvantage prevents them from competing within the political and economic frameworks of society.

The 'Iceberg' Syndrome

The problem of racism is a major issue. Its institutional and structural features can only be resolved by engaging the larger society on this one issue, rather than primarily the minority groups who are the 'recipients' of this racism. There is a dangerous lack of concern about this social malaise, compounded by a tendency to scapegoat the visibly different and powerless. Salman Rushdie has maintained that the crisis is not simply economic or political. 'It is a crisis of the whole culture, of the society's entire sense of itself. And racism is the most clearly visible part of the crisis, the tip of the kind of icebergs that sinks ships' (Rushdie 1982: 417).

As Britain moves away from its colonial past to the point where the younger generation of Britons do not see the colonial legacy vividly, or at all, it is crucial that the issue of racism is contextualised from within the British frame of reference. For one persistent force in British history has been the state's categorising people on the basis of 'race'.

Historically it has been used to exclude large groups of people – Celts, Jews, Blacks, Roma – from the British historical past and contemporary life. Hence the masquerade of using it as the only significant marker of divergence in British society. As just indicated, the realities of diversity are of a very different order. Yet the state finds 'race' an overwhelmingly powerful category because of the way it has permeated the consciousness of all peoples at all social levels. Its use to identify scapegoats for all social ills at times of crisis is a pervasive historical force. Now increasingly conflated with anti-Islamic feelings a new enemy is in the process of being constructed to replace communism now seen as dead.

At the same time, those who articulated the anti-racist struggles and movements within Britain in the 1980s did not take cognisance of the broad historical, socio-political and national contexts and structures within these struggles and allowed anti-racism to develop. Anti-racism, with its privileged Black voices, tended to marginalise and peripheralise the movement, because of the way in which it constructed whites and Blacks as holistic groups – accepting the construction created originally by white racists.

THE NEW IMMIGRANT COMMUNITIES

Immigrant Status

The Nationality Act of 1948 created the status of 'Citizen of the United Kingdom and the Colonies'. However, the status thus acquired was undermined by subsequent immigration legislation which gradually restricted immigrants' right to settle in Britain. The 1962 Commonwealth Immigration Act started this process by requiring employment vouchers from the Ministry of Labour to enter the country. The 1968 Immigration Act denied British nationals of East African Asian origin the right to enter and settle in Britain. The 'patriality' clause of the 1971 Immigration Act, allowing entry to those who had had a British grandfather (a clause designed to allow in white citizens of the former Empire), widened the racial grounds on which citizenship rights became increasingly restricted. The 1981 British Nationality Act introduced the concept of *jus sanguinis* (law of blood), and undermined for the first time in British immigration history the *jus soli* (law of the soil, i.e. place of birth) principle. The legislation from 1962 to 1981 ended primary immigration – but paradoxically did not lead to integration, as politicians had asserted.

By 1979 immigrants from the ex-colonies numbered about two million and constituted 3.7 per cent of the total population. The 1991 census showed that they constituted 5.5 per cent of the population. They settled in large urban clusters rather than dispersed in conurbations across the country, with large settlements of all groups in the southeast, particularly the Greater London area.

Politicians have, however, argued that there were high levels of Black immigration, most notably Margaret Thatcher in her 'Swamping' speech of January 1978. Moreover the existence of racism at all levels of society has meant that the positive effects of the 1976 Race Relations Act and the actions of the Commission for Racial Equality have been minimised.

Over the last twenty years the level of debate, discourse, policy and action to tackle racism has been considerably undermined. Those who have worked assiduously towards greater levels of equality have been marginalised or dispensed with. This type of undermining has happened systematically at the national and local state level. The expertise acquired by local government through their various initiatives, including their mistakes, has been lost to the current practitioners.

In the last two decades, qualitatively and quantitatively, the means for dealing with racism have diminished. The Commission for Racial Equality (CRE) and the local Race Equality Councils operate with reduced resources and personnel. Within the European Union Britain had been developing a critical edge to its expertise in public and social policy fields. This is now lost. The CRE maintains its national overview, and through its overworked staff maintains contact with flashpoints in the country, but it requires increased powers to ensure equity in all levels of the state, including powerful public and private institutions which continue to discriminate. The Institute of Race Relations does, however, still continue to provide a radical voice.

The radical right obviously did an enormous amount of damage over these years. But restoring the damage does not receive political priority. Most politicians do not regard it as a vote-winning issue. The real challenge at the political level remains how to articulate an anti-racist agenda which is not viewed as a minority field but is realised to have implications for the whole British body politic.

'Black' Immigration

Confusion has been spread and maintained by the way British usage has conflated differences of origin and nationality, drawing on the vocabulary of racism. Those of Indian, Pakistani, Bangladeshi or Sri Lankan origin are subsumed under the category 'Asian' – which excludes Chinese, Japanese and Vietnamese. Those of African or Afro-Caribbean origin are categorised as 'Black'. But at the level of political articulation of struggles against racism the term 'Black' has come to include both. In popular English speech it may refer to either, a usage some Asians deeply resent.

The Black presence in Britain dates back to the Roman-British period, witnessed by Latin texts and archaeological evidence. Emperor Septimus Severus (born in North Africa, died in York) visited Hadrian's wall in AD 200 and saw African troops based there. It is an interesting irony that there were Africans living in Britain centuries before the English invaders arrived from Europe. There are references to Africans (called 'blue men') in the Icelandic sagas, and once Europeans had made contact with Africa in the fifteenth century, they found their way to Europe, many as slaves.

With the development of a slave economy in the Caribbean, slaves were regularly brought or sent to Britain by their owners. Recent research estimates that by the turn of the eighteenth/nineteenth centuries there were about 5,000 in London and another 5,000 in other parts of the country (Myers 1996). Their numbers declined during the nineteenth century but there were always marginalised Black communities, chiefly in London and the seaport cities, and a few who were able to advance themselves to middle-class status (Fryer 1984; Green 1988; Visram forthcoming).

The Afro-Caribbean Community

The post World War II Black population in Britain is largely a result of the decolonisation of the British Empire and the demand for unskilled labour in postwar Britain. Large-scale immigration from the Caribbean began in 1948, offering men and women opportunities of steady employment unavailable at home. Welcomed as a labour force they met social hostility and ostracism and were forced to live in run-down housing in deprived inner city areas. Nevertheless many brought their families over and settled down in their own neighbourhoods, forming self-contained communities in conditions of social deprivation. Though the massive re-housing schemes of the 1960s gave them better living conditions, they tended to be housed in the less-favoured locations where it was difficult for more than a minority to give their children the educational advantages that would enable them to rise socially.

Their white neighbours tended to remain hostile, and in 1958 and 1959 Blacks were viciously attacked by gangs in Nottingham and in Notting Hill, London, where one was killed. Feeling against them was inflamed by Enoch Powell's notorious 1968 speech with its reference to the 'River Tiber flowing with much blood' which set off public demonstrations demanding they be deported to the Caribbean. Grudgingly, however, the white public came eventually to realise that their presence in Britain had to be accepted. But they remained the victims of police and local government harassment, and as the national economy slowed down many lost their jobs and found themselves unemployed.

The younger generation felt increasingly embittered at the lack of recognition and opportunities. There were severe outbreaks of frustrated Black violence in Brixton in 1981 (followed by the Scarman Inquiry and Report), and again in Handsworth, Birmingham, in 1985. Their indignation was particularly inflamed against the police which persistently victimised them, notably in 1981 when the police authority refused to investigate a fire in Deptford, London, in which thirteen young Black people lost their lives in what was plainly a racist attack. In 1998 the police were accused of institutional racism in the Macpherson Report, because of the way the murder of Stephen Lawrence was investigated. The inquiry gives force to the issue of institutional racism, with major implications for all areas of public and social policy in Britain.

What the white British public particularly came to recognise was the cultural contribution the Afro-Caribbean community was making. The annual Notting Hill Carnival, despite initial police harassment, developed into one of the great cultural displays and tourist attractions in the country. Some individuals achieved national esteem in the fields of sport and entertainment – the fields traditionally opened to African Americans in the days of official discrimination against them. And some of those who entered the professions eventually achieved eminence in their fields. Some were elevated to the House of Lords. Thus gradually, after some fifty years, they are largely seen to be and have become an accepted part of British society.

The Caribbean-origin population of African descent has been joined of recent years by a growing African immigrant population, chiefly those disillusioned by prospects in the newly independent states of Africa, or refugees from political persecution. Many have skills or professional qualifications and middle-class lifestyles. Their children, if born in this country, are entitled to British citizenship and many now identify with Britain rather than with their parents' African homelands.

The Asian Community

The economic boom in the 1960s brought an even greater demand for labour. The partition of India in 1947 led to the displacement of millions of people, particularly in the Punjab and Bengal, and large numbers of Indians and Pakistanis, Muslims, Hindus and Sikhs, from these regions emigrated to Britain to work, soon followed by wives and children. Once established as family groups they moved out from rented accommodation and purchased homes of their own to facilitate a family life, settling in inner city areas where housing was cheaper, and founding their own places of worship.

Most were members of the working class and peasantry who came from rural areas. In Britain some remained part of the working class communities, albeit becoming more skilled. Others became small traders and shopkeepers. Some, building on British imperial memories of the Indian cuisine, opened restaurants. Those who came as professionals, or were educated in Britain, entered the professions. And some flourished as entrepreneurial businessmen, some of them becoming millionaires with global interests.

From the mid-1960s Asians from East Africa, many of them British subjects, finding themselves displaced from their employment or opportunities by the Africanisation policies of the new governments, began settling in Britain, usually in family units. Their numbers were dramatically swelled in 1972 when President Idi Amin expelled them all from Uganda. Those who were able to use the cultural capital of their links with Britain could establish themselves as functioning members of society within a very short time without becoming a social burden on the British state. Instead of settling in the inner cities, they concentrated on the East Midlands and Greater London, establishing themselves in newer areas or creating their own communities.

The Asians, unlike Jews or Turks, face the particular aversion in British society to diversity of physical appearance. Those concentrated in inner city residential areas have their mosques, temples and Gurdwaras as well as their own shops and cinemas, to provide a social community focus. To resist discrimination, and insulate themselves, they maintain a strong sense of family, which helps to keep away unnecessary intrusions by the social services. Similarly house ownership protects them from discrimination by landlords. Such insular communities tend inevitably to adopt a 'siege mentality' against the perceived and actual hostilities which emanate from the dominant communities. The strengthening of traditional or patriarchal values may also help to strengthen their resistance, as well as inhibiting any dynamic interaction with neighbouring English communities. It may lead to demands for separate schools, invoking what has been called 'the politics of recognition' (Taylor 1992).

Though young and old stand together against racism, those born or socialised in Britain may have very different perceptions and experiences from their elders. The younger generation, particularly young women, may have strong views on issues of patriarchy, separate schools and rigid belief systems. Asian women have demonstrated by militant action in the workplace that they cannot be stereotyped as a supposedly traditional and passive section of the community. The strikes at Mansfield Hosiery, Loughborough (1972), Imperial Typewriters, Leicester (1974), Grunwick Film Processing, London (1976), Chix, Slough (1980) and Hillingdon Hospital (1995–98) were mainly based on the resistance of women. The supposed generation gap between the older and the younger women whether from the Indian sub-continent or from East Africa proved irrelevant in the context of their larger unity. This struggle at the workplace was not sustained by sympathetic white co-workers but by the support accorded by the home and the community (Gundara 1982: 54).

Moreover there is no unity over national and religious issues. Bangladeshis and Pakistanis are not necessarily united by their common Islamic faith – though all were able to unite over the Salman Rushdie affair, which gave the Muslim community, most notably in Bradford, the dynamic militancy and self-confidence that it had lacked. The Sikhs too are divided politically.

Yet the Asian communities tend to be perceived from outside as one group, and interpreted by simplistic, often xenophobic, stereotyping. It is, for instance, widely assumed that Asians have a high reproduction rate. In fact the numbers of births remain constant, and women's fertility has fallen. Thus whatever their social status, they remain marginalised with incalculable consequences for British society and the nation state.

The Chinese Community

Few Chinese found their way to Britain before the twentieth century. The 1851 census records seventy-eight. By 1931 there were about 2,000, chiefly employed in Chinese laundries, but they were put out of business by the large steam laundries and launderettes and the community faded away. Then in the 1950s British people, freed from rationing and wartime recipes, developed an appetite for exotic food. In 1951 there were thirty-six Chinese restaurants in Britain, by 1967 more than a thousand. Chinese men came in from the rural hinterland of Hong Kong to staff them.

Originally they arrived as sojourners, without their families, sending back remittances, and hoping to return home eventually. But, by a strange irony, the Commonwealth Immigration Act of 1962, which limited the numbers of Commonwealth immigrants, and was designed as a brake on immigration, inadvertently turned them from sojourners into settlers. For as the demand for restaurant labour soared and single men could no longer be recruited, wives and other dependants came instead, creating for the first time a permanent Chinese community.

It remains concentrated in catering, which is estimated to absorb 70–90 per cent of the population. They live in isolated family groups, working in restaurants scattered over the country. Their long working routines restrict their social life. Many, particularly the women, can scarcely speak English. Socially they are the most marginalised of the immigrant communities. Only with the growing into adulthood of a British-educated younger generation are they becoming less isolated.

BLACK YOUTH

Constructions of Black Youth

In the past two decades there have been dramatic changes in British society, particularly in relation to the economic and social systems. There have been high levels of unemployment in general, but particularly amongst the Black community and more particularly the Black youth. This economic insecurity has influenced their attitudes not only to life, but to the society they live in and the diminution of their life chances. Michael Rutter suggests that amongst the youth in general: 'economic loss has been associated with entrance to deviant subcultures during adolescence' (Rutter and Smith 1995: 16).

There are particular problems associated with minority cultures, particularly with the Black community. Black adolescents are extremely sensitive to evaluation by the majority culture, and to how their cultural background is represented.

When their culture is represented in the mainstream of society there is a greater level of security and belongingness. But as they mature cognitively, and realise that their culture is not evaluated positively by the majority culture, it leads to greater feelings of marginalisation.

Their schooling only tends to reinforce this feeling. At school they may have to face verbal and physical abuse from students from other communities. They may even receive them from their teachers. Hence for many of them schooling is a continual fight against innumerable acts of discrimination. For while they feel the pressures of their families and communities to adhere to their 'ethnic' cultures, teachers and peer pressures propel them away from their cultures of origin.

Young Black women are especially vulnerable to pressure, particularly from their parents, to conform to social and cultural patterns. The older generation are still generally from abroad but as primary immigration has closed, a much larger number are born in this country. This leads to complex realities for young people, the types and levels of pressures depending on their social class and types of family structure. It would seem that multigenerational families may not only be stronger but, if they are supportive, they can mediate the influences of media, school and peer group to conform. Given the high levels of Black youth unemployment, familial and cultural dimensions can become protective.

But if they are not supported, young people may doubt their own competences and may have a lower self image during the difficult period of adolescence. In single parent or nuclear families there are chances of stronger peer group relationships and of youth culture, because parents have reduced opportunities to monitor the preoccupations of adolescents. Moreover the levels of insecurity brought by immigration restrictions have impeded family unification, while rapid social change, low levels of social security and bad housing have led to insecurities and behavioural problems.

Secure young Blacks mature fast and can provide their parents, if they are not literate or speakers of English, with contacts and insights into the outside world. But lack of employment opportunities can mean that, while still remaining dependent on their parents, they retain a measure of autonomy and links with their own age group, which leads to strengthening aspects of youth culture. There is probably a lengthening of this youth phase for a larger number of young people, except for Asian girls who tend to get married off younger in certain sections of the community. Nevertheless there is a growing level of friendships, relationships and marriages across cultures. These powerful bonds obviate the influences of the older generation and parents on the lives of the younger generation, born, or else largely socialised, in Britain.

The lack of familial, parental, social and community control or cohesiveness not only contributes towards stronger youth cultures, but also to greater levels of illegal, criminal and resistance cultures – although there is no clear evidence that youth culture or changes in usual sequences of life events in the adolescent period are among the causes of the rise in crime (Rutter and Smith 1995: 480)

There is, however, a clear division between the older and younger generation.

There is, for instance, less religiosity amongst young people, which makes for a parting of the ways between generations. This raises the issue of different value systems between the parents and the younger generation. However, these values may vary among different sections of young Blacks. Not all are positioned in the ghetto and in the underclass. Those located in other social strata have different social realities. To use the North American equivalent, the 'downtown youth' have lower social positions and life chances from those of the 'uptown youth' who have higher social status and different educational outcomes. The disjunction between family, community, school and workplace is greater for downtown youth.

J. T. Gibbs described African American youth as an endangered species because of its 'high rates of social and behavioural problems, welfare dependent families and crime ridden communities'. Can one say that Black British youth are likewise an endangered species? Some of the experiences of African American youth apply to them as well. As Gibbs continues, 'they have been miseducated by the educational system, mishandled by the criminal justice system, mislabelled by the mental health system and mistreated by the social welfare system' (Gibbs 1991: 73).

Secondary school expulsions and drop-out rates are higher among young Afro-Caribbean Blacks than among other groups. They have significantly higher unemployment rates, particularly in the conurbations; higher levels of juvenile arrests; higher usage, sale and distribution of drugs – which are associated with the higher drop-out rates in school and unemployment; higher unwed teenage pregnancy rates; higher rates of homicide; and a range of physical and mental health problems. While there are qualitative differences between the situations of Black American and Black British youth, some of the above do apply in both contexts, particularly for those whose cultural base has been historically demeaned because of slavery. In both contexts, inner city manufacturing jobs have disappeared, and lower levels of educational performance have prevented them from taking up the highly skilled jobs in the high tech industries.

Young Black Women

The position of young Black women differs in the different communities. While matriarchal systems may have powerful resources within the Caribbean community, amongst the Asians it is patriarchal influences which attempt to keep them separate. Young Muslim women particularly tend to be more subject to patriarchal control than Hindus and Sikhs. The patriarchal notion of family honour (*izzat*) has strong sanctions on young Asian women generally, and has denied some of them career opportunities outside the home. It is also manifested by aggressive young Muslim males, who brutalise Muslim women who go out without scarves or in short skirts, or have left their homes to live on their own. And young women may be forced into marriage with unwanted partners, and threatened with not only family but community reprisals if they try to escape.

In both cases, Black and Asian, they may face parental sanctions against relationships with males and thus create tensions with the older generation. Severe sanctions may be used in the event of a pregnancy, and shame on the family leads to young single mothers leaving home. The shortage of sheltered homes, and the lack of kinship support systems, presents them with further misery. Many young Blacks, understanding these problems, have opted for careers to insulate themselves.

Despite evidence that young Black and Asian women do better in school than young men from their respective communities, they are still not able to obtain appropriate vocations and employment. Mirza points to a strong sense of agency among those with high aspirations. But despite their attempts to obtain jobs in social class 1 and 2, she found they were only successful in obtaining jobs in social and welfare 'caring' fields. They nevertheless fared better than young Black males (Mirza 1992: 189–94).

Schemes to get unemployed young people into employment lack the capacity to provide skills which actually lead to employment. Nor have they had the links with employers to ensure employment after training. Hence they are not seen as critical to improving their life chances. As Brah writes about young Asians:

> They question, resist, challenge and repudiate the social and cultural mechanisms which underpin their subordination. Their political consciousness is marked by their first-hand experience of the processes of exclusion/inferiorization, and their responses are embedded within ideologies developed and elaborated in dialogue with a variety of political discourses, with Asian peer groups and increasingly in discourse with young Afro-Caribbean blacks and anti-racist young whites
>
> (Brah 1996: 65–66)

The Family

The strength of peer group relationships and youth culture is contingent on the type and strength of families. They are weaker where family structures are strong, stronger in lone parent or stepfamilies. Hence, as families in the Black communities reconstitute, as do families from the dominant communities, in a climate of high unemployment, the transition to adult life, what Bob Coles has called the 'staged progressions' from childhood to adulthood, may be shortened. It may be shortened by leaving the school or families at short notice, which can lead to serious consequences to themselves. As he writes:

> There were differences between different ethnic groups in terms of the amount of control of behaviour and the areas where control was most likely to be exercised. Asian families proved to be more strict and especially so with regard to smoking, drinking alcohol and going out.
>
> (Coles 1995: 89, 71)

In legislative terms, parental and family obligations to children are strengthened by law in the Children's Act 1989 which codified children's and young people's rights and responsibilities in fairly extensive terms. In law, outside agencies can only assist parents through voluntary partnership with them. The rights, needs and interests of young people and their parents are specified in greater detail in the Guidance and Regulation documents. A second major Act of Parliament, the Criminal Justice Act of 1991, again highlights the obligations of parents to their children. Courts now have powers, mandatory for children under the age of sixteen, over the parents of young offenders. The legal and moral obligations of parents are further highlighted in the Child Support Act which came into effect in April 1993. The Child Support Agency was set up to enforce this responsibility. Its work has led to major disputes with the increasing numbers of divorced parents who claim that they are severely penalised.

Young Blacks from homes susceptible to economic vicissitudes have been made even more vulnerable because their benefit entitlements were eroded by the 1986 Social Security Act. Their eligibility for housing has been affected by the Housing and Homeless Persons Act 1985. Given the higher rates of unemployment amongst young Black people, and the insecurities of their parents and families, the impact of these legislation enactments by the Conservative governments has been to further erode their social rights under the presumed guise of empowering parental obligations. Here, the extreme cynicism of these policies is manifest, because the government's own economic policies eroded and corroded parental and familial capacities and structures.

While all youth in Britain are vulnerable to these measures, those from the Black communities have been particularly placed at risk. Even the traditionally organised Asian family structures cannot sustain the pressure under which they are placed. The climate outside the home is rife with exploitation, discrimination and abuse of Black youth who confront the forces of the market, particularly the labour and housing market, with little or no bargaining power.

This demands that the state provide a better care system for children, particularly as impoverished Black families live in sub-standard housing and can neither support nor house them. In many of the inner city care homes, 'Black children were over-represented' (Coles 1995: 131). These children suffer grave educational disadvantages and acquire few or no educational qualifications to enable them to join an increasingly competitive job market.

The expectations of 1997 that with the change of government there would be a change in social policy have not been realised. Social policy expenditure in proportion to indicators of national prosperity has declined. And the fragmentation of the familial and social fabric inherited from the previous Conservative governments has led to more blighted areas and to an increase in the numbers of marginalised groups and families. As support systems have weakened families have grown poorer (Walker 1998; Glennerster and Hills 1998). For all the rhetoric on 'the family', there has been little increase in the momentum for constructing a broader social and family policy, and the focus on social security fraud is still very strong. The new government, like the old, still sees the family as providers of income although it has no control over loss of jobs and consequent family breakdown.

The aim of getting more people into jobs and off the benefit systems is to be welcomed. But it must be able to provide training of a kind that will lead to employment, and have the massive infrastructure for child care and pre-school education integrated into it. Poor Black and white families cannot begin to live lives of hope, of greater equality and better intercultural relations unless this complex issue is re-examined.

Education

Those classified as having learning difficulties have their right to knowledge further diminished. 'Afro-Caribbean boys were three times as likely to be defined in these categories than their white contemporaries' (Coles 1995: 154). This over-representation of young Blacks, sometimes through misdiagnoses or for disciplinary rather than educational reasons, also diminishes their chances to become educationally qualified. There are gaps in the procedures on how children are statemented through a multiagency and needs oriented approach, as recommended by the Warnock Report (1978). The practice of local education authorities in providing guidance to Black parents in general is minimal.

Nor are the educational needs of young Blacks, especially those with special needs, enhanced by the Education Act of 1988 which was supposed to provide an entitlement to a national curriculum. Indeed the National Curriculum, and the Anglo-centric values underpinning it, diminishes the right to knowledge for all Britons in a multicultural society.

Many schools tend to exclude children who have special educational needs, which include language. In a competitive environment in which schools need to compete on the basis of better examination results, such children are less acceptable, not only because they require extra resources, but because they are seen as lowering the school's position in the league tables which are based on examination results. Hence those with special needs are not equipped to function effectively in mainstream society as they reach adulthood.

Neither within the youth care provision, the schools, nor the other state institutions, have children's cultural, religious, linguistic and racial backgrounds been rationally recognised.

Young Blacks Under Threat

The social conditions in inner cities, with large numbers living below the poverty line in sub-standard housing with bad care, lead to bad health. As the social policy props have disappeared, and equality of opportunity policies are denied, by the privileging of the market, the cycles of disadvantage have been further exacerbated. The closure of early nursery education programmes, as well as other programmes which support youth socialisation, has led to the worsening of educational outcomes of those from the underclass. As the alternative of better education, which would reduce school exclusions, disappears, social equality becomes more remote.

The discriminations and exclusions young Blacks face, which diminish their rights within the public domain, also raise the question of their responsibilities within it. Since they are not accorded their rights, there are resentments at being expected to accept public responsibilities and obligations. This negation of their civil, political and social citizenship rights, and the undermining of the social policy provision, makes those in the underclass particularly vulnerable, and subject to poverty and crime in the ghetto.

To these dilemmas in the public domain are added those in the private domain where parents and families may demand deferral to patriarchal, familial or religious values – dilemmas made worse by their being made more dependent on their families through unemployment and insecurity. Hence increasingly in the 1990s they have seen an erosion of their autonomies and rights in the private as in the public domain.

During a period when prospects of employment have decreased, and the market principles hold sway, young Black people are vulnerable to consumerist pressures without the capacity to earn a livelihood. Indeed, as factories and mills have closed, and adult Black and white workers have lost their jobs, their children have no direct experience of work. Nevertheless they are in thrall to consumerist pressures, particularly as the symbolic value of music, style and fashion has increased. Moreover, it is consumerist consumption patterns, the purchased manifestations of their own distinctive life-styles, that enable them to display their own distinctive identities. The symbols of their Black identity exact a heavy market price.

This disparity between ferocious market pressures to consume and being unable to earn money through productive work poses a major paradox. Their responses are varied. Some conform to market demands and innovatively attempt to acquire incomes to consume. Hustling has been used as a survival tactic by many young inner city Blacks, an indication that they are streetwise at a time when jobs cannot be found.

Others have cut off from consumerist pressures and developed mentalities of resistance. There have been rebellions in various shapes, forms and intensity in the 1980s and 1990s which researchers like Cashmore have referred to as 'innovative'. In 1981 there were riots in Brixton, Bristol and Liverpool. 1995 saw a series of riots in Brixton, Ealing, Manchester, Bradford and other inner city areas. These latter riots had inter-ethnic dimensions. Young Asians, who had been scapegoats over two decades for young whites, now experienced violence from young Blacks, some of whom belong to the skinhead culture. They, in turn, have organised into protective networks and vigilante groups.

The structural influences on Black youth culture include their social class, gender and ethnic affiliations and their intersection in different localities. The networks of friendships, parents and families, and the peer group mediate these influences. Broadly speaking, the range of options presented to them in contemporary Britain is remarkably limited. It is only those who come from socially and geographically mobile backgrounds whose life chances and job prospects bear some reason for optimism.

For the rest, not only do the general disabilities of poor locality and social class act as inhibitors, but institutional racism further damages their future potential.

Many schools, rather than dealing with racism, construct young Blacks as a problem, and some researchers recommend strong anti-racist policies. The most vulnerable groups in terms of jobs are the Afro-Caribbean and Bangladeshi youth. Yet none of them can be seen as being passive victims, because they have developed their own strategies to deal with racism. Males obviously have different strategies of resistance from females.

They are also regularly constructed as criminals. Convictions for criminality have been higher among young people of Caribbean origin, with 39 per cent of age seventeen boys, than those of Asian origin, 24 per cent and Cypriot, 21 per cent. This is compared with 28 per cent for those of English or Irish origin. There is, however, a major problem of assessing the incidence of criminality or criminalisation of Black youth. On the one hand there are assertions that young Blacks in poor inner city areas are overwhelmingly involved in criminal activity. The representation by the media of young Blacks as being criminalised was also taken up by white working class young men in South London. These assertions were made despite the fact that police statistics did not support the evidence.

On the other hand, there has been work by Stuart Hall and others at the Birmingham Centre for Contemporary Cultural Studies on the 'moral panic' caused by the rise of mugging in the early 1970s, which was associated with young Black males (Hall 1978). Also Stanley Cohen, discussing the rise of mods and rockers in England during the 1960s, has examined how reportage shapes certain subcultures as 'folk devils' and provokes 'moral panics', thus articulating and containing anxieties in society. He characterised them as arising in a certain pattern, and then construed them as beginning with warnings of a catastrophe facing society, followed by the event itself and its impact. The events and their impact were then used by the media to depict an exaggerated and threatening picture which had symbolic meanings, and were articulated to provide an equally consistent and uniform response (Cohen 1992).

Enoch Powell's 1968 'River Tiber flowing with much blood' speech helped fuel the moral panics about the Black community which, in the 1970s, focused on the issue of Black mugging. And the emergence of more complex identity structures and the rise of a distinctive youth culture have been continually thwarted by reactivation of moral panics either by politicians or the media, or by young people sympathetic to the National Front or the British Movement.

BLACK CULTURE

Defining 'Black Culture'

The cultural dimension of the Black community's life reflects belongingness in legal terms, and negation and discrimination in virtually every other aspect of their lives. Their belongingness means that there is a cultural presence in all the arts and media that cannot be denied. Yet, paradoxically, their cultural output remains marginalised. Oppression and subordination inform the community's cultural output, yet its strong presence is based on its specificities and not on any legitimation within the body politic

The two main components of Black culture, Afro-Caribbean and Asian, have in common an opposing stance and resistance to racism. These are the only common features of their cultural identities and output, and to it they bring to bear different strengths, experiences and histories. The total erasure of African languages and cultures in the New World, and the resultant development of opposing cultures to the dominant culture, has empowered the Afro-Caribbean community with overtly intellectual and political messages about oppression. In particular, the cult of separateness of the Rastafarians made them visible to the police and therefore more susceptible to harassment. The arrest of Blacks in Mangrove Restaurant in 1970 marked the beginning of confrontation with the authorities, and especially at the Notting Hill Carnival in 1976, 1977 and 1978. Police harassment of the black population was devastatingly revealed in 1998 in the Stephen Lawrence inquiry.

The Asian cultures in general terms are not overtly political and have complex linguistic and religious legacies which are largely traditional. As these exclude 'outsiders', to whom they are incomprehensible, they tend to resist any changes. Where changes are found is among Asian youth who can identify with the racial and class oppression that Afro-Caribbean youth also experience. As we shall see, the identifiable 'Black culture' in Britain is Black youth culture.

Multiple Identities and Culture

No single Black culture covers all age groups. But a syncretic Black youth culture, cutting across the specific identities, has emerged. There are, however, inhibiting factors as well. The exclusionary effects felt by the older generation of Blacks are also felt by some of the younger generation. This tends to strengthen the ethnic, religious and patriarchal values. In many inner city areas the Black churches and other fundamentalisms are a sign of 'siege communities'. Yet, as second and third generation Blacks become socialised here, their cultural moorings are a syncretism of the cultures they breathe and live in Britain. They have no lived memories of Africa, Asia or the Caribbean. Only the messianic visions of Rastafarianism or of religious fundamentalisms act as psychological props to protect against the exclusions, racism and xenophobia of the larger society.

Exclusions by the dominant group and increased ethnically based media influences have also heightened religious identifications amongst young Asians. Though the roots of the religious systems lie outside Britain, many young Muslims and Sikhs have embraced their faiths with greater fervour. The resurgence of Islam, and the perceived threats against it from the atheist and Christian west, is one force. The Sikh identification with the Khalistani cause (a Sikh state) has also strengthened Sikh religious identity. Some young people have activated religious conflicts in certain neighbourhoods. Tensions between young Hindus and Muslims, or Sikhs and Hindus, have been evidenced, resulting in violence in Ealing and Manchester in 1995.

But examples of cultural mixing are everywhere: Tizard and Phoenix (1993) estimate that 30 per cent of people of Caribbean origin have a white partner. But how it is perceived by a conservative establishment and society delimits its value and impact. For instance, children of mixed racial or cultural backgrounds are described as 'half-caste'. Apart from the negative attributions to Black people because of slavery and colonialism, this is perpetuating the myths of 'scientific racism' which asserted that racial mixtures led to 'hybrid degeneration'. Despite the statement by geneticists and biologists issued by UNESCO in the early 1950s that such beliefs were scientifically not valid, young people from mixed backgrounds continue to suffer from discrimination.

Large proportions of those from mixed backgrounds have a complex view of their identities. Tizard and Phoenix found that about half think of themselves as Black (Tizard and Phoenix 1993: 159). Twenty per cent are confused. Others identify themselves with fervour as whites and join racist groups to assert their identity. Such conflicts point to the complex problems related to acceptance of cultural mixing. Hence some young Blacks feel marginalised, distanced from other young people, propelled into a twilight zone by religious identities, isolation from their parents, educational disadvantages and lack of employment prospects. Others, from all sections of the Black community, have improved their socio-economic status and are now part of the middle classes.

Young people's use of language illustrates this cultural crossing. Most young Asian migrants from the Indian sub-continent had little knowledge of English. Those who came from East Africa were reasonably proficient in the use of it but it was not their first language. Many have retained some understanding or knowledge of their first languages, and this has added to their linguistic repertoires in and out of school. Ben Rampton has analysed this phenomenon among young Punjabi-speakers in the Midlands. His ethnographic study of youth culture in the multiracial Midlands demonstrates how adolescents of Afro-Caribbean and English backgrounds, as well as young Asians, are using Punjabi. They also use stylised Indian English, and engage in what is called 'heretical discourse' in an attempt to break with the ordinary order and to establish a new common language (Rampton 1995).

The common-sense understandings in conservative establishment circles that linguistic diversity would lead to social fragmentation are seen to be untrue. Here these young people's linguistic diversity seemingly leads to inter-group friendships. Different aspects of ritual, serious or playful, lengthy or fleeting, are used by these British-born adolescents. These interactions are based on trust, and come out of attempts to establish shared understandings.

This analysis of the use of Punjabi and of Indian English develops the pioneering work of Roger Hewitt on the use of Creole. Young Afro-Caribbeans have been seen as speakers of English, yet they have largely been Creole and patois speakers. These hybrid Caribbean languages, brought to Britain by their parents, remained as languages of resistance and incorporation. In the British context Creole has undergone further transformation. Young Afro-Caribbeans have been using it as a language of resistance, particularly in the context of the school, police and other cultural contexts (Hewitt 1986).

The use of localised black cultural forms has also led to inter-racial friendships, using London English, local Creoles and Black music, because of their opposing stances, with which many young whites also identify. These friendship patterns have been ethnographically researched in social locales which move beyond notions of individual friendships, despite the existence of strong local racisms in areas of south London. Their complexity and circumspection has also been explored in other contexts. Helena Wulff has conducted a study of Black and white girls in south London which provides further examples (Wulff 1995: 63–80).

Black Youth Culture

Young Blacks who are either largely socialised or born in Britain have less recourse than the older generation has to a cultural map into which they can fit. The older migrant generation has totally different reference points in cultural terms. While the Black youth may draw on parental culture they also have some 'cultural commonality with white youth' because of 'their shared conditions of life – common experiences in the same streets and schools mediated by many of the same creative tasks' (Willis 1990: 8). They are therefore engaged in the complex role of defining themselves in the context of dominant British identity as well as their identity as Black persons in Britain. Within the public domain there are no symbols which validate their identity. So they have had to create their own.

The development of a separate youth culture in postwar Britain went through different stages, all drawing on Black cultural resources. The mods during the mid 1960s were influenced by Black American and Afro-Caribbean models which they admired for their music, their dancing and their coolness. The 1960s phenomenon was transformed in the 1970s when the punks were influenced by reggae and its Rastafarian inspiration – the Rastas' vision including a change of the whole system in what was seen as Babylon.

The young Blacks' identity was reinforced by the prevalence of racism, and provided a strong opposition to the power structure. They were given a sense of their history, their identity and a millenarian future. Their lack of hope for future employment made this view stronger. The punks used the same analysis and articulated a position of youth being oppressed. 'Rock against Racism' allowed punk and reggae musicians to campaign against racism as manifested by skinheads, the British Movement and the National Front.

Both groups, but particularly the Blacks, did badly at school which further lessened their chances at work or in future education. They drew an inspiration from the Jamaican Rude Boys and a Rude culture of impoverished youth took root in Britain. Its regional variations included Two Tone based on a record company in Coventry. One of the bands which recorded with Two Tone was Madness which 'captured the rude boy ethos' (Willis 1990: 55). The music was rooted in Britain, using London and Midland dialects, and did not draw on American styles. The

Black British, having initially initiated Black American styles, had gone on to develop its own.

To quote Paul Willis:

> Songs can be a source of political ideas and development when focused around particular issues such as gender relations, war, apartheid, unemployment, nuclear weapons or ecological questions.

(Willis 1990: 70)

Songs also tend to have a moral sense and dispense wisdom. Young British Blacks have used music, particularly the Jamaican reggae and American soul, to construct political understanding of the issues around them. While the Jamaican reggae provides the political message and has a cultural dimension, Black American music speaks to the marginalised lives in the metropolitan conurbations. Those young people who still attend church, especially the Black churches, have access to spiritual music. Young Blacks have not only increasingly internalised these genres of music but have also made a significant contribution in writing and recording music in Britain. Indeed this new syncretic music, rooted in Britain, has made a powerful contribution to youth music in general. For instance, the substance and context of youth culture, language and music speak to the much larger audience of white and Asian youth.

Funk, soul, disco, rap and hip-hop have now established an enormous intercultural following amongst young people of different ethnic groups in Britain. Willis continues:

> White youth too continue to find in black music a language and a set of symbols with which to express their own age, gender or class-based experiences. Thus some young whites relate strongly to reggae, hip-hop and rap.

(Willis 1990: 71)

The role and function of music is in many cases all encompassing. It includes the personal tape and CD players which are listened to everywhere, as well as social listening in youth clubs, dances, socials, at work while studying, and at home. Young people have used such music to appropriate an enormous amount of space, particularly as the range and scope of sound systems has become more sophisticated electronically and in terms of sound system technology.

The difference between private and public spaces has become blurred. A creative use and customisation of sound systems is no longer restricted to classical music and upper social classes, but has become increasingly, even largely, used by young Blacks. It has also become a focus not just of consumption but of production of sound, which has extensively proliferated into the distribution and retail networks and mechanisms. This commercially viable institution has had a firm basis in the Black community, and has changed the nature of community-based leisure, through the recording of sound, and creating new labels, in shops, in discos and clubs, as well as the audio and broadcasting media.

One of the more interesting issues represented by Black youth culture, particularly as it relates to language, literary and musical cultures, is that the stronger the discrimination against their output from becoming part of the mainstream, the stronger and more identifiable the output in these cultural productions has become. Homegrown language and literature in postwar Britain is not as vibrant as the more discriminated against African, Caribbean and Asian literatures, written in first languages as well as in English.

In as much as youth culture, Black and white, is in opposition to the school and the official and mainstream systems, these musical Black youth cultures have provided an obvious focus for developing a syncretic oppositional culture. The notion of sufferation (oppression) in Black youth music has relevance to young whites, particularly from Bob Marley's songs. The young Asians in Britain are also producing their distinctive cultural forms. This is evidenced by a British version of Punjabi Bhangra music which has now developed into Bhangra pop.

Some young Sikhs are now moving beyond Bhangra culture into Sikhi culture, retaining the fundamental core of Sikh doctrine, but with syncretic orientations, including a concern with environmental issues, and being ready to engage with young whites. Meanwhile others are turning to narrow scriptural study of the religious texts and are reverting to notions of religious piety.

Finding themselves excluded, or made unwelcome, in white leisure institutions, young Blacks have developed their own with their own autonomous cultural forms. This has helped to develop street level cultural norms. DJs, for instance, introducing music, improvise on lyrics and make interjections and exhortation. Hence music rhythm is linked to words and rhythms. The grounded aesthetic of the DJ results from articulating everyday experiences/vocabulary/language.

Young women are also moving into reggae and breaking it as a male preserve. They want to keep it as music of Rastafarians which is not commercially mainstreamed, so their music is largely not on vinyl but on tapes for circulation amongst friends. But as aspects of the music have more commercial potential it is produced and distributed outside the private radios, specialist record shops, clubs and dances. This also explains the importance Blacks attach to clubs and dances.

The music making and playing is a collective activity based on good time and public recognition. It gives the unemployed leisure which allows them to move away from state control. It also acts as a psychological defence mechanism for them. As Willis puts it:

> Grounded aeshetics developed here are essential to the ways in which young people make sense of the social world and their place within it. Music, in short, is not just something young people like and do. It is in many ways the model for their involvement in a common culture which provides the resources to see beyond the immediate requirements and contradictions of work, family and the dole.
>
> (Willis 1990: 82)

Good appearances are also important: the fashions impinge on young people. A priority is the making of clothes, so that fashion is more specific and cheaper, and provides further strength to the 'grounded aesthetic'. Black hairstyles/aesthetics, based on the 'Black is Beautiful' slogan from the 1960s, has the symbolic function of giving their hair different attributions from those ascribed by whites. In the 1980s, however, according to Willis, these forms of cultural resistance drawing on a grounded aesthetic of naturalness and authenticity have been informed by another set of cultural strategies in the medium of hair. These turn around a grounded aesthetic of artifice that works in and against the codes of the dominant culture through hybridity, sycretism and interculturalism (Willis 1990: 92–7).

An innovative Black youth culture has now created a new identity with its own symbols and culture, appropriating elements of the dominant culture which have then been marked off and differentiated.

FURTHER READING

Ghassan Hage (1998) *White Nation: Fantasies of White Supremacy in a Multicultural Society*, Annandale NSW: Pluto Press Australia and West Wickham, Kent: Cornerford and Miller Publishers.

Jeremy Paxman (1998) *The English: A Portrait of a People*, London: Michael Joseph.

Montserrat Gubernan and John Rex (1997) *The Ethnicity Reader: Nationalism, Multiculturalism and Migration*, Cambridge: Polity Press.

2

Basic Issues in Intercultural Education

THE THEORETICAL CONTEXT

This chapter assumes that good citizenship is not something that accrues without political understandings. It is important that young people have an access to good political education both formally as well as informally. In diverse societies the need for such education is greater because the complexities within them can be misrepresented. Populists can acquire mass support by simplistically representing both historical and contemporary aspects of diversities. Vulnerable and discriminated groups can be stereotyped and since they have little voice they may not have recourse to challenging the reasons why they have been disadvantaged or are represented as having psychological, racial and social deficits.

The differences of educational performances and achievements between different communities need to be viewed with caution because many communities, like the Asians, cannot be seen wholistically as a successful group different from the other subordinated groups.

Politics in Education

The role of politics in education is predicated on the fact that political education itself is necessary for all sections of society. As it is, the skills, knowledge and understanding of the political nature of society are ambiguous to large numbers of people. Such politically uneducated or undereducated members of societies are dangerous, because they can misrepresent human and societal complexity and may opt for simplistic solutions based on populist policies which encourage authoritarian and undemocratic solutions to difficult societal issues. Political awareness, knowledge and understanding are necessary if people are to grasp the inherent complexity of society and their rights and responsibilities within it.

The rationale for not engaging in political education is that ordinary people are not capable of understanding issues and are susceptible to propaganda. Sometimes political leaders and elites also suggest that because human nature is largely negative it is better not to inculcate interest in political issues among the masses. But such assumptions about the negativeness of human nature require scrutiny and comment.

If indeed human nature is considered to be basically negative, then selfishness, conflict and violence are so deeply embedded in human consciousness that educational and other socialising influences have no role to play in changing patterns of behaviour and social relations. There is, however, no scientific evidence to show that 'human nature' has been investigated extensively enough for definitive statements to be made about it. Indeed, given the absence of firm evidence, no firm views about human nature can be made. Human nature can be seen to be neither good nor bad in itself. The human capacity to be social or selfish is an open issue: the capacity and potential for both exist among people. Human nature may be neither Hobbesian nor Rousseauistic but have the potential, the proclivity and the capacity to be both.

Nature and nurture give individuals social as well as selfish instincts. Minds are not *tabula rasa*. They encode both personal and larger historical legacies which make the issues of equitable socialisation very complex. Confucian thinking sees human nature as something open and perfectable through education – that indeed the potential for good in human beings is infinite (de Bary and Chaffee 1989). And new thinking by biologists like E. O. Wilson are now bringing the sciences and humanities into an ethical framework to promote human rights and progress (Wilson 1998).

The role of political education is to enable the evaluation and the establishment of a healthier balance between the selfish and the social by accepting the learners' sanctity and autonomy thus enabling them to negotiate some of their society's complexities. Education systems with a political education syllabus would enable the emergence of thinking citizens who would be more likely to seek solutions to conflicts based on negotiation and resolution of differences rather than through violence.

The education of the young also ought to involve unpacking the underpinnings of evil in society. However, this is a broader task of public and social policy and requires an inter-agency approach. If truth and veracity are inherently human values so are lying and deception. Hence broader social and public policy measures are necessary to deny the roots of evil, lying and deception. Such policies include the curbing of cruel treatment of children. Here the 1998 judgement of the European Human Rights Court outlawing beating is a good example.

Pluralism

In the 1960s an American scholar, M. Gordon, postulated that the United States was a plural society and that there exists in it a structural and cultural pluralism (Gordon 1964). Structural pluralism can be demonstrated by the existence of diversity among minority groups which are separate on linguistic, religious and racial lines. At the minority group level it exists in the form of institutions which are relevant to specific communities. The existence of their media (minority group presses), religious organisations (temples, synagogues) and educational institutions (Jewish schools) is an indicator of their recognition.

Cultural pluralism, in the context of the state, focuses on the ideologies and institutions of society within the 'structurally assimilated' schools in the public institutional framework, exemplified in Britain by the comprehensive state school system. It may take the form of (1) segmentation and dominance or (2) the autonomy of groups which demand or already posseses a high degree of equality.

One society which has continued to represent aspects of segmentation and dominance is South Africa where the politically dominant white minority until recently autocratically governed the majority black population. The new South African political institutions are attempting to radically transform the context of these hierarchical relations but socio-economic divisions continue to exist. In Britain and the United States the trend is from segmentation and dominance towards a situation of group autonomy within a context of equality. Here, over time, the distinct cultural groups within this institutional setting maintain their distinction. If, for instance, the majority or minority groups are not allowed certain levels of autonomy they may then make demands for separate institutions, be they on racial, linguistic or religious grounds.

A major theory of cultural pluralism views integration as racial assimilation, e.g. the socialisation of black children with children from the dominant white community. If and when some elements of the minority communities accept this postulation they may do so on the grounds that if their culture comes to resemble that of the dominant group they may become more acceptable. Or they may feel that failure to accept the dominant value system would leave them open to oppression and persecution in the future. Or those who experience self-hatred may adopt the dominant norm and reject others of their own culture. The contemporary school curriculum in Britain and the United States retains a traditional nationalistic Anglo-Saxon and Protestant orientation. Because of this, integration as racial assimilation is merely 'token desegregation' (Rist 1978). It involves no change in social structure and the content of education, nor does it reflect the presence of diverse cultural groupings. British models of the 1960s and 1970s, including Roy Jenkins's ideas of cultural pluralism, were basically integrationist. For instance, translated into educational terms, the policy of 'dispersal' of immigrant students was based on the assumptions of integration.

Most minority communities reject this form of assimilation or integration and favour the cause of diversity which allows for the affirmation of values which are other than Anglo-conformist or Anglo-centric. A school which accepts diversity in racial terms presupposes that pupils, parents and teachers have equal status based on equal power – though in practice the dominant group will often not allow power to slip from its hands. In the United States there has been a tendency to ask for community control, while in Britain demands for separate schools based on religious (Pentecostal, Muslim, Sikh) grounds, for what Charles Taylor has called the 'politics of recognition' (Taylor 1992), are increasing.

Such schools face factors such as diverse social classes and languages which complicate the pedagogic issues. Moreover, local communities and religious groups control them, although young people who study there have yet to face national examinations to legitimise their knowledge. Furthermore, these minority groups do not possess the economic resources or political power to become independent of the majority (Carby 1980: 34, 64–5). Nor do such separate schools necessarily have further intercultural links or relations amongst pupils.

Plural Deficit and Disadvantage Models

The debates and discourses about intercultural education and education in multicultural societies do not have a linear and uniform trajectory. Much of the earlier research and many of the earlier publications were firmly based on deficit and disadvantaged models of subordinated groups. This especially applied to research about African-Americans and the Black British. Even a scientist like E. O. Wilson was accused of racism because he had earlier used a biological basis to write about social behaviour. His work on sociobiology and human behaviour (1975) and human nature (1978) brought disapproval from the American left, which accused him of being a eugenicist even though his 1978 book had won a Pulitzer prize.

Hence the complex research by sociologists and psychologists needs to be outlined to provide the backdrop to the political and educational policies of the conservative right which emerged in Britain in the late 1970s and were paralleled in the United States.

The reality of social classes means having to assimilate on a class basis and raises issues for those who are poor or 'disadvantaged'. In Britain this means that those from social classes 4 and 5, using the Registrar-General's classification, are considered to be 'culturally deprived' or 'culturally disadvantaged'. The conservatives in this debate tend to postulate an inferiority based on genetic factors. The liberals tend to stress that disadvantage is really a result of past discrimination based on sex, race, class and ethnic or territorial grounds which has resulted in the existence of a disadvantaged section of the community. A combination of these forms of discrimination, so runs the argument, may contribute to a family breakdown which may then have led to the inadequate socialisation of individuals, accumulated deficit and a resistance to schooling. In other words, what children from the poor classes needed was an initial dose of socialisation to acquaint them with the values, behaviour and ideals of the middle-class population (Carby 1980: 17–18)

Educational researchers and teacher-training courses have used such theories to explain poor performances in schools: they form the basis of various remedial or compensatory programmes. In the United States such thinking determined the initiation of programmes like Head Start. It should, incidentally, be remembered that those who argued that Head Start was not successful in the long term assumed that its programmes were on the scale of the Marshall Plan, designed to alleviate centuries of economic, cultural and social exploitation, ignoring the fact that educational responses to such multiple disadvantages are not adequate on their own.

The IQ Debate

The liberal reforms of the 1960s failed in most cases and evoked a conservative backlash in education. In the United States Jensen wrote an article from the University of California in 1969 arguing that intelligence was about 80 per cent determined by genetics and that differences in IQ reflected genetic differences, thus reversing the postwar psychological theory of compensatory education. He asserted that since intelligence was largely determined by genetics the efforts to raise the intelligence of people with low IQ scores by compensatory education were bound to fail. Intelligence, as such, he only defined by reference to intelligence tests (Jensen 1969: 1–23).

Jensen focused on the racial differences in IQ scores and gave a genetic explanation that blacks, on average, do not possess the same innate intellectual qualities as whites. His research was swiftly supported by Eysenck, an influential member of the Institute of Psychiatry in London (Eysenck 1971). These arguments found favour with right wing politicians and those who favoured cuts in educational budgets. This was illustrated by the Black Papers episode which brought together practising teachers under this same conservative umbrella. Their stance, under guise of demanding higher standards, resulted in a negative appraisal of the liberal curriculum content and urged the withdrawal of financial support.

The whole position was, however, shown to be suspect because any psychological analysis which deals with individual differences and ignores ideology does not provide a fair analysis and only compounds issues of disadvantage (Hogan and Emler 1978: 534–748). The data used by Jensen and Eysenck were also criticised. Indeed it was eventually shown that Sir Cyril Burt's evidence had actually been fabricated (Kamin 1977). Sir Peter Medawar, a biologist and Nobel Prize winner, pointed out that 'intelligence' cannot be summarized by a single IQ score, and that human capabilities and potentialities are far too diverse for this type of simplification (Billig 1979: 8–9).

The important issue to remember is that Jensen's and Eysenck's work was picked up without using the details of their argument. Fascist groups saw them as vindicating their racist ideologies. Eysenck's books went onto the reading lists of groups like the National Front in Britain and have been widely used in the training of psychologists in many countries. Their work received further stimulus from work done by Herrenstein and Murray which advanced these arguments with greater force (Herrenstein and Murray 1994).

Obviously the hypothesis of IQ test scores and the so-called rigorous testing and measurements that supported it must be firmly rejected, or those groups who are labelled with genetic inferiority face disaster educationally and socially. As Kamin has argued, the research involving IQ testing is inherently political:

With respect to IQ testing, psychology long ago surrendered its political virginity. The interpretations of IQ data has always taken place, as it must, in a social and political context, and the validity of the data cannot be fully assessed without reference to the content.

(Kamin 1977: 11–30)

Academics have to play a positive role in rejecting these theories which revive race-science in a milieu which is susceptible to fascist ideology and create a culture of racism. Their educational implications mean a worsening of ethnic relations between groups since they justify the way the poor continue to be marginalised in educational systems.

Social dimensions

The social dimensions of the deficit debate have even wider implications than the individual-oriented psychological theories. It can be postulated that both the liberal and conservative approaches to this issue are incorrect and that people are disadvantaged because of *present* forms of racism, *present* forms of structural inequalities and *present* barriers to choice (Claydon, Knight and Rado 1978). While older forms of inequality might be removed, new forms of inequality are being instituted. Until institutional forms of inequality are removed, the education of those who are considered disadvantaged will not improve. Potential for inter-ethnic conflict and demands for separate institutions would remain.

Within other disciplines, the anthropological and sociological models of 'cultural deprivation' and the 'poverty of culture' have taken as their evidence the low-level social organisation of minority communities, and their intellectual and cultural resistance to the norms of the dominant group. This emphasis on client behaviour and the need for its modification for entry into middle-class cultures is similarly not valid when basic and causal issues such as the elimination of poverty are not tackled.

One of these approaches is the environmental deficit model   that lower class children where the family provides no intellectual or social stimulation fail in schools through a lack of literacy and social skills. Similarly, restricted language codes, lack of books at home, and non-intellectual life styles contribute to stimulus deprivation, and, in terms of performance in school, this leads to an inability to delay gratification and sustain attention, resulting in failure to develop perceptual discrimination skills.

In English-speaking countries there is considerable research to support the thesis of the functional inferiority of black and working-class children. Moreover aspects of special education, including units for 'disruptive children' and remedial education, serve to replicate existing racial and class differences and ensure that they have unequal schooling and end up without the paper qualifications to improve their economic status.

Psychology as a profession has also contributed to this debate by formulating the issue as one of inadequate socialisation. Disruptive family patterns, single-parent families and the lack of adequate adult models are held responsible for interrupted social growth. The classic environmental version of this determinist model of social behaviour was propounded by Patrick Moynihan in 1965 in his Report to the US Department of Labor on the black family in which he held that the matriarchal black family derived from the emasculation of the male by slavery and was inconsistent with the patriarchal norms of American society. In the British context, however, the matriarchal argument has been used to explain higher achievement among girls from matriarchal single-parent families (Driver 1980).

Moynihan's assumption of the pathological condition of the black family gained currency in Britain in another form. In 1974 Keith Joseph, Minister of Health and Social Security, alleged that 'eugenically transmitted deprivation' made the poor family an agency for perpetuating poverty so that poor families 'threatened the balance of our human stock' (*The Sunday Times* 1 June 1981). The Department of Health and Social Security jointly funded an extensive research programme on 'transmitted deprivation' with the then Social Science Research Council. These projects were carried out at various British academic institutions and produced recommendations about compensating for the debilitation of the child's personal family life. The structural and institutional reasons allowing the schools, as part of the state system, to replicate parental occupational inheritance and socio-economic backgrounds were not examined.

These theories of inherited psychological deficit and disadvantage derive their apparently scientific basis from the doctrines of eugenics articulated in the latter half of the nineteenth century by Francis Galton and held by prominent British intellectuals like Sidney and Beatrice Webb, John Maynard Keynes, Harold Laski and Marie Stopes. In Scandinavia between 1935 and 1976 more than 60,000 Swedish women were sterilised in an effort to create a 'purer and stronger Nordic race' (Freedland 1997). Similar policies were carried out in some of the states of the USA. Though such views were largely abandoned in the shadow of Auschwitz, Treblinka and Sobibor, and have been effectively countered by such scientists as Stephen Gould (1981), they have survived in Singapore and China. They also survive, implicitly or explicitly, in the way Roma suffer discrimination in much of Europe (Kohin 1995; see also Monee Project 1998: 41–61).

The educational implications of such discrimination are compounded by assuming the linearity and singularity of intelligence. Totally different conclusions can be drawn by focusing on multiple intelligences as favoured by Stephen Gould and used by Howard Gardner in devising complex educational programmes (Gould 1981).

Different Approaches

These personality-oriented and eugenic models of analysis only continue the long process of deflecting attention away from the larger social system as a determinant of social inequality. They focus on individuals and families in powerless positions, and not on powerlessness itself. Because of this, cause and effect are not clearly demarcated. It can, for instance, be argued that in the pursuit of 'equal' opportunities for education through compensatory and remedial programmes, the more we do the worse the students get. This only compounds and further entrenches the powerlessness of subordinate groups.

What we see is that the various deficit theorists on whose work policy has been based have deflected their analysis from the real issues and, as a result, resources have been misdirected. Rather than schooling a population to accept a lower status in social terms, the real issue is how to educate a society that no longer requires a disadvantaged class of people. The structures and institutional practices of the school should seek to minimise the inequalities between different groups of children. The curriculum could be used to analyse the reasons for disadvantage and offer proposals to redress the present forms of inequality. That would necessitate giving schools a measure of autonomy which would allow educators who recognise diversity to alter the curriculum.

The critical issue of racism in education must be viewed in terms of the dynamics between dominant and subordinate groups. Racism would then be seen to be a problem for the dominant group. Here inter-agency responses and social policy measures may be needed. Obviously in a diverse society teachers have to expect conflict. They have to expect that racist feelings will be derived out of direct experiences – limited opportunities of employment, housing problems, or racial problems caused by geographical proximity in the inner city. This means acknowledging class diversity in a society without a unified value system and the affirmation of the values of the working class and its culture. The legacy of the British colonial connection also needs to be taken into account (Street-Porter 1978). As it is, schools are not very good at validating the cultures of the oppressed and the subordinated. The implicit denigration of these cultures leads the children affected to reactions which may be irrational, exclusive and violent. The schools must therefore be able to present these cultural variations as neither good nor bad in themselves.

THE POLITICAL CONTEXT

The Legacy of Tory Rule

Substantive educational, academic and knowledge issues have been subverted in this country since the Conservative administration took power in 1979, as a direct result of political onslaught, aided by the media. The privileging of the market principle has placed an unusual reliance on the power of the market, not just to regulate inefficency, but to benefit and assist the creation of wealth from which, it is supposed, all will ultimately benefit. Though it is admitted that certain forms of inequality, particularly economic inequality, are a necessary part of the market's regulatory power, as Sir Keith Joseph, at one time Minister of Education in the Conservative administration, put it:

> The blind, unplanned, uncoordinated wisdom of the market ... is overwhelmingly superior to the well-researched, rational, systematic, well-meaning, co-operative, science based, forward looking, statistically respectable plans of government.
>
> (Lawton 1989: 35)

The opposition to all aspects of the political and social consensus that had prevailed since 1944 could not be made more clear. From this perspective, if there were problems over educational attainment, untrammelled market forces – as in, say, a voucher policy where parents could pick and choose an education to their liking – would quickly restore efficiency to the system.

There was, however, another element in this conservative restructuring – the old style conservatism, often associated with even more forces of reaction, whose supporters wanted to interfere with the market. Sometimes it was to maintain the greater values of national sovereignty. But also, where the workings of a free market might encourage temporary in-migration, this strand of conservatism wished for ever stronger immigration controls to keep 'visible' minorities from entering the country. Many went even further, encouraging the 'repatriation' of those already settled, whether British black or immigrant – indeed making little or no distinction between the two. If they had an educational policy it would centre round the defence of white English culture, and the need to promote its ascendancy and to enforce assimilation into it.

Until the late 1970s such educational views were seldom considered outside the narrow confines of those concerned. But they gained wider support within the Conservative administration and in the mass media as a right wing counter to what was increasingly seen as the 'loony left'. Their particular ire was directed at anti-racist education, particularly as espoused by Labour controlled local education authorities such as the Inner London Education Authority and the Boroughs of Brent and Haringey.

Moreover these authorities' policies on gender were seen by conservatives as threatening. With the enthusiastic and prurient support of a significant proportion of the national press, they presented policies relating to gays and lesbians as being intended to turn all children into gays and lesbians. As the Hillgate Group asserted, in a document that clearly influenced the 1988 Education Act, there was a real worry that 'traditional' values were being destroyed with schools 'preaching on behalf of homosexuality, sexual licence and social indiscipline' (Hillgate Group 1986: 4).

On religious matters they were slightly more tolerant, perhaps because they recognised similar reactionary tendencies within the range of religious faiths which were now such a feature of British inner city schools. However, religious tolerance went against the spirit of assimilation, and the 1988 Education Act showed that their tolerance was no more than provisional.

A third element, in conflict with the traditional right wing element of conservative thinking, and by no means limited to those in the Conservative party, is meritocratic. Its proponents assume that if the race is fair, the losers deserve to lose, and the winners deserve all the prizes. Tradition is worthless unless it supports efficiency, modernisation and the development of meritocracy. Such a meritocracy is not egalitarian, but within it people – and by implication school children – get their just desserts. It assumes an unquestioned 'level playing field' of advantage for all children.

Clearly there is much here in common with the market-led element of thinking, although the two differ on the degree to which government should intervene in the process. It meant that nothing in education was to be left unquestioned if it could not demonstrate its contribution to the economic growth of the society. Given the innate conservatism embodied in most education systems, it was astonishing how enthusiastic the government became about root and branch reform.

From the early 1980s it began to remove huge areas of educational activity away from the Department of Education and Science, and also away from schools, as the huge expansion of vocational education and training, partly induced by political worries about the high levels of youth unemployment, was initiated, and run from a rival ministry, the Department of Trade and Industry. This was later reversed, and the Department of Education and Employment was given these issues.

The Local Management of Schools (LMS) following the 1988 Act gave schools greater autonomy, thus reducing local authority influence. This increased school control over budgets which has had serious consequences for reducing in-equality.

While this has made transparent the manner in which funds are allocated to schools, it severely limits scope for positive discrimination on the part of the LEA to counter disadvantage (Whitty, Power and Halpin 1998).

Curbing local education authority policies to provide equity has left a major gap between those who were doing well at school and those who had fallen behind. Added to this, the grant-maintained schools programme began in September 1989. About one thousand schools opted out, teaching about 700,000 pupils, about 10 per cent of the school-age population in England. These schools, rather than being progressive institutions, tended to hark back to traditional values and adopted teaching and learning strategies to support them (Whitty, Power and Halpin 1998: 89–90). These changes and strategies contributed to marginalising intercultural education.

Moreover, children who require special assistance because of language or learning difficulties tend not to be acceptable to schools where good examination results are needed to ensure the school's position in the educational market. Hence a more exclusive and segregated schooling has continued to take root. These individualistic, market-oriented policies have resulted in a culture of winners and losers which undermines social cohesion and citizenship values.

Opposition to these dynamic new elements in Conservative educational thinking was belated and often equally disastrous. There was a demand to return to the educational consensus policies of the 1960s and 1970s with their stress on relevance, mixed ability teaching, and the value of the non-selective comprehensive seondary school.

As this system had not worked for many minority school students, it was not a strategy likely to gain a high level of their support. But earlier alternative strategies had had even less to offer, the nostalgia for grammar schools disguising their never having really been a significant instrument for working-class social mobility. In practice they would have offered very little to minority communities, in terms of either access or outcomes.

Even the policies on 'Race, Gender and Class' of the Inner London Educational

Authority before its demolition by the Thatcher government were suspect. The race and gender dimensions were given some superficial empowerment because Black and feminist groups were vocal, and campaigned vigorously for their cause. But the white working class, who felt that their children's educational needs were excluded and negated, felt extremely bitter. Inevitably any positive action which is seen to empower certain groups in society at the expense of other disenfranchised groups is in peril. Once it is directed in favour of certain identifiable minority 'ethnic' groups, they become hostages to fortune of the similarly disenfranchised dominant groups whose underachievement remains unrecognised.

In general, the DES persistently saw the immigrant groups as creating 'problems' for the educational system. In the early 1960s its response was to assimilate immigrant children into schools. The main emphasis for their education was confined to teaching English as a Second Language. Its response was to react to pressures and demands from the Black community. This led inevitably to uneven responses by the local education authorities.

In 1977, in a government consultative document, 'Education in Schools', the DES replaced the assimilationist model by referring to the country as having become multicultural. It declared that:

> our society is a multicultural, multiracial one, and the curriculum should reflect a sympathetic understanding of the cultures and races that make up our society.
>
> (DES 1977)

And the major government document, 'The School Curriculum', published in 1981, stated:

> First, our society has become multicultural and there is now among pupils and parents a greater diversity of personal values
>
> (DES 1981)

– a statement that, with its use of the words 'has become', totally ignored the historical diversity of British society and the major issues raised by such an understanding of society and its implications for education.

The New Labour Approach

The nearly two decades of Conservative governments effectively dismantled educational policies devised to bring about equity in education in an unequal and socially diverse society. So when Tony Blair pronounced 'education, education, education' as a key basis for 'redistribution of possibilities' (Giddens 1998: 109) the public was given hope.

David Blunkett's New Deal in education has indeed at long last struck a positive note. Moreover, its promises are backed up with massive financial support. He is now pledged to tackle the 'cycle of disadvantage' which leads on from disadvantaged education to permanent unemployment. One of his first initiatives has been to transfer responsibility and increase the funding for ethnic minority teaching, from the Home Office to the Department for Education and Employment. This followed alarm at the figures published by the Commission for Racial Equality showing that within the ethnic minorities more than one in five have no qualification, and that unemployment for 16- to 24-year-olds is three times higher than in the comparable white population. In addition, he has urged more black and Asian employers to get involved in the New Deal strategy.

Indeed a new era seems to open with his recognition that 'Children from ethnic minorities are an important and vibrant part of today's Britain, and it is vital we ensure they have the same opportunities to succeed as everyone else' (*The Guardian* 13 November 1998).

The establishment of Education Action Zones targeting areas and groups requiring special attention is particularly to be welcomed The initiatives linking education with employment, and the substantial increase in funding for sixth-form and further education colleges to encourage those who leave school unqualified to enter post-school education programmes, is also welcome. So is the Crick Report on Education for Citizenship which offers a chance to negate some of the xenophobic and racist ideas rife among young people (Education for Citizenship 1998).

But the three agencies created by the Tory governments to implement their educational policies – the Qualifications and Curriculum Authority, the Teacher Training Agency and OFSTED – have remained largely unchanged and the comprehensive principle of education has failed to receive the support one might have expected from a Labour government. Selection and choice continue to be the governing principles. A comparative study analysing devolved and marketised education found that there was still 'overall emphasis on devolution, diversity and choice' (Whitty, Power and Halpin 1998).

It needs to be realised to what extent cross-cultural themes have now become marginalised by teachers and schools. They work today under pressure to focus on the dominant school subjects, driven by examination league tables which are based on a range of specific subjects and not on cross-cultural themes. Issues of intercultural curriculum and citizenship education need not only to be taken seriously and highlighted but given the importance they merit by the enforcement agencies.

The new government has failed to recognise the nature of multiculturalism in British society. It has tried to focus on exclusions within it but without recognising the wider implications as outlined in Chapter 1 of this book. There is the same old stereotyping of 'ethnic minorities' and 'ethnicity' as categories, with their familiar assumption of there being a dominant English nation. There is little recognition of the multilingualism within British society and the need to develop models of teaching first and second languages formally in the schools. There is no provision for a bilingual education which builds on second language (that is to say, English language) acquisition. 'Other languages' are not seen as fundamentally part of the school's work, not only to enable young people to learn their first language better but to acquire greater competence in English as a second language.

There is the Ethnic Minority Achievement Grant (EMAG). There are, however,

Dominant.

ambiguities about EMAG, how it works in schools and local authorities.

The issue of intercultural education still remains to be faced seriously – seriously, because Blunkett, on a visit to Dublin, announced that the Irish language is to be introduced into the English national curriculum so that English schoolchildren can have lessons in Irish (*The Independent* 29 October 1998). In Irish – but not in Punjabi, or Urdu? Is multilingual education only to be seen as a little weapon for use in international power politics, and not as a potentially enriching cultural force?

While this book was in preparation came the news that Blunkett has promised government finance to a London Muslim school – a disastrous surrender to the 'politics of recognition'.

THE ASIAN COMMUNITY – A CASE STUDY

Attainments of Pupils

In general, educational research on Asians is not extensive. What exists is comparative research with a focus on African-Caribbean attainment levels (Gilborn and Gipps 1996). The 1991 Standard Assessment Task, for instance, made detailed assessments of African-Caribbean, White, Pakistani and Indian pupils, and reported that the Pakistani children obtained lower levels than other groups in English, Maths and Science. The usage of English at home has an impact on the performance in these three subjects. However, the lower performance of Pakistanis is problematic because Indian students also do not use English at home extensively. Closer analysis of the figures may reveal social class to be one additional factor. South Asians from professional classes have done better on average exam scores, though female students have not done as well as the male cohort groups.

It is possible that for analytical purposes the Asian category may be meaningless because it is too broad. In Bradford (1994), Indian pupils were ten points higher than Pakistani and Bangladeshi pupils – equivalent to two Higher Grade C Level passes at GCSE. In terms of employment Indians were least represented in GE manual classes, and this may be one explanation for their higher educational achievement.

The issue is complex. London Pakistani pupils do better than those in Bradford or Lancashire. The additional barriers against Bangladeshis require further explanations However, with the Bangladeshi groups in the Tower Hamlets area there has been an improvement in their average scores from 16 points in 1990 to 24 points in 1994. This does represent a dramatic improvement in examination results, despite economic disadvantage. One explanation could be that Tower Hamlets has 25 per cent of the British Bangladeshi population and has targeted the use of EM 6 Funds. The argument is that when funds are targeted they are used for that specific objective and not only can the expending of funding be monitored but the outcomes can be measured. It is worth considering how such targeted support and tuition can be generalised as good practice. Also in the long term how can a more rationalised funding system of EM 6 be devised to replace Section 11.

There are various ways in which value added calculations and multilevel modelling are used to judge school effectiveness (multilevel modelling is a statistical technique which demonstrates the effectiveness of schools). However, there is a danger of reducing analysis to simple input/output measures – which ignores complex measures requiring attention as far as all minorities are concerned. For instance, pupils may be classified as having learning difficulties when in fact language learning may be the issue.

The focus on the backgrounds of pupils is one variable, because schools may be differentially effective for different groups – yet there is little statistical or other information on these differential factors. The regional variations are in themselves important, because evidence from Brent and Birmingham suggests improved results in examinations, while in Lancashire they remain lower and unchanged. The differentials are partly dependent on the complex relationship between pupils, their families and of course teachers and schools. Lower expectations of teachers, bullying and racism remain issues of continuing concern. Much credit is due to the way in which Asian young people have responded to the influences of the values of teachers and parents. Hence the role of good teachers and schools, supported by parents, cannot be ignored. Their efforts in this respect ought to be recognised.

One of the issues which requires further and concerted action is the stereotype that Asian girls do not need to study hard or go on to further and higher education. The unequivocal opposition of Pakistani parents to their daughters' education is strikingly featured in a study of interviews with fifty-five young women. The Punjabi Sikh parents' response was the opposite (Brah and Shaw 1992). Despite these problems, higher numbers of Asian girls (Indian, Pakistani, Bangladeshi, Chinese) participate in full-time education between 16 and 19 years of age than white girls.

The result is that by the age of eighteen Asians are the most highly qualified national group. This places them in a very strong position for entry into higher education, though fewer gain entry to traditional universities, and far greater numbers to the new universities. Fewer still get into high status faculties.

Nevertheless the Asian success myth needs to be treated with caution. It might be rash to expect subsequent generations to perform as well as the first. In a winner/loser society there will be larger numbers of poorer Asians who will become marginalised like the Irish in the 1840s. They will, however, be part of a 'new type of poverty' which will have little in common with the old respectable and deserving poor. As new victims, they will be blamed for their own impoverishment and ineducability – and the Asian meritocrats will not disagree. These young people, it will be said, have become the new rabble who merely breed and therefore cause their own poverty. As we have just seen such notions of 'transmitted deprivation', nurtured by the late Sir Keith Joseph, have now received new impetus in Britain from American research (Herrenstein and Murray 1994).

Dilemmas and Policy Issues

There is a need to construct an academic discourse which draws on various disciplines to inform a better map of the complex Asian community in Britain. The current modalities of analysis, based on the ethnic focus, are not adequate. Just the notion of Indian, Pakistani, Sri Lankan or Bangladeshi 'ethnic groups' is nonsensical because these are national categories which consist of various ethnicities. Issues raised by an Asian presence have a national significance and are not merely an ethnic dimension of a narrow and dominant construction of the British nation.

Since the period of Asian settlement, a very diverse British Asian community, or communities, has emerged. They range from conservative groups who have developed 'siege mentalities' to more mobile and hybridised identities. The second and third generation obviously have more complex notions of themselves. In educational terms, the social structuring and class affiliations could have tended to depress educational outcomes, yet, as the improved educational outcomes of numbers of Asian students demonstrate, this is not necessarily the case. They have not totally conformed to their stereotyped roles. Their sense of agency has also played a role in allowing them not to be negatively stereotyped or positioned in British social structures and hierarchies. Part of this structuring is not dissimilar from the differential outcomes of New York Chinese, where there are marked differences between 'downtown' and 'uptown' Chinese.

Also, because of exclusionary mechanisms and racism, Asian men and women may have different views on the issues of patriarchy, fundamentalism and religious schools. Rather than be locked into the double exclusionary mechanisms of the dominant group, and to the conservative sections of the community, girls and women may have more imaginative ideas of broadening access to the educational system. This has relevance to providing access to school curricula and higher educational institutions, as well as basic education for Asians. The need for education for survival, as well as for social reasons, especially in regard to women, is a priority.

British Asians need to adopt a more critical stance towards the educational system which would enable them to make constructive proposals for changing the system. For instance, according to the Third International Maths and Science Survey (TIMSS), Britain is twenty-fifth in league table terms in learning science and maths. Since British Asian children do well in both these subjects, it could be argued that they would be better placed at age thirteen if they were studying these two subjects in Singapore, Japan, Hong Kong, the Czech Republic, Belgium or the Netherlands.

How the Community Could Help

British children, including British Asians, form part of what Wendy Keys of NFER suggests is a 'long tail of low achievers', and teaching methods which include 'whole class interactive teaching' may be more appropriate for teaching and learning maths and science. Here the British Asian community should assist in improving the educational system as a whole.

Broadly based interdisciplinary research about the British Asians would in turn inform better their educational positioning. They have to rise above the question of how the community is to be defined, described and positioned by dominant disciplines, especially within the educational domain. The educational future for British Asians would be mediocre indeed if, to quote W. B. Yeats,

> The best lack all conviction, while the worst
> Are full of passionate intensity.

In educational terms the picture is so fluid that research gets easily dated because changes in education lead to changing and differential outcomes.

A principled but forthright position on educational issues is necessary because the Asian migration and settlement process has been a painful one. The settlement in Britain has not led to mere replication of the old country, but an adaptation and dynamic replication of culture, religion and customs.

This social dynamism can only retain its vigour if, as a people, we are able to make it part of the mainstream of life. The continual marginalisation of Asian knowledge systems, languages and cultures would lead to polarised communities who would fight to keep alive their imagined pasts through patriarchal and fundamentalist notions of self. This invocation of the 'politics of recognition' has an educational corollary, i.e. 'curriculum of recognition' – leading to demands for an Asian-centred or Islamic-centred school and curriculum.

Here we have a major challenge – to turn the construction of Asian educational experience from deficit and disadvantage models to ones based on difference. Part of this process entails the consideration of a genuine entitlement curriculum which is not narrowly Anglo-centric, but is inclusive of Asian and other knowledges, histories and languages. In other words – a pluralistic curriculum.

An inclusive and shared system has a two-fold pay off. One is to give the British Asian community its citizenship rights, in the course of which the members can also accept its responsibilities, because they would have a genuine stake in both the educational discourse and society generally. The second and more important pay off would be to strengthen notions of common and shared value systems for all those who attend school. Such a common value system would strengthen both the civic culture and the civil society. Given that the public domain and its institutions have been battered, it is paramount that they are strengthened. The British Asian community has an obligation to the whole society as well as to its own self-interest to ensure that it contributes to strengthening public education and public institutions, and helps in developing a system in which all have a stake.

But at a time when society has seemingly evaporated and the market and meritocracy rule, another issue is raised. How does one construct school, local authority, and other anti-racist or Single Regeneration Budget policies which do not cast Asians and other excluded groups as 'special beneficiaries'? There are lessons to be learnt from the failures of Affirmative Action in the USA so that one can devise educational and social policies which meet the needs of excluded groups (see Chapter 4). There are also lessons to be learnt from the failure of previous anti-racist initiatives. The Burnage School Inquiry Report can be one such source.

Another very negative issue which needs to be countered by a broadly based inclusive school policy and curriculum is the rise not just of ethnicised peer group cultures, but of racialised and religious, or narrowly nationalistic, youth gangs. Asian youth also share this gang culture which has negative features. This is a matter for an inter-agency approach, but Asian adults have a major responsibility to counter these narrow ethnicisms.

Although the age-old bullying by white youngsters and black youth continues, there are now more complex religious exclusions – for instance, Muslim girls wearing scarves or Sikh boys with turbans. The CRE report *Learning in Terror* bears an apposite title because Asian school children are particularly vulnerable. Another issue is the rise of fundamentalist groups at schools and universities who have threatened not just gays and lesbians but Jews, as well as Asian girls who are seen to be modernised.

When the Gillborn and Gipps review was published, the African-Caribbean community in Leicester blamed the Asian school presence as the main reason for depressed African-Caribbean children's performance (*The Guardian* 10 September 1996). This issue of African-Caribbean and Asian division has resonances from across the Atlantic where African-Americans, instead of casting racism as cause of their children's education failure, blame the Asian-Americans for causing their school failures. These divisions ought not to be allowed to drift into Britain.

Strategies ought to be investigated to build coalitions to bring about greater equity in education for the Asian communities from the Caribbean, and from East Africa and the sub-continent. This coalition should then explore ways of building links with poor whites and African-Caribbean groups. With changes in the economy and the rise of new technologies, links between education and meaningful training necessitate a more consistent and systematic development of continuing education. Second chance learning for younger and for older Asians is very necessary.

Finally, as the Asian community begins to get older and to retire, an emphasis on education for the elderly requires attention. Education for retirement is necessary, and with attention to the University of the Third Age and to relevant local government provision. There is a need for particular emphasis on the basic and survival education of older Asian women, including widows, to enable them to cope, for as the Asian family system changes, the support systems tend to get undermined.

FURTHER READING

Peter Mortimore (1998) *The Road to Improvement, Reflections on School Effectiveness,* Lisse, Netherlands: Swets and Zeitlinger B.V.

Joseph Lo Bianco, Anthony J. Liddicoat and Chantal Crozet (1997) *Striving for the Third Place, Intercultural Competence through Language Education,* Melbourne: Language Australia.

3

Practising Intercultural Education

INTERCULTURAL EDUCATION

A National Concern

The critical issues of intercultural education, and the promotion of a sense of belonging rather than of being excluded or marginalised, need to be addressed as part of a national concern for educational progress. For if intercultural education is not fundamentally integrated into the mainstream educational system, the main social policy provision can be counter-productive and have racist consequences. It can also lead to disillusionment amongst the subordinate communities and tend to their balkanisation within the state.

Education takes place within a broad societal and political context. On its own it cannot solve all society's problems – political action and economic measures are needed, to maintain peace, social stability and political integrity. What is being considered here is not the politicisation of education, but the recognition of the broader political context in which education takes place.

Tackling racism in schools, for instance, requires a multi-agency approach because schools alone cannot deal with this critical issue. The inability of a school to devise strategies to combat racism can lead to pupils 'learning in terror' – to quote the title of the 1988 Commission for Racial Equality Report. It also raises the possibility of more dangerous conflicts based on ethnicisation of young gangs, based along racial, religious and narrow nationalistic lines. A strategy at national level is imperative, to ensure strong school–community links in all major cities. Meaningful school–community links are essential to consolidate the good work of teachers.

Children develop multi-dimensional identities as they become involved in families, peer groups, schools and other socialising activities or organisations. The success of this development process, however, depends on the meaningful involvement of parents of both dominant and subordinate groups in the educational programme. Unless schools have strong community links, chauvinistic and fundamentalist parents can undo the work of schools and reinforce racism and narrow ethnic identities.

Therefore the key question remains – what can the education system do, both in the early years of school, and later at secondary school level, to broaden the choice of identities for young people which can transcend ethnic or narrow nationalistic roles?

The Potential of Multilingualism

Britain is part of a multilingual Europe and world. Over 300 languages are spoken in London alone – and these languages represent an extremely rich resource which can be harnessed for academic, literary and economic purposes. My own life has certainly been enriched by having grown up fluent in four languages. Yet, because of the international status of English, most of them are being allowed to disappear within a monolingual mainstream.

There are in fact 307 languages spoken in London by children. Only two-thirds of London's 850,000 school children speak English at home. While the largest group of languages used are from the Indian sub-continent, the lexicon of languages runs from Abe (an Ivory Coast language used by children in Lewisham) to Zulu, with 47 speakers in Haringey. There are no current comprehensive records within the inner or greater London areas and the number of languages used may be far higher, especially if dialects are included. These include at least 100 African languages although some are spoken only by small groups of children.

Schools obviously cannot teach them all: it is the linguistic communities that have an obligation to teach most of them autonomously. But they must not be seen as 'ethnic languages' for 'ethnics'.

Literature written in first languages survives among the older generation, but those born in Britain are losing it. Meanwhile some of the best writing in English comes from those who use it as an additional language, enriching it by other linguistic and literary imaginations. A more relevant multilingual national strategy requires fresh thinking, policies and support. I shall return to this issue in Chapters 4 and 6.

Cultural Distance and Disaffection from School

Many present generation students suffer the basic disadavantage of a poor socio-economic origin compounded by cultural distance. Social background, size of family (including single parents), non-attendance at nursery school and parental interest all have a bearing on performance at school.

Cultural distance is, however, a complex issue which may be independent of the issue of nationality. For example, in France national origin in itself is not a significant factor, since Italians, Spaniards, Belgians and Germans appear to achieve better than their French counterparts. But for those of North African origin, and in Britain Afro-Caribbean, country of origin is a discriminating factor, indicating the importance of cultural distance.

There is a complicated pattern affecting school achievement which includes factors such as linguistic proximity of the national group, the existence or non-existence of a common cultural base, and the compatibility of school systems.

1	English	608,500	21	Igbo	1,900
2	Bengali & Sylheti	40,400	22	French-based Creoles	1,800
3	Punjabi	29,800	23	Tagalog (Filipino)	1,600
4	Gujarati	28,600	24	Polish	1,500
5	Hindi/Urdu	26,000	25	Kurdish	1,400
6	Turkish	15,600	26	Swahili	1,000
7	Arabic	11,000	27	Lingala	1,000
8	English-based Creoles	10,700	28	Albanian	900
9	Yoruba	10,400	29	Luganda	800
10	Somali	8,300	30	Ga	800
11	Cantonese	6,900	31	Tigrinya	800
12	Greek	6,300	32	German	800
13	Akan (Ashanti)	6,000	33	Japanese	800
14	Portuguese	6,000	34	Serbian/Croatian	700
15	French	5,600	35	Russian	700
16	Spanish	5,500	36	Hebrew	650
17	Tamil	3,700	37	Korean	550
18	Farsi (Persian)	3,300	38	Pashto	450
19	Italian	2,500	39	Amharic	450
20	Vietnamese	2,400	40	Sinhala	450

Approximate totals rounded up or down to nearest 50

Figure 3.1. Most common mother tongues for London children
Source: The Times, 21 January 2000

In Britain a larger proportion of poor English, Afro-Caribbean and Bangladeshi children perform badly at school, partly because of the gap between the school culture and that of home. Cultural distance may result in alienation from school, low educational performance and disruptive behaviour. The school in turn may have various responses to this disaffection, from rehabilitation to temporary suspension and permanent exclusion. It may be useful to focus on some of these factors to help minimise excessive alienation from school.

In today's society, with its diverse cultural groups, the lack of a secure identity, knowledge, skills, and ability to see the world in complex ways, can all lead to a sense of displacement for young people. Schools have an important role in enabling young people to understand the social diversity around them. Those who have not done well in school during their late adolescence require second chance learning. Though the younger generation in poor urban neighbourhoods often lack educational attainments and vocational skills, the school should be able to build constructively on the survival and street skills which are part of the lives of many urban young people. One of the real challenges for schools lies in developing cross-cultural peer group solidarities, and replacing negative aspects with a more constructive value system.

Rutter and Smith (1995) demonstrate that low educational outcomes are influenced by peer group cultures throughout Europe. While the authors present no simplistic solutions, parents, youth workers and teachers have an important role

LANGUAGE		LANGUAGE	
Bengali	20,113	German	296
Gujerati	3,904	Serbo-Croat	230
Urdu	3,822	Other European	627
Punjabi	3,062		
Hindi	593	Chinese	4,242
Tamil	398	Vietnamese	1,573
Singhalese	167	Tagalog	1,102
Other IPBS[1]	274	Malay	163
		Thai	144
Turkish	4,625	Japanese	133
Arabic	3,427	Other Far East	211
Farsi	613		
Hebrew	525	Yoruba	2,941
Other Mid-East	113	Twi	1,111
		Ibo	779
Spanish	3,095	Ga	346
French	2,342	Somali	267
Greek	2,241	Fante	213
Portuguese	1,939	Luganda	147
Italian	1,619	Tigrinya	145
Polish	682	Swahili	123
Gaelic	318	Other African	1,244
Maltese	311		
		All Languages	70,221

Figure 3.2. Languages recorded in ILEA schools in 1989
(1) IPBS = India, Pakistan, Bangladesh, Sri Lanka etc.
Source: 1989 Language Census (RS1261/891) ILEA Research and Statistics Branch. London: ILEA. Cmnd: November 1989.

to play in countering youth cultures which are averse to education. The real issues are how can young people learn to be an asset to society by being integrated and how can teachers effectively reduce alienation from sections of the community not interested in the alienation process?

A reduction in alienation from school may in turn lead to a reduction in social alienation, and a greater social and economic cohesiveness in British society. As we face the challenges of the next millennium, schools can no longer afford to ignore the institutional aspects of racism, and marginalise the potential of good intercultural education.

Teacher and School Strategies

A major problem in education systems is the distance between teachers and students. This gap between teachers' and students' culture has many manifestations, ranging from language, religious, social class and age differences to differing views about the role of education. Teacher education needs to address these issues. Unless appropriate education policies are implemented by teachers, the marginalised groups will continue to be blamed for their failures rather than viewed as victims of educational and social exclusion. Intercultural policies at national, local and school levels ought to be devised to ensure that they include all groups, and that their impact leads to practices which can be monitored. To focus on specifically disadvantaged groups only stigmatises them further.

This demands that teachers are well educated on issues of intercultural education. Good intercultural education is one of the greatest challenges which this country faces. As a minumum teachers should not be overtly or covertly racist. They should also be equipped to deal with xenophobia and racist behaviour and they ought to organise their classrooms so that children with different competencies and levels of cultural distance can learn from each other. Regrettably, the narrowly defined notions of teacher 'training', which preclude any broader intercultural understandings, skills and knowledge, are a major barrier – an issue considered in Chapter 4.

School policies should qualitatively and quantitatively monitor excessive levels of exclusion of pupils from certain communities, and take measures to minimise them. An analysis of how complex classrooms and modern schools work should be part of this practice. Dysfunctional mechanisms should be reformed as part of school management.

Schools should work in coordination with youth and community workers and should provide an in-service education for teachers on the importance of this aspect.

Playgrounds, Games and Styles

Formal leaning in the classroom and the school do not take place in isolation from what happens in the corridors and the playground. Organised games can provide discipline and rules that help intercultural relations. However, informal interactions in the playgrounds may reinforce racist prejudices (Cohen 1991). This is especially the case where play is beyond the influence of stabilising adult cultures.

Much of young people's peer culture revolves round oral cultures, music as well as styles. Clothing and fashion are also complex issues which carry deeper meanings than is ascribed to them. These meanings may have political messages. Camouflage clothing, battledress jackets, combat trousers may work as a symbol of political rebellion, reflecting notions of an 'urban guerilla' or the 'commando chic', as well as of reactionary stability. Dr Klaus Martens boots– 'Doc Martens' – have become an international symbol of fascistic young people as have the rebellious skinheads' red 'bovver boots'.

The masculine underpinning of much of this fashion and its inspiration for racist, fascistic and intercultural relations amongst young peple is an un-researched question (*Warriors* 1994). It is also something which many schools disregard. Perhaps simple and cheap school uniforms which poorer families can afford would be a partial answer.

The role of education in teaching games and sports as a way of ensuring fair play or rules of play is of critical importance. This became very apparent during the 1998 World Cup. Football and the game itself are used as symols of war and play has become secondary to nationalistic considerations. Young people's violence, largely on an ethnicised or nationalistic basis, subverts the positive and intercultural dimensions of the game. Educators have a role in using sport for intercultural relations. Schools are also obvious sites where the stereotyped association of certain groups with certain types of sports needs to be dealt with. The focus on bodies and the labelling by young people constrains the development of intercultural sports: for instance, the assertion that blacks cannot swim because of the peculiar relationship of their shoulders to the rest of the body.

A Non-Nationalistic Curriculum

A genuinely national curriculum should respect the principle of diversity. Peter Newsam declared in 1988 that the National Curriculum entitled all children to 'a common set of educational experiences pitched at a high level'.

The stress on entitlement implicit in the National Curriculum is a genuine advance. Yet if it is to become a reality, all children in Britain ought to have access to a common curriculum based on universal principles. Entitlement to an ethnocentric English curriculum does not constitute such an entitlement, since such a curriculum would be based on fantasising, or on an ideological construction of the 'others'' past. Indeed it would assume that there is a monocultural future. Such an assumption is a fallacy: a multicultural future is already with us. To deny it presents students with distorted values and endangers the polity.

A previous Secretary of State for Education said that students from African, Caribbean and Asian backgrounds ought to be taught Western classical music. What he ignored was that it is equally incumbent upon an English child to understand and enjoy the icons of Oriental and African traditions. This is particularly the case with music, when contemporary youth culture is influenced by music from such a very diverse range of backgrounds.

Similarly Britain's reservoir of universal knowledge includes a vast range of languages spoken in urban areas. Optimum policies should draw together that vast linguistic knowledge so that children can acquire mastery over a second language. And in developing the students' oral and written skills in English language, it is important to build on their own linguistic experience and skills. The English curriculum can help them develop a critical edge to their thinking.

Moreover, taking Bakhtin's conception of language as a socially plural construct, in which our own speech is never entirely and exclusively our own, but always heteroglossic and polyvocal, language and culture are at the borderline between oneself and the other. As Clifford states, the word in language is 'half someone else's': it is never all one's own (Clifford 1988: 237) It is therefore important for a National Curriculum to avoid dominant monologues and establish dialogues which would give a stake to all.

The rationale for establishing such a commitment is not merely to demonstrate tolerance to diversity, but to overcome the dichotomy between 'them' and 'us'. This approach presents immense challenges, not only for the institutional pedagogies and curricula within schools, but for teacher education as well.

Having been schooled myself in the rigidly Eurocentric and culturally crippling curriculum of British Kenya, I am only too aware of the dangers that a Eurocentred curriculum can bring, and of the need to replace it with a curriculum in which questions and criticisms are welcomed, not suppressed. The history curriculum in particular represents a site for questioning local communities and British society. Issues of societal diversity and migration can help students to enlarge their understanding of the complexity of the underlying society, and enable them to re-interpret history and make connections. British history cannot therefore be taught merely as a story of England. Understanding 'Englishness' must entail an understanding of its symbiotic relationship with the more complex and larger aspects of 'Britishness'. This ought to be seen as a genuine attempt to engage with the complex diversities of all groups within British society.

Educational initiatives which lead to making diversities cohere are important in a period of fragmentation. A curriculum which de-emphasises racism and narrow ethnicisms can nurture and assist the development of healthily rooted but dynamic common cultures. Students and teachers ought to be enabled to negotiate critically core values to which all can subscribe, and which result from a broader understanding of the commonalities in a socially diverse society. From this perspective the shift is not towards a mindless cosmopolitanism (Krupat 1992: 232–480). It is, in fact, a constructive engagement with progressive specificities, and particularities of diverse cultural groups, without the parochialism which is bound to grow if exclusion, racism and ethnicisation of cultures continue.

A curricular development which engages with such questions presents teachers and students with a very large canvas, involving the possibility of the genuine negotiation and development, both of the students' critical faculties, and of the teachers as professionals. It means disengaging from such moralisms as privileging notions of 'sovereign unitariness' or superficial 'celebration of diversity'. It should involve the development of whole school policies to establish a climate for positive learning where all feel equally valued (National Union of Teachers 1992). Such policies need to cover all aspects of school life; they need to involve everyone so that they feel 'ownership' of the policy.

Introducing a non-Anglocentric curriculum to enhance learning and reduce alienation from school means re-appraising the canon of knowledge that is relevant for all children. Yet the National Curriculum, as it is currently understood, does not build on the diverse origin of knowledge which ought to constitute a curriculum to build a shared and common value system. For instance, the notion of a British culture connected with Greek civilisation, but detached from other cultures and civilisations, is a myth. Yet it is being perpetuated in the English context by the Qualifications and Curriculum Authority (previously School Curriculum and Assessment Authority).

It is a myth created by nineteenth and early twentieth-century racism and anti-semitism, which ignored the contributions to the arts and cultural knowledge of Ancient Greece made by the Egyptians, and by the Phoenicians and other East Mediterranean peoples. It presents Greek culture in isolation, as if it were uncontaminated by other influences, and not as the dynamic hybridised culture which it was. And the emphasis on the spread and influence of Greek culture over Europe, as if this were a unique phenomenon, ignores its spread eastwards to Central Asia and India. Its influence is apparent, for instance, in the development of my own ancestral Gandhara culture, as exemplified by some beautiful sculptures in the British Museum. This should form part of a national curriculum designed for a country whose diversity of cultures has been so regularly enriched from outside.

As it is, a Eurocentric curriculum has unleashed a reaction from those who feel that their knowledge, histories and languages are excluded from the mainstream discourse of the school. Students' refusal to learn and disruptive behaviour may be partly the result of an approprite curriculum. Oppressed groups who have experienced exclusion of their knowledge and educational outcomes are making separatist demands – demands within polities which may embody various indices of diversity but still continue to be governed by hegemonic state apparatuses, the 'politics of recognition', demonstrated by the demand for Black or Islamic schools.

The next step has been a 'curriculum of recognition' which has included courses like Black, Irish, South Asian and women's studies (Gundara 1996a: 27–28). Such courses have been under-resourced and hence marginalised, which has led to demands for Afro-centric or Islamo-centric knowledge to counteract Eurocentrism.

But as Said explains:

> The whole effort to deconsecrate Eurocentrism cannot be interpreted, least of all by those who participate in the enterprise, as an effort to supplant Eurocentrism with, for instance, Afrocentric or Islamocentric approaches. On its own, ethnic particularity does not provide for intellectual process – quite the contrary.
>
> (quoted in McCarthy and Critchlow 1993: 311)

Separate schools or curricula do not assist in bringing about intercultural understandings. They reinforce misunderstandings, and by negating the children's knowledge and educational potential, they negate the whole concept of intercultural learning. What is important within our complex societies is to develop cross-cultural negotiation and learning, and develop common and shared core values. A rigorously selective but intercultural curriculum, which may necessitate a reappraisal of what is the relevant canon of knowledge for children, can play a critical role in helping shape such values. The curriculum/classroom do not work in isolation from the community.

SCHOOL AND COMMUNITY

School/Community Relations

There is a certain problem in the usage of the term 'community'. Those who use it assume that it has some coherent, consistent character. But this may need to be created. Schools need to develop a common strategy which engages not only all the parents but the members of the community in which they are located, so that there is a consistency in parental and community involvement across cultural lines, soundly based within the community.

An African expression states, 'it takes a whole village to educate a child'. Education is not merely the concern of parents and their own children. Though parents are responsible for their children and their welfare they do not own them. In the widest sense the education of adults and children is potentially a concern of the whole community. Hence the school has a basic task of getting to know the whole community around the school, above all those who have been educated in schools at an earlier period or in different cultural contexts and cannot understand the schools in this country. Now the 'village' itself needs re-educating.

Democratisation of education, and community control, only becomes meaningful if local communities have the political understanding to implement meaningful policies. Without political knowledge and skills, community control of education only becomes populist in nature, incapable of making meaningful changes in the educational process.

Many small and major initiatives can ensure the involvement of communities and parents in the life of the school. It is obviously much easier to involve parents than the wider community. But even amongst parents, the most needy and illiterate remain excluded from the life of the school, and from the learning and education process as a whole.

And here I must be honest enough to recall my own school years. My parents would have been astonished at the suggestion that they had anything to teach the school, while I, for my own self-interested reasons, was unwilling that they should become involved in it. But somehow, with tact and understanding, the barrier between school and parents has to be broken down, and parents be enabled to see that their own insights and experiences can enrich the life of the school.

Those in the wider community should also be enabled to feel that they too are needed, that they can play a positive role, and that adults can make their views and feelings known to the school and staff and be taken seriously. In multicultural communities, their linguistic, religious and cultural backgrounds should be valued. They should be shown that schools and communities are organically linked. This is easier in the early years of a child's education, and more difficult in secondary schools as peer group culture becomes powerful and home, community and school become more distanced.

Until recently the teaching profession has not faced the issue of parental links.

Schools and teachers did not provide appropriate information for parents, make links with them or gain their confidence. Then in 1991 the government enacted a Parents' Charter to substitute for the customary 'deference, puzzlement and helplessness' felt by parents 'a formal right to information and access concerning their children's schooling, and to share in decisions regarding this'. The Parents' Charter legalises a joint commitment and common purpose in educating future generations of children. Schools ought now at least to draw up a clear policy of parental involvement.

The conclusion of the Plowden Report (1967) could not decide whether 'performance is better where parents encourage more' or whether 'parents encourage more where performance is better'. The Catch 22 still remains. But the common-sense solution is that the issues are interrelated and that home/school interaction is an important issue in the education of children.

Parental Choice

The issue of parental choice of schools has also been simplistically presented – indeed it is a myth because it is the schools who do the choosing. Parental expression of preference can lead to social segregation with schools being classified as 'good, adequate or sink schools'.

How can schools in poorer areas, marginalised communities, rural as well as urban, constructively activate parental links when they do not have the means? It is there that the need for parental and community links is greatest. In many such areas, particularly in socially mixed communities, parents have long realised that their children were not doing well in school. The Haringey Black Parents Group, for instance, formed in the late 1960s, published what has become a seminal pamphlet, Bernard Coard's 'How the West Indian Child is made educationally subnormal in the British school system' (Coard 1971). These parental concerns led to campaigns against the poorer educational performances of many children and resulted in two enquiries being set up by the government (Rampton 1981; Swann 1985).

Subsequent administrations have paid scant attention to their recommendations. And the decline in understanding these issues, and the dismantling of existing practices and structures, only encourages further efforts to re-invent the wheel.

The differing educational outcomes of middle class children and children from families with limited 'cultural capital' illustrates a critical factor in improving children's performance. A Coventry study showed that parental involvement with 1,000 children from disadvantaged backgrounds was able to improve their performance to the educational levels of middle class children. In language and reading these eight-year-olds could do as well as their well-off counterparts. When the group was retested the following year the data had in fact hardened (Kruger 1990).

Whether it is a traditional school or a community school, parental involvement is an important factor (Widlake and McLeod 1984). Parental participation is easier in a community school because community educators recognise the value of such work. The work of Eric Midwinter in England, and Ettore Gelpi, the Italian educationist working in UNESCO, has promulgated similar notions of what Gelpi calls *educatione permanente* (life-long education). However, the present legislation in England militates against such parental involvement through community schools in which both parents and children are learning.

In the traditional school, where teachers and support personnel are the only adults seen to be involved in the educational process, it is easy for the child to assume that the process terminates as you leave the classroom. Teachers need parental support in carrying out their professional job. Parents and community as a resource can help teachers improve children's academic performance as well as their school attendance, retention and behaviour and reduce school exclusion. The school can provide a framework for parents to help their children's education, particularly in homework (Vogler and Hutchins 1988).

It could include homework assistance centres run by volunteers, career information sharing by volunteers, problem-solving skills development classes, enrichment programmes after school, tutor assistance for students with learning difficulties, guest lecturing in classes, mentorship for students interested in specific careers and volunteers teaching technology to students.

In developing such strategies a school can establish a partnership with parents. It provides a positive relationship which ends the customary practice of parents and schools only coming together when there are problems, a practice in which the measure of trust tends to disappear. The school's priority should be to obtain community and parental trust, and to help parents value their role.

Parents should be made to feel that they are needed and can play a positive role, and that when they make their views and feelings known, the school and staff will take them seriously. In multicultural communities the parents' linguistic, religious and cultural backgrounds should be seen as of positive value. Parents in poorer areas may neither be confident of their own ability nor have the confidence to help in educating their own children – mothers particularly may feel isolated. Their isolation can be reduced by being involved in the school with other mothers. Traveller and Roma families may have a totally different set of unmet needs and concerns which can be developed within the common schools or on sites where they live. As it is, they are usually judged by the norms of settled people, norms whose unversality is taken for granted

'Community' Schools

Distinct from the idea of an inclusive, organically linked, community and its school, there is a trend, set in motion as part of the 'politics of recognition', in favour of so-called community schools. Twinned with the idea of marketised education, they would have a far narrower scope. Their aim is set either in commodified form, to lead to jobs, or like the City Technical Colleges (CTCs), they are specialised schools catering for students with specialist academic interests. This has increased the demand for Muslim, Christian or other faith schools under the provisions of the 1993 Education Act (Walford 1995). The power it gives to parents, all the greater when they are organised on the basis of their faith, has strengthened the demand for such schools. So far the Labour government has not taken their demand on board.

Obviously this narrow definition of 'community' only fragments further the comprehensive provision of education. Indeed, narrowing down the focus to include only particular groups, even individual parents, makes nonsense of the definition. What we are now seeing is a reversal of the gains won in the 1960s and 1970s and the continuation of unequal relations between groups. Selective education gives benefits to young people in a privileged class position. Those who need the help to improve their performance that a mixed-ability, comprehensive school would provide drop behind even further. 'Choice' and 'diversity' are of no value to these children. They do nothing to improve their educational outcomes. Rather 'they seem to be further disadvantaging many of those very groups who are disadvantaged by the present system' (Whitty, Power and Halpin 1998).

Thus poorer children from both dominant and minority communities would suffer from these changes. If the schools were also to become racially segregated, as the introduction of faith schools would in practice virtually entail, the downward spiral of poverty and race would only divide existing mixed communities or localities further.

Differentiated school systems can only reinforce divisions within communities. Parents, it is true, obviously have responsibilities towards their children. But the local education authorities and the central government also have a responsibility to develop a more cohesive and egalitarian society.

School and Parent–Community Partnerships

One of the main educational concerns should be the education of adults and children within the framework of community education. While adults' identities are already formed, children's are in the process of being formed. Issues of belongingness, as well as of exclusion, should be part of the educational concern and process, and should enable students to transcend narrow definitions of identity. Community education is difficult because communities are fragmented, and the educational systems have a very difficult task in activating such complex educational initiatives. Now also there are pressures for re-skilling for jobs, not just for community education.

Children are able to construct a broader understanding of life based on their own personal concerns and experiences. These understandings underpin what may emerge as multi-dimensional identities. They grow up and develop different identities as they begin to get involved in different types of collectivities, ranging from family to peer group, school work and other socialising influences, including the media. Yet unless parents and adults are also part of the educational process, racism and the narrow ethnicised identities are likely to be reinforced. This is as true for the dominant as for the subordinate groups.

Chauvinistic parents and adults can undo the work of the school, and unless the schools have a strong community link, negative spillovers can undermine the work.

The uniqueness of belonging to a particular nationality ought not to exclude identification with other nationalities. The school curriculum has therefore the further challenge of enabling young people to understand culturally and socially diverse neighbourhoods, and to reduce levels of insecurity and uncertainty. Those young people who do not acquire good educational outcomes have a greater need for second chances of learning.

Partnership with a school requires that parents and communities do not feel alienated from it. Many parents feel that education is the job of the teachers and that they should not interfere in their professional domain. Nor may they understand the differences between informal pre-school and formal education in which schools are engaged. In multicultural communities they may feel cut off if languages other than the dominant ones are not understood.

All professionals, doctors and lawyers as well as teachers, find it difficult to share skills, decision-making or accountability. This position detracts from mutual understanding and partnership between schools and communities, parents and teachers. But links between the two can be enhanced by regular and effective communication, sharing information, with teachers showing visible manifest respect to parents, as well as listening and explaining. For instance, parents' advice can be sought on curriculum as well as assessment issues. Equal opportunity and intercultural policies should be made clear to them. In general, the teachers should ensure that they and the parents have similar or shared goals.

At school level these dimensions ought to emerge particularly within Parent-Teacher Associations and within governing bodies. Parents who may speak another language, or may be only partly literate, find it difficult to follow communications through the written word. Therefore personal links with staff are important, because through informality meaningful links can be made. This is not a substitute for 'social events' or formal meetings, even though some parents may find it difficult to understand or follow them, or to feel empowered enough to contribute. Schools need to explore ways of enhancing parental 'voice' in the social events and formal meetings.

Formal meetings, particularly those of governing bodies, are intimidating, and many parents do not have the skills, confidence or information to take part. Ways should be found to restructure meetings to allow them to participate. The use of jargon, which normally inhibits participation, should be eliminated. Governors should receive some training. Where the agenda is determined by a clique of partisan or politically active governors, parents are inhibited from participating, because they feel disenfranchised. The openness of agendas and meetings can help to bridge the home–school and home–community links.

How important are training courses for governing bodies? If they are useful they should perhaps be organised by consortia of schools – though some current courses organised by private consultants may not be very helpful, because their prime purpose is to make money. Parents need to understand the legal basis of the complex current legislation as well as the rules and regulations under which the governing bodies and schools operate. Parent involvement must not be limited, as it normally is, to matters like fund-raising. Parents must be allowed parity of 'voice'.

School/Community Strategies

In multicultural school settings there is a need to avoid the dangers of bullying, particularly since parents themselves may be 'learning in terror' (*Learning in Terror* 1988) and unable to be involved in their children's education. The schools therefore need to understand the complexities and the delicacies of the situation to ensure that children, parents and isolated members of the community all feel safe within the school. This issue again highlights the role of school–community links – not merely a role restricted to links with parents. The school also needs to deal with racist incidents sensitively, so that no children are left feeling insecure and vulnerable. This includes strategies to integrate into the school culture the children of travellers and Roma whom other children may exclude. If the school develops as a 'safe school' its positive ethos will spill over into the community.

School language policy needs to encompass the linguistic diversity within the community. Positive strategies for teaching languages to children and adults should be developed to ensure that non-English-speaking parents can be involved in the education of their children, as well as seeing their children understand and actively participate in their own education.

All the school staff must together develop a 'collective school ethic'. This is a difficult issue because the staff are part of a complex institution: it may be easier to develop in primary than in secondary schools, which are more difficult to manage. Communication within the school is essential because, for instance, good work in the classroom can be undone by school welfare staff if there is no coordination between different parts of the school.

Parental involvement in their children's education might entail combining it with education of adults, and thus contributing to the continuing educational process within the community to ensure learning across age groups. It must also take into account the changing role of families and work patterns. The school has to accept not only the diversity of cultures but also of parental and familial life styles. Privileging the two-parent nuclear family tends to pathologise the rest, particularly as female-headed families are increasing in all communities. In 1973 one in twenty parents were separated and now it is about one in three. The Major government's 'back to basics' in family values was cynical in the extreme, given the way its economic policies have fragmented the family. Lone parent families, and dual career families, provide special challenges to schools in establishing successful school involvement. This is particularly true of parents from minority communities, and other people who have to work long hours in poorly paid jobs to keep their households solvent.

The School and Value Issues

Issues of cultural diversity and their impact on schools go beyond issues of political correctness. Schools have a complex role which is not just cosmetic, particularly in developing a common curriculum based on a shared value system which would subsequently inform the functioning of a civil society (a theme to be developed in more detail in Chapter 7).

As children grow older they naturally want to keep parents away from school (as I did myself in my Kenya schooldays), particularly in teenage years, as school culture can be different from the culture of family influences. Youth and peer group cultures assume a more powerful role in social relations, language use, styles, musical and consumer tastes. Moreover the media have a critical role in marginalising local and family values. Rituals of inclusion and exclusion in the playground are part of developing more insular and autonomous peer group cultures. These rituals include ways in which both physical and verbal harassment exacerbate other levels of marginalisation. Children use images, jokes and commonsense prejudices, and exclusions based on them are passed from older to younger children. Does the growth of autonomous young people's cultures arise partly from the failure of education to successfully socialise children and partly from the 'dumbing down' of young people?

Teachers and schools therefore face young people who have other preoccupations (consumer goods, style, music, sex), and are often under pressure to become less academically inclined. Some schools are excluding pupils from certain minority communities because the greater cultural gap presents major problems. The tripartite relationship of parents, school and community should ensure that such expulsions are minimised. Excessive exclusion rates, particularly if associated with specific groups (for instance, young black males), indicate bad relations between parents and children. There should be institutional policies to consider teachers' perceptions of behaviour and why pupils behave badly and disruptively.

At a time when the rise of extreme right politics, and the reaction in the form of 'politics of recognition', and separatist demands by subordinated or marginalised groups, is threatening to polarise communities, it is imperative to create spaces where parents and communities can have a 'voice' in education. This can help to avoid polarisation, particularly in places where the parents and disenfranchised communities have come to feel that reaction and separation are the only solution.

This is something that education in England and Wales has ignored as a critical issue in the polity. The rise of narrow identities and reactions (whether nationalistic, 'ethnic', religious or racial) obviously requires commitment from the education system as a whole. The role of the school in strengthening civic culture as well as public values is something that has been weakened and requires strengthening, particularly given the high unemployment and the undermining of social policy provision.

A school ethos based on moral, spiritual, cultural and social values therefore

	1994/95* No.	1995/96** No.	Increase No.	%
White	8,765	10,096	1,331	15
Black Caribbean	768	867	99	13
Black African	148	216	68	46
Black Other	182	241	59	32
Indian	98	109	11	11
Pakistani	208	255	47	23
Bangladeshi	46	58	12	26
Chinese	11	14	3	27
Other	241	366	125	52

*Excludes 181 pupils whose ethnic origins were not known. The figures were based on the 1991 census.
**Excludes 10 pupils whose ethnic origins were not known. The figures were based on information from schools.
Sources:
Department for Education and Employment (1996) Youth Cohort Study: Trends in the activities and experiences of 16–18-year-olds: England & Wales: 1985–1994, in *Statistical Bulletin*, Issue No. 7/95, June.
Department for Education and Employment (1997) Youth Cohort Study: The activities and experiences of 16-year-olds: England and Wales: 1996, in *Statistical Bulletin*, Issue No. 8/97, June.

Figure 3.3. Increase in permanent exclusions in England, by ethnic group, 1994/95–1995/96

raises issues not just for 'social and personal education', but across the structure of the school and indeed community. It must not be consigned to one particular area of the curriculum. The obvious linkages and connections in developing citizenship values, and a commitment to rights and responsibilities within civil society, are the responsibility not just of the school but also of the community.

Community and school links are particularly important because negative or positive aspects from each domain spill over from one to the other. Violence in the community can affect life in the school. The tension in London Borough of Greenwich schools after a murder in the Thamesmead estate in 1998 is a case in point. In this instance different interpretations and stories worked their way from school to community and vice versa. The school gate is therefore not the end of a school's role or policies. The schools can obviously control children's behaviour through school policy. However, the important aspect of children's imagination in both positive and negative terms still remains to be tackled. This is particularly true of 'racist imaginations'. As a negative phenomenon it requires action by the media, teachers, youth workers and the community.

Many communities are trapped between the imagined pasts of home, and the alienation they experience when the dominant groups assert notions of the 'imagined ownership' they have of 'their' cities in 'their nations', thus reinforcing the exclusion of these already marginalised groups. Cities, however, embody notions of belongingness as well as of alienation. They enable some to form new identities, though others may just retreat with 'siege mentalities' into siege communities.

These issues of belongingness and exclusion should form part of the educational concern and process developed between school and community. For though the identities of adults are already formed, those of children are in the process of being formed. Such an educational process should enable them to transcend narrow definitions of identity, and construct a broader understanding of life based on their own personal concerns and experiences.

4

Post-School Intercultural Education

This chapter deals with aspects of interculturalism as they impinge on continuing, professional and higher education studies in Britain. But the issues are raised in an introductory manner because there is very little substantive analysis of the way in which exclusivities and xenophobia operate within professional and higher education programmes. North American research in the field is more extensive but has little direct relevance because of the qualitative differences between British and American education or professional programmes.

The very low take-up of higher education studies and postgraduate studies from certain sections of the British and overseas student body is made worse by their higher costs. Positive measures are needed to ensure that the higher reaches of academe do not become the preserve of those who can afford it.

Multicultural student bodies and intercultural practices present new challenges to professional higher education studies. The older universities with a longer tradition of study and research ought to become more flexible in refining their skills, knowledge and practice. This would allow them to raise academic standards for higher education research with a diverse body of students and a more universalised basis of knowledge. It is, however, the new universities which may be more open to these ideas and able to acquire the skills to help students from different backgrounds.

Issues of an inclusive and an intercultural curriculum present a very positive challenge to the professional and higher education institutions. They have the potential to make academic work more dynamic and positive at a time when these institutions confront dual challenges of globalisation and a culture of management.

Affirmative action programmes to correct previous disadvantages and inequalities require a critical examination to ensure that they do not have negative consequences. This chapter examines consequences of such measures with some circumspection.

CONTINUING EDUCATION

The Role of Continuing Education

The continuing education sector is presented with a unique opportunity to study the complex map of British society, within a historical as well as a contemporary social science perspective. Here the customary focus on 'ethnic' and 'migrant' groups, and their educational needs, marginalises the educational initiatives for the community. Not only are their educational needs seen to be separate from the rest of society, but also the adult community in general remains ignorant of how diverse and complex society is. Continuing education provision for adults should provide for the whole community. Concentrating provision of continuing education on 'ethnics' and 'migrants' tends to peripheralise the very groups who are supposed to benefit from it.

Not only does such an emphasis categorise them as problems, it deflects attention away from issues of racism and xenophobia within the wider society. For instance, the Nationality Act (1981), the Immigration Acts (1962, 1968, 1971) and the Race Relations Act (1976) are all indicators of racial discrimination – not discrimination based on 'ethnicity'. For those involved in adult and continuing education, stress on 'migrant' or 'ethnic' provision detracts from broader concerns about the curricula – from institutional practices and structures of adult and continuing education in relation to the education of the whole community.

Given the social basis of the adult education movement, there is a great deal that educators can do to provide broader-based education about society for a large number of British adults. A holistic approach to studying it, including its positive and negative features, would have the advantage of enhancing the personal and intellectual development of the adult population (Gundara, 1988). Analysing negative features like racism and xenophobia has the advantage of being socially relevant – a major rationale for the education of adults. A contextual and wider social science approach, which adults see as relevant and is widely accessible to them, is preferable to narrowly based courses on race relations and racism awareness which may not only be counter-productive, but may legitimise the category of 'race' within the social sciences.

A real challenge for adult and continuing education lies in developing constructive approaches to inter-group relations within the social sciences. These should be accessible to the whole community, while at the same time distanced from a narrow, socially constructed category of race, which has no scientific basis. Furthermore, issues of appropriate continuing education for a multicultural society are relevant to all parts of the country, whether or not 'ethnic' or 'migrant' groups live there, even in catchment areas that are totally white. A permeation model, which ensures that multicultural and anti-racist perspectives inform all courses, should underlie the educational content.

There are two barriers to be surmounted. First, the lack of an institutional commitment or policy which would provide an educational ethos for such work at the institutional level. Secondly, the lack of educational experience on the part of the staff. This can be addressed through staff development courses ensuring that staff are competently trained and capable of dealing with these issues. There is the further issue of the tutors expecting 'a customary degree of academic freedom in devising their courses', an issue answered as long ago as 1987 by Horace Lashley :

> First there is a need to negotiate a policy framework for each institution which envisages the inclusion of multicultural anti-racist perspectives into all subject areas. This will encourage permeation to take place. Second, there is a need to include a discussion of the policy framework in tutor training at all levels and in all subject areas.
>
> (Quoted in Hampton 1987: 8)

Nor must such educational issues be brushed aside because they are said to water down continuing education, particularly in arguments in which excellence in education is opposed to justice in education. James Lynch argues:

> that it is only through the structural and ideological inclusion of currently excluded groups in discourse about a new national covenant, that current hostility, anomie and intergroup conflict can be assuaged; new national ideas will have to provide the philosophical foundations and agreed ideals identified, which are accepted by all legitimate cultural groups.
>
> (Lynch 1987: 13)

Such negotiated and agreed ideals will have to provide the philosophic foundations for continuing education, so that excellence and social justice for all groups in society can be pursued. Only then can sound educational grounds for the curriculum as a whole be devised. Knowledge of oppressed groups who are defined as the 'other' by the dominant groups is generally excluded from the curriculum. Including their knowledge is a fundamental educational question, and would enhance the excellence of all continuing educational provision, rather than detracting from it. Such a perspective would provide a relevant educational provision at continuing education level for the whole community, and would indeed make the role of tutors and students of continuing education more interactive and dynamic.

Continuing Education Policies

As we have seen, in the early 1960s the Department of Education and Science response to what was seen as the 'problem' created by the immigrant groups was to assimilate the children into schools. The main emphasis for adult education was the teaching of English as a second language. Then, in 1977 and again in 1981 government consultative documents declared that the country had become 'multiracial' and 'multicultural' (DES 1977, 1981).

There were two main consequences of this change for adult educators and for all their pupils: first, that multicultural objectives have relevance to the education of the population as a whole, and, second, that the onus is not, as in the earlier assimilationist model, on the various communities to adapt to the system.

The system itself had to change in relation to the broadly based diversities in society.

Strict cash limits on local government spending in the 1980s made choices for adult education increasingly difficult. Yet those engaged with adult education, particularly tutors, not only had to cope with these difficulties, but also had to meet the conceptual and practical challenge posed by the increasing recognition that all students should be educated for living in a multicultural society.

Changes in the educational map of Britain have continued to ensure that the adult and continuing education sector remains a poor cousin of the educational system as a whole. Its position as a 'Cinderella Service' has been further reinforced in a prevailing educational context where the needs of the whole community were not seen to be relevant to the market forces. Within this 'Cinderella Service' the concerns of educating for a multicultural society have been largely ignored, and the educational needs of those who are disadvantaged and disenfranchised have been even further marginalised.

The number of initiatives which have been undertaken by providers in the adult education field still remain very patchy. There is certainly very little evidence to show that the enabling role of continuing education to provide a critical understanding of this society, the broad basis of human knowledge, and skills to function in a diverse society has been fully tested.

Political Education for Young Adults

The articulation of their political interests by certain sub-groups is more than counterbalanced by the political illiteracy, uninterest and apathy of the majority. Given the way in which society is structured, a 'hidden curriculum' operates within adult education which, by its very inattention, perpetuates the status quo. The very fact of stating that a more encompassing political education is not an appropriate subject for adult education is in itself a political statement.

Therefore, the challenge for continuing education is how to meet the needs of the wider community, while working with those who have easier access to the political system. One way is by refining the political management skills of this interested sub-group. But, while it is easier to provide for the needs of this politically motivated group, the continuing education sector needs to address itself to the needs of the total population so that they can become politically aware and participate in political processes which affect their lives.

Given the social basis of the adult education movement, it is important that major attention should be given to the issue of racism in British society. A political dimension of the study of race relations would have the advantage of enhancing personal development and, because of its social relevance, addressing social problems. This focus is in tune with the major rationale for adult education, namely an emphasis on personal development and on social relevance.

The intransigence of attitudes formed at a young age, with little political knowledge, requires political education for those already in school. This can then be built upon by institutions of further and adult education. Attempts to

Rank	Language	Courses
1	English language[1]	497
2	French	474
3	Spanish	389
4	German	279
5	Italian	276
6	Japanese	86
7	Arabic	81
8	Russian	79
9	[Modern] Greek	75
10	Portuguese (Brazilian 6, European 60)	66
11	Putonghua (Mandarin)	65
12	Turkish	37
13	Hindi/Urdu (Hindi 13, Urdu 17)	30
14	Dutch	28
15	Polish	18
16	Bengali (15) + Sylheti (1)	16
17	Cantonese	13
17	Irish Gaelic	13
19	Swedish	12
20	[modern] Hebrew	11
20	Welsh	11
22	Czech	10
23	Punjabi	9
24	Gujarati	8
25	Danish	6
25	Fasi (Persian)	6
25	Norwegian	6
28	Malay (2) Indonesian (3)	5
28	Swahili	5
30	Hungarian	4
30	Serbian/Croatian	4
32	Scottish/Gaelic	3
33	Catalan, Cornish, Korean, Somali, Thai, Vietnamese, Yoruba	each 2
40	Albanian, Amharic, Basque, Belarusian, Bulgarian, Estonian, Hausa, Kurdish, Latvian, Lithuanian, Romanian, Shona, Slovene, Tamil, Ukrainian, Yiddish, Zulu	each 1

(1) This is the total of courses offering 'English language' (150) and 'English for speakers of other languages' (347).
Source: Multilingual Capital – the languages of London's schoolchildren and their relevance to economic, social and educational policies (eds.) Philip Baker and John Eversley, Corporation of London, Battlebridge publication 2000.

Figure 4.1.   Number of part-time day and evening courses offered in particular modern languages at all levels of public sector establishments in Greater London 1999–2000

introduce race relations to young adults without any prior political knowledge may be counterproductive. This was illustrated by Miller's research with young adults at a London college of further education which found young apprentices were more prejudiced after three hours of work than before it (Parker and Raybould 1972). Plainly, teaching these issues needs careful planning, preparation and integration into the curriculum.

The real challenge lies in developing constructive approaches to teaching about racism issues within the framework of political education. These courses can range from those devised for adults in general to those tailor-made for social workers, teachers, managers, trade unionists, administrators or the police. But they will prove inadequate if they simply stress a sociological perspective while ignoring the dimensions of political education. Tailor-made courses on race relations legislation, if unaccompanied by a component of political education, or a social science framework, may merely allow officials who know the legislation to evade it.

Another approach would be to start with the students' own specific attitudes and experience and use that as a basis for defining issues and problems. Questions about racism may lead to studies of ethno-centrism, prejudice, discrimination, bigotry, stereotyping, nationalism and fascism, which would necessitate a historical exploration of the roots of racism. This approach involves a fair amount of reading, because students would have to follow social and economic developments as well as examine the development of racist ideas. An examination of the development of racism might well lead them to study literature on the theories of immigration, as well as Britain's own imperial and colonial past, as being responsible for the presence of Blacks in Britain. As Sivanandan (1982) has said, in another context, 'We are here, because you were there'.

Such explanatory frameworks from various disciplines (history, economics, psychology, politics) can be used to examine critically the contemporary situation with reference to housing, employment, trade unions and education. In the study of racism within this broader, multidisciplinary framework, tutors may start with the stock of political information that students may have, and build upon it. It would entail a critical view of society, and relate to the real world and the experience of adults.

The use of a multidisciplinary approach which encourages a 'critical awareness' may also lead to the examination of another strategy for political education. The whole curriculum may need to be appraised for its suitability in the context of the wider diversities in society. The reappraisal of courses may allow political education to be taught across the whole curriculum, particularly with reference to racist and sexist bias. This approach would, of course, require continuing education of all tutors, not only those concerned with the specific subject of 'political education'.

The Russell Committee described political education as

essentially a task for adult education rather than for school alone, requiring as it does from its students a background of practical experience, maturity of judgement, and the serious motivation that comes from the challenge and responsibilities of adult life.

(DES 1973, para 58.3)

Groups of Blacks and women acquire political education as adults by resisting oppression and discrimination. This does not mean that they are devoid of political values and awareness. Quite the contrary. Their political values are informed by their experiences of defined roles, political processes and committee structures which they find inadequate. For instance, Black women have resisted the stereotypical roles and functions allotted to them in their places of work. Asian women workers have had to engage in struggles with management, white workers and official trade unions to redefine their roles as the underpaid, underemployed and overworked segment of the working population.

The young unemployed Blacks in Brixton, Toxteth and Southall have demonstrated another, violent dimension of resistance because they do not experience equity after leaving school. Schooling and the street provide a political education that is not recognised as being valid even when they are involved in the process of second chance learning. Tutors who work with all these self-politicised groups need to be aware of these broader political issues. Those who work on role issues not only need to be aware of the system as it is, but also have to have an idea of what the system 'ought to be'. They must also learn to present issues of race in a way that divorces fact from fiction. Similarly, those who teach development education must include issues of colonisation and continuing dominant/subordinate relationships between the so-called 'developing' and the third world.

The success or failure of political education ought to be measured by how well it is able to reverse the larger inequalities of society. Survival skills in literacy, or in English as a second language, ought to be reappraised in view of how effective they are in improving the students' life chances. Access to education in this sense goes hand in hand with access to resources for life. Do courses on housing rights lead to a better chance for the homeless to acquire homes? Unless adults see such education as also leading to a shift of power in their favour, it will be seen to have failed.

INTERCULTURAL ISSUES AND HIGHER EDUCATION STUDIES

Students and Academic Work

The academic community is constituted of different groups, disciplines and domains and in principle the presence of culturally different groups and the knowledge they bring should not be seen as presenting any problems. There is, however, a range of questions arising from social inequalities endemic within social differences and minority status which have a bearing on higher education institutions.

The first is that of variances in access to higher education from different communities. Of recent years there has been an increase of, chiefly middle-class, African and Asian minority group students, 60 per cent of them studying at the new universities, many of whom do well. But the representation of Afro-Caribbean men and of Pakistani and Bangladeshi women remains low (Higher Education Funding Council 1996).

These differentials lead to lower levels of take-up at higher education levels by students from marginalised sections of society. Students from these communities may not only have low levels of representation within the student body but also have higher proportions studying technical and business subjects and fewer in the pure sciences or in the arts and humanities – the higher status curriculum subjects.

This is not simply a correlation between different academic cultures and those of the minority communities. Attitudes, experiences and perceptions of learning, for instance, of middle-class Asian and Afro-Caribbean families may have much in common with those of middle-class English families. On the other hand, the differences in attitude between middle-class and marginalised sections of the three communities in relation to higher education may be great. Academic institutions at formal and informal levels of their functioning may need to take measures which diminish cultural distances between different groups and improve institutional access for students from the marginalised groups. At one level friendly and supportive relations between staff and students may help to bridge some aspects of cultural distance for all students in higher education.

	White	All ethnic minorities	Black	Indian	Pakistani & Bangladeshi	Other
25–59/64 years	%	%	%	%	%	%
Degrees	14	16	14	19	10	19
Higher below degree	9	7	11	7	2	8
A-level	23	12	15	11	7	11
GCSE grades A–C or equivalent	20	13	19	12	8	11
Other qualifications	15	29	25	30	26	36
No qualifications	20	23	17	20	47	15
16–24 years						
Degrees	7	6	*	9	*	8
Higher below degree	4	2	*	*	*	*
A-level	27	24	24	29	19	26
GCSE grades A–C or equivalent	37	34	37	38	30	30
Other qualifications	10	15	15	*	17	19
No qualifications	10	17	18	12	24	15

*Numbers less than 10,000; estimated percentages not reported.
Source: Office of National Statistics (1997), Labour Force Survey, Spring, data made available by DfEE.

Figure 4.2. Highest qualification held among people of working age, by ethnic group and age, Spring 1997

There may, however, also be institutional customs, practices and procedures which overtly and covertly discriminate against students from racially and culturally different backgrounds. At this level formal policies might need to be enacted to ensure that institutional arrangements and practices do not discriminate against groups defined as being different. Monitoring such policies ought to ensure that student admissions, staff appointments and promotions are transparent. This is essential both for the optimum functioning of higher education institutions and in ensuring quality control in relation to equity in higher education.

One of the positive aspects of a diverse student body at higher education level is that students bring different ways of thinking, behaving and interacting with each other and their tutors. Some students may be reticent: openness on the part of staff can allow them to engage with members of the faculty and other students. However, in certain Asian and African cultures appropriate behaviour towards those who are learned and academic is to demonstrate respect and to maintain what is seen as a proper distance. The hierarchical character of an academic institution in certain cultures prevents some students in Britain from treating members of the faculty informally or from challenging statements made by staff, even if that is the norm in Britain.

Where the academic and support staff are from non-minority backgrounds themselves, this may enable the student to fit into an academic milieu more congenially. An intellectually and materially supportive environment is a prerequisite to establishing collegiality. A structured orientation programme is also of great importance. This enables students to meet each other, the faculty and support staff, and to understand the structure of the institution, so that they can engage personally with the institutional culture. Such an orientation programme is useful not only for out-of-town students, but especially for students from overseas, who have little understanding of British society, its culture and its institutions. Such students generally feel lonely and need friends to begin to feel familiar with the institution, the place and the people.

Advantages of an Orientation Programme

The orientation programmes of some North American universities perform an excellent role in ensuring that there is a collegial, friendly and welcoming higher education community. Such an orientation in no way detracts from the academic nature of higher education studies or the intellectual rigour expected of students who attend these institutions.

The traditional British model of higher education work, which used to rely on autonomous student research and study without necessary participation in additional course work especially at post-graduate level, can be a solitary exercise for students who belong to minority communities or are from overseas. Such students normally receive assistance from their tutors soon after beginning their studies to help them design their study programmes and prepare collection of data and analysis, as well as developing their writing skills. However, many students would benefit from advice on a range of matters which, though unrelated to the strictly academic issues, would enhance their performance. This kind of supportive structure can enable students to optimise their scholarly contributions and their academic potential, thereby lowering the number who fail to complete their studies.

Such preparation can also help address certain weaknesses in study and research skills that students may have acquired from institutions with pedagogies different from those in British universities. For instance, some South Asian students take for granted what a tutor states in a seminar. Lectures are vested with an authority which British students, because of earlier education, may question. They may, therefore, need to be enabled to adopt a stance critical of whatever modes and voices they read or hear.

Special problems are presented by those who have to undertake academic work on a part-time basis. While the desire to learn and to become academically qualified is very high among certain categories of students, they typically have complex living circumstances. Some may have full-time jobs and families, but may nevertheless wish to improve their professional qualifications and future prospects.

If they are more mature than the other students and some staff members, then delicate handling may be necessary.

Most university faculties are not organised to deal with the specific needs and support requirements of such students, some of whom find great difficulty in orienting themselves towards a learning situation after long absence from educational institutions. Though their tutors may have very high expectations of them, it may be extremely difficult to acquire the intensive high levels of reading, writing and learning that their work requires.

This is particularly a problem if they are studying or researching into fields which are totally unrelated to their earlier education or if they have full-time jobs. For instance, a history teacher who might find it easier to write about teaching history in an intercultural way may instead be undertaking a more difficult dissertation on questions of epistemology in relation to the curriculum, or an examination of the historiography of the subject as an intellectual issue. It is only the most committed and motivated who will undertake the challenge of shifting from their field of work to another. For such students, attendance at conferences, courses or seminars can provide contacts with other students and academics which represent an important way of inculcating and inducting part-time students into the culture of learning and higher education institutions.

Understanding Women Students' Problems

The involvement of women from minority communities presents a rather different set of potentials and problems. Such students may be even more motivated than some men from their communities and are perhaps more disciplined and committed. Their focus and concentration may partly arise from their involvement with carrying out chores in their personal capacities at home. They may not take education for granted. Such a situation may not only provide the impetus to learn but also a personal discipline in undertaking and completing tasks. In certain cases they may, however, have a lower order of academic skills and knowledge, resulting from the inadequacies of the previous learning institutions they may have attended.

Ideally faculties taking on women students from diverse backgrounds should create a friendly academic structure to enable them to make intellectual contributions at tutorials, lectures and seminars. They can in turn ensure a supportive context in which other students from similar backgrounds can make positive intellectual contributions. Such a structure ought to enable students who are expressing different views to be confident and comfortable in doing so. Tutors must recognise the contribution that a student's previous skills and experience can bring. Their different perspectives can immeasurably enrich the pool of ideas that they and their teachers are exposed to and their levels of intellectual discourse.

As stated earlier, some students from minority backgrounds, and women in particular, may feel deferential towards their tutors. Tutors' perceptions and students' own responses may not cohere. Tutors need to be sensitive to the different value systems such students may bring. These divergent values may be beneficial in broadening the ways in which faculties operate and students are tutored. When students have low levels of confidence during certain periods of their studies or research, tutors need to demonstrate support in improving it.

Students may lose confidence, because they perceive the poor quality of their own work, or because of misunderstandings arising from cultural reasons. Unless the problems are resolved quickly, it might be difficult for them to re-acquire the capacity to produce work of desirable quality. The tutors, in addition to their direct role, should also facilitate student collaboration. A cohort of students may be able to support each other's work, particularly if there are problems of cultural distance.

Student Interactions

The differences between home and overseas students is in itself a complex issue. The complexities are reflected in the way in which students from European Union countries may be seen to be closer to home students because of British proximity to Europe. But paradoxically they may be more distant than higher education students from the Commonwealth who, because of former colonial links, can work in English, and may also have an understanding of the British university system, based on their experiences in universities which have been developed on the British model.

Both these groups of students will have varying levels of competence in English, and be familiar with different types of English. A major challenge for higher education institutions is to build upon the different linguistic repertoires, knowledge systems and intellectual understandings that both categories of students bring. The problem of language will be discussed below, but tutors need to acquire competence to draw upon the different modalities of thinking, conceptual frameworks, and knowledge of students from diverse backgrounds.

The differences between home and overseas students can also emerge in another way. Universities earn a higher rate of fees from overseas students, and accept students with large scholarships or from wealthy families, which can lead to tensions between home (whether from minority or dominant communities) and overseas students. Their resentment creates more problems for the overseas students, inimical to the mutual support systems and structures they require, and may alienate them.

Where home students are white and those from overseas are not, racial tensions may be increased, thus negating the positive aspects of intercultural learning and connections. Such tensions may also put to the test institutional mechanisms to deal with xenophobia and racism when they arise. These resentments can be especially exacerbated when overseas students are accepted for studies with lower academic qualifications than those required for home students.

There may also be problems of different cultural interpretations which can lead to lower achievements by overseas students or those from cultural minorities resident in Britain. The cumulative effects – unless there is a supportive environment – can lead to further distancing which may be exacerbated by inappropriate contributions to seminars, or pieces of work submitted. Moreover where tutors do not read students' work immediately and critically, they may continue to address issues, and go on with study and research, which only distantly relates to the core of their work.

Working for Degrees

Patterns of organisation and methods of teaching and research vary across different disciplines and faculties. It is possible that general guidelines may not be relevant to all situations, but the organisation of an individual, or collective, ethos of enquiry may facilitate the capacity of students to optimise their learning and research potential. While some of the issues raised below have relevance for undergraduate studies, it addresses those involved in postgraduate studies.

A community of scholars can develop if collaborative work leads to working collectively, engendering the development of critical audiences and providing articulate feedback (Eggleston and Delamont 1983: 663). Collaboration needs to be structured properly so that such activities are not competitive and can assist in establishing close working relations. The creation of a collective ethos which instils in all students, whether from dominant, minority or overseas cultures, and between men and women, the desire to establish a common and shared understanding could be a useful and important starting point.

There is also a need to provide for the development of study and English language skills required for their work. Students can establish common sets of skills and shared meanings and help each other through different problems they come across. The tutors' role in this context is of paramount importance. Establishing mechanisms during the early phase of students' work reduces problems for students and tutors at later points in their studies. These mechanisms can include regular tutorials where written work is submitted prior to the tutorial discussions. Following tutorials, a written report on points agreed upon, as well as future work to be undertaken, is often very useful. It can also form a record or guidance to work for the next tutorial.

Tutor feedback should be critical in nature to ensure that students can renegotiate the specialist aspects of knowledge and of their subject. Tutors ought to avoid flippant, personal, arrogant or ideologically laden comments that make it immensely difficult for students to continue to improve their work. Delicacy and balance are far more valuable to the student, especially as it is difficult for tutors to help their students to write well. For students with different first languages, writing in English has different cultural manifestations. They also face the complex task of establishing a relationship between the discourse and their discipline. Tutors have an important role in helping their students to understand the subject by opening gates rather than guarding them.

A preliminary orientation programme can help to ensure that students from patriarchal communities can relate to women tutors or fellow students without any problems. In the absence of such a collective ethos both students and tutors can confront awkward situations and misunderstandings. In general, however, higher education students from minority backgrounds or overseas universities are imbued with egalitarian and modern values and tend to reject the authoritarian or patriarchal values of their families.

It is more likely that those British students from dominant groups who do not take the intellectual functions of universities seriously may hold on to the hierarchical and patriarchal values, but may be better able to disguise them. Racism in various forms is likely to be experienced by students from non-dominant communities. Strong institutional policies and sanctions ought to regulate behaviours of all staff and students, whether in dealing with racism or sexism, to ensure that no student feels excluded or victimised. An institutional policy, and named equal opportunity consultants in academic contexts, ought to prove supportive of tutors and students.

Such institutional policies are far more important than the recommendations of writers like Phillips and Pugh who suggest that students should learn 'assertion techniques' (Phillips and Pugh: 1994). Such an approach leaves the onus of change on the students when, in fact, it is the institutions which need to change, and facilitate diversity of staff and students. The intellectual dimension of 'assertiveness' would negate any openness of mind to the issues being studied or researched, particularly if students also became intellectually arrogant. Rather, both tutors and students ought to develop an element of openness and humility in their interactions.

Academic institutions may construe certain types of difference as a deficit. For instance, students from other cultures may not previously have used English in specialist discourses within higher education, but they may bring different conceptual frameworks, knowledge systems and, largely, a respect for learning and knowledge. If the institutions do not develop strategies to build on these diverse experiences, then the notion of institutional change to accommodate diversity can only be negated.

One of the mechanisms for ensuring that conceptual and theoretical constructs can be usefully built into the study and knowledge framework students bring is to ensure that the language courses on offer enable them to expand their repertoires so that they can express complex ideas. The Institute of Education in London has pioneered quite elaborate ways of developing academic English, and these may help in connecting students' knowledge with their expression in English. Supervisors and tutors in turn need to grasp the complexity involved in the transfer of conceptual frameworks from one linguistic system to another.

Some students from minority communities, like those in social policy and educational studies, who have taken the diploma route, may have greater knowledge, and more facility for work within professional fields. However, students from these professional routes may not bring the scholarly orientation and knowledge of certain academic disciplines or research methods to their work, compared with those who have studied humanities, social sciences and sciences. Institutions which accept students from these backgrounds ought to consider providing adequate preliminary support

Those home students who have used the access routes to the new universities may be limited to understanding the type of intellectual engagement in which supervisory competence is available. Similarly those who move for further study from new to old universities may bring a totally different understanding of the intellectual cultures and traditions they find there. Such students may bring fresh insights. It is important that refining their study skills does not undermine the freshness or vivacity of their ideas.

The types of study or research undertaken also influence the levels of student competence and the nature of the teaching or supervision students may require. For instance, those from overseas who undertake analyses or fieldwork in their own home countries would require an expertise in the necessary techniques, but will be familiar with the culture of the country. This will obviously be an advantage. Those who register to undertake theoretical work with some component of fieldwork would obviously require higher levels of bi-cultural and bilingual competences. The teaching or supervision of such students also needs to have a different dynamic because they will be trying to make sense of complex literature, and to construct original arguments of their own. Minority community students who engage in analysis or research of unfamiliar fields may bring fresh insights to their areas of inquiry.

Students from different backgrounds and universities bring different strengths and weaknesses. Academic departments and tutors may need to acquire resources and expertise at an institutional level to deal with the complex levels of understanding and skills – as well as the lack of them – that students bring with them. Tutors, therefore, require greater 'resources and capabilities so that the student, once accepted, does not fail for want of adequate tutorial support'. Teaching and supervisory functions enable an individual student from a disparate background to shift from being a relatively 'ill-informed and undisciplined thinker to the author of a limited but definitive enquiry' (Eggleston and Delamont 1983: 62–63).

Constraints on Postgraduate Work

The current institutional pressures on doctoral student completion rates, and the pressure to complete the research in a prescribed time period because of the students' own financial constraints, is seen by some as leading to students undertaking 'safe' projects for their research. As Phil Salmon suggests:

> a narrow time scale can mean a narrow scope. This narrowing would also, perhaps, inevitably be the effect of a doctoral programme which adds in a training element at the expense of original work.
>
> (Salmon 1992: 3)

Salmon raises the issue that generic taught courses at doctoral level are not necessarily being useful, and suggests the need for research workshops which are 'firmly grounded in the needs and perceptions of students themselves'. Here, emphasis on the original contribution to knowledge arising out of the creative personal endeavour, which in turn leads to a transformative role for research, has particular significance for intercultural contexts. Students from 'other' cultures, bringing 'other' knowledge systems, can only engage in intellectually bold and imaginative research if there is institutional and tutorial support for it. Academic supervisors who function within narrow fields may not be able to assist in this process unless they themselves have an intellectually open mind, are well informed and are involved in their own professional, intellectual and academic development.

The British model of postgraduate research, where a student ploughs a lonely furrow, has greater potential for the students breaking new ground and uncovering new knowledge if they are well supervised. The North American model of taught courses only presents somewhat limited potential for developing students' exploration or imagination. Yet, paradoxically, the British model requires greater commitment on the part of staff and resources. The students' intellectual journey requires the tutors' academic and scientific expertise, as well as their own personal confidence, to help define the exploration. The supportive function of tutorials, seminars and conferences is to ensure collaboration and co-operation, and not competitiveness, amongst students.

At this juncture there is a difference between Salmon, who relies on prolonged and intimate involvement without direction of the student, and researchers like Bourner and Barlow who recommend a more sustained tutor direction (Bourner and Barlow 1991). Currently there is a danger of total routinisation and bureaucratic direction of doctoral work, which can sap the excitement and detract from its creative solitariness. Moreover, in the intercultural context, there is a need for genuine partnership between tutor and student to bring about a commitment to the field of enquiry. A median between the two positions may be more productive for students in intercultural contexts, to optimise their autonomy as well as to give them support.

Good tutors can engage with students' notions of deference for knowledge, to develop greater levels of student autonomy through interaction with them. Supervision can also help in retrieving certain situations before a student has gone down a counter-productive route.

The total routinisation of postgraduate work can be further exacerbated if it is commodified and linked to the job market. Such research work may undermine not only student autonomy and genuine commitment to the intrinsic value of education and research, but also the possible new directions within an intercultural context. The ways in which doctoral work can be transformed through intercultural directions would be aborted and retarded even further.

INTERCULTURAL EDUCATION FOR PROFESSIONALS

Issues of Professional Education

To get the best educated and optimally qualified public and social policy professionals, professional education should be undertaken at universities or institutions with comparable standards. This would ensure some parity with education for legal, medical, architectural and other professions. Public and social policy workers should, therefore, as autonomous professionals, join a professional education institution after an undergraduate degree, and have a professional status and autonomy similar to those in other professions.

To raise the profile of the profession, a high level of rigorously educated professionals with accredited postgraduate qualifications is essential. As a part of this accreditation, intercultural course dimensions need to be built into the formal education process. At present, students from the smaller nationalities and minorities who have done well at university tend to qualify for high status professions, not at the social policy institutions which are seen to have a lower status. Yet to make intercultural education effective the education institutions need to have diverse students and teachers. Not only do the professions have to be made attractive, but education of the minority and smaller nationalities needs to be improved, and measures instituted to ensure that a number of them do join the public and social policy professions.

An accredited professional competence, which is validated and includes an integral intercultural dimension, is needed to ensure that what is at heart an essential educational issue is not marginalised. Nor should intercultural education be seen as an issue relevant only to urban culturally diverse institutions, but to all institutions, including suburban and rural ones.

Defining the Levels of Knowledge and Skills

The issues for professional education in general, and for its intercultural dimension, are twofold: what do professionals need to know in terms of knowledge, and what are they able to do – the skills dimension? The role of professional institutions should be to ensure that the professionals' understanding of knowledge issues and their skills are of a high order. They ought, to begin with, to bring to the field a learning experience from their undergraduate education, to ensure that at the postgraduate level there is systematic study of teaching and learning, as well as planned clinical experience in local areas which is closely supervised and monitored. As it is, those who study to become teachers in Britain or America complain that education courses fail to prepare them for teaching. If asked about intercultural education they smile and shake their heads. Professionals not only need a command of the fields in which they practise and a sound grasp of the techniques of their work, but must also have information on research and development, and an understanding of the differing intercultural needs.

The status and structure of the public and social policy professional institutions are critical for the role and position of professional education itself. If educators of professionals are seen as consisting only of previous practitioners, whose understanding of the field and knowledge of public and social policy issues and research is in itself of a low order, then the education they provide cannot be adequately rigorous.

Professional education should be an integral part of the university – and should establish good links with local institutions, in the same way as medical schools are linked with hospitals. This would create the possibility of cross-fertilisation of ideas across knowledge systems and its practice, generally in public and social policy issues, would benefit the development of intercultural education. There is, therefore, a need to enhance the expertise of those who educate professionals, giving them a sound academic background and an ability to work together with others to develop a sound intercultural dimension of education. One of the accusations is that intercultural education 'waters down' the educational process and is not able to raise educational standards. This accusation requires serious attention, to ensure that all those professionally qualified have had a rigorous education which at its core is intercultural.

Structuring Intercultural Professional Education

Professional education is poorly placed at present to implement effective intercultural policies and measures, if it is to provide these necessary postgraduate, research-oriented, courses, and establish links with other university faculties and with local communities where practical experience is required. The structuring of intercultural dimensions would be marginalised if professional education institutions themselves have a lower status than a university institution. A further issue is how intercultural issues are located within these institutions.

If they are left to a few interested staff, without any structural arrangements to allow for a more integrated approach, they would then be marginalised. Each field has to acquire and develop its own expertise. It may also require development of interdisciplinary and cross-institutional frameworks to implement the changes. This therefore requires the involvement not only of a few enthusiasts, but of an institutional structure – resources, mechanisms and infrastructure – to ensure that changes will take place.

Such changes are necessary because, as institutions, they will have customs, procedures and practices which, directly or indirectly, discriminate. Such discriminatory practices may not be evident at the surface level, and can only be eliminated if institutional structures bring about greater openness in their operations. They may, moreover, have not only relevance to intercultural education, but also general implications for educational equality, including the issue of gender equality. The subtleties of discrimination in higher education institutions are very difficult to tackle because they are camouflaged in many ways.

Policies for intercultural professional education cannot be effective unless they have the support of all the staff, and changes are seen to be made in (a) student admissions, (b) staff recruitment, development and promotions, and (c) initiation of research and curriculum developments. Moreover such changes require an evaluation of their effectiveness, and cannot be of a tokenistic nature. Hence methods of monitoring the implementation of strategies and policies are necessary.

Professional educators cannot themselves initiate changes unless there is staff development which allows all the staff to update their knowledge and skills. Professional education institutions ought therefore to ensure that the intercultural competencies of these workers include their personal and professional development. These should include expertise in their field, but ought also to give a more academic, as well as a practical, dimension to their education. This entails a complex evaluation of values, standards and methods across a range of their activities (Gundara 1997).

Professional education has therefore theoretical as well as practical dimensions. Obviously there will be a continuing tension about the balance between these conflicting demands, and about how much time should be devoted to theory as opposed to practice.

Teacher Education and the Culture of Racism

Racist imaginations cannot be dealt with by only tackling behaviours. It requires greater concern with developing complex strategies, and ability to deal with individual as well as institutional racism.

Research and development entail not only work in educational institutions but also in the communities from which the institutions draw their staff and students, particularly where racism is overt and can spill over into local institutions. Likewise there are instances where the culture of racism within an institution can spill over into the community. Educators cannot ignore this complex linkage which they tend to deal with by using 'common sense'. Yet sometimes being given, for instance, the correct facts about refugees or immigration is not sufficient to make those with prejudiced minds abandon their views. At this level a totally different engagement with the negative and racist imagination is required.

This issue of xenophobia and racism is riddled with 'inventing the wheel' – which may be avoided through institutional cooperation. Intercultural developments at the local level and at the professional education level can only become effective if they demonstrate more effective meeting of needs and delivery of service.

Professional Educators

As there is a need to recruit professionals from diverse social backgrounds, there is a need to recruit from different minority backgrounds. Some institutions do have equal opportunity policies, as well as policies against racism, but the recruitment of minority background professional educators is not yet a reality.

Not many professional educators are bilingual, and, because of this, many of the linguistic repertoires could disappear from the linguistic map of Britain. Professional educators have not taken seriously the potential of this linguistic diversity to provide a good service to their students and clients who do not speak English. It would not only enhance understanding between the different cultural groups within Britain but contribute to British understanding of the world which it once colonised, but learnt very little from or about. The learning of languages spoken in so many local communities would also enhance the learning of other European languages which has now become essential to membership of a multilingual Europe.

Finally, in what are essentially multicultural societies with diverse value systems, educators or professionals could contribute to the construction of meaningful values for the whole community. Yet, because there are so few from diverse backgrounds, there is hardly any erudite level of discourse, or even discussion, of this major issue.

When secular democracies are under threat in many parts of the world, social policy education in multicultural democratic states ought to engage with others in countering this malaise. Here the contributions to discussion and debate are mainly from the Christian, agnostic or humanitarian quarters, while developing a more meaningful discourse, involving greater sections of a very diverse population with differing values, is not taking place.

In dealing with these issues, professional education institutions, along with others in the social sciences, humanities and cultural studies, ought to construct a more imaginative and meaningful understanding of contemporary societies. They should engage in discussions with philosophers and those working on values education from a variety of backgrounds, to make the ethical issues within the professions more relevant and meaningful in the contemporary context.

Status of Institutions

There are complex issues in relation to the status of higher education institutions and the representation of students from different social classes and communities. The creation of new universities from polytechnics was not accompanied by changes in resource bases, structures, status of academic staff and standards of education. This has led to universities in name but not in status. This also means that students from minority communities remain largely barred from high status older universities. It is largely the new universities which accept students from these communities as inner city young students.

Status difference between universities and lack of clarity about affirmative action do not necessarily help students and institutional equality. It may exacerbate differentials between institutions seen to be academic and also status differences between students.

AFFIRMATIVE ACTION

The US Example

On its own, affirmative action cannot be expected to bring about, nor has it brought about, better inter-group, caste or race relations. Complex and multi-layered approaches may be necessary, particularly to enable the dominant communities to understand its importance in resolving potential conflicts. Similarly suppressed and oppressed groups must be made aware of the basis on which it is founded, and be in agreement with it. If affirmative action and consensus are to be legitimised, political and educational initiatives are needed to establish a common ground for all citizens in society. These measures may need to precede, or to be carried out alongside, affirmative action programmes.

The United States offers us a warning. In March 1961 President Kennedy issued Executive order 10925 authorising the enactment of affirmative action to counteract discrimination on the basis of race, colour, creed and national origin. A subsequent decision of the US Supreme Court made affirmative action unconstitutional. Though this decision had grave implications for the social cohesiveness of American society it was not challenged by the legislature. Indeed critic after critic added their voice in support of what is plainly the dominant mood – reflected in the decision of the California Board of Regents to end affirmative action within the university system of the State of California where it had originally been championed.

But the decision needs to be questioned. One of the assumptions made by critics and supporters of affirmative action alike is that the established political order, and the construction of a dominant polity, is the best way in which American society can be constructed and that it should continue to function in that manner. The question can be raised in another way. If American society is basically multicultural and multilingual, how can a state system with a dominant monocultural and monolingual norm be considered best for all groups in that society?

That brings us back to the rights and responsibilities which derive their inspiration from the Enlightenment. The issue can be illustrated as follows: one can argue that the African-American community constitutes a truly American community because, as Fukuyama (1995) has argued, unlike the 'white', Asian or Jewish communities, the African-Americans have not asserted an ethnically based identity. It can therefore be claimed that the African-Americans can be construed as 'true' Americans, with a belief in the American constitution, because they did not construct their 'other' from amongst the diverse groups of America.

This constructed Americanisation of the African-Americans has been referred to as deracialisation or deculturalisation. In fact, however, it is the other groups who, by preserving their narrow group identities, have detracted from optimising and realising the true potential of being an American, instead of lending their weight to the rights and obligations accruing to them under the constitution. It is particularly invidious when Dinesh D'Souza (1992), himself an East Indian, goes on to construct the African-American community in pathological terms, as the result of slavery – though if indeed the deculturalisation of the African-Americans were the result of slavery would there not be a historical burden which would require consideration and recompense?

The continued victimisation and marginalisation of the African-American community have now been capitalised upon by Louis Farrakhan and reinforced by the Republican right including some black middle-class (Marable 1998). Such a reactive nationalism which establishes common features with other ethnicised and racialised groups in American society can only help to undermine the constitutional principles and notions of equity and shared belongingness. It will also contribute to the balkanisation of the American polity. This balkanisation is enhanced because inequality is pervasive, and rights guaranteed under the constitution are continually being denied or subverted by emphasis on narrowly defined ethnic group values which disallow the emergence of a generally accepted value system within civil society and the public domain.

Why, in discussing affirmative action, is the issue of a shared value system within the public domain so important? The reason is because without it affirmative action can lead to greater conflict rather than reducing it. If social redress is not based on a shared historical imagination but on dominant constructions of it, it can exacerbate rather than resolve conflict. When the University of California, Berkeley, originally introduced affirmative action it was an attempt to bring about parity between blacks, whites, Asian Americans and Hispanics. The university felt it was correcting the inequalities accruing from the past as they were reflected in contemporary society. Yet it led to groups of Asian Americans accusing the university of being racist. If these ethnicised groups had believed in the larger goals of equity in American society they should have been ready to accept affirmative action. Plainly such ethnicised solidarities are detrimental to developing the social cohesiveness of American society.

Implementing Affirmative Action

We should heed the American warning. Affirmative action on its own is ineffective unless there is a general level of agreement about the need for equity, based on the shared values of the civil society. If there is no agreement on the common good or on shared goals in the polity, universities and employers will be accused of compromising merit and achievement. Hence, government, schools and other social institutions have the major task of creating requisite political awareness, and of strengthening the notion of rights, as well as responsibilities. Then, when affirmative action decisions are implemented it will be generally accepted that they are made for the individual, corporate and democratic good of society.

The polarisation of society in the last two decades undermined the 1960s agendas of a liberal society with its conciliatory and reconciliatory gestures. These new polarities cannot, however, simply be bought off by an uncritical liberal response. They require a rigorously argued and sustained position which is able to make a difference, not only to greater equalities of opportunity, but to educational and employment outcomes for all, however identified. The education of advantaged children needs to advance in tandem with improvements in the education of the disadvantaged. Yet the disparities of differential social and cultural capital that children bring from disadvantaged backgrounds will still lead to differential outcomes unless schools are effective, and are seen to be effective, in improving the life chances of all children.

In the prevailing climate of the last decade and a half demands for affirmative action as a way of avoiding social crisis fell on deaf ears. Affirmative action programmes based on collective obligations, compensations and redress could never be substantiated in a climate in which Thatcher, in a speech to the Church of Scotland, talked of relationships as being only a contract between individual, family and the market. Or when the policies of the 'New Right' reaffirmed her belief that 'society' does not exist. But once it is again accepted that the concept of society, and of a society based on social justice, is important, we have a basis for providing redress to the disadvantaged which would lead to greater equality.

We must therefore try to reinstate an affirmative action agenda in which issues of social justice and individual rights are balanced. This is particularly important at present because of the previous failures and critiques of affirmative action. One of these options is to institute preparatory or access courses for affirmative action students to ensure that they acquire the required qualifications and that their formal entry is based on academic credentials. This would obviate the present high drop-out rates. An effective affirmative action ought to ensure that members of disadvantaged groups can function in all professions, no matter how rigorous or demanding. Hence, access courses are essential to ensure that cognitively demanding jobs are within the competence of all sections of society. Many minorities complain that only 'soft option' careers are open to them.

However, institutions cannot implement affirmative action programmes without appraising what goes on inside them. The customs, practice structures, pedagogy and curricula ought to be critically reviewed regularly, to ensure their relevance for all students. This should ensure more effective and rigorous, but also universally relevant, curricula, so that there can be a genuine possibility of learning across cultures. Such measures would counteract the criticism that the quality of education would be lowered. It would ensure matriculation of affirmative action students and guarantee graduation and learning, as well as acquisition of competencies. Higher education institutions would therefore enhance both quality as well as equality of education.

Another criticism of positive discrimination in India, and affirmative action in the USA, is that the dominant scheduled castes and the bourgeois blacks assimilate within the existing structures. In both contexts there are accusations that there is a vested interest within them to perpetuate affirmative action. These accusations further state that the gaps between those few who benefit, and the large underclass who do not, have widened. Yet other programmes like the US Headstart may bring social gains, acknowledged even by parents. Life chances have improved, and nearly a million children and parents have acquired a better quality of life.

How can such policies be made to work effectively and lead to greater levels of equality – and lead ultimately to their dismantlement? The various minority groups are not homogeneous categories. They do not constitute a single undifferentiated stratum of society. Only a coordinated effort in all areas of economic and social policy would lead to greater levels of equality. Action in, say, education may not be effective if other disadvantages are not alleviated through multi-agency approach. This is therefore not just a matter of politics, but also of public policy, and has issues for the public domain. An effective affirmative action would be a matter not only for private institutions which rely on private funds, but also for public funds which are used in an atmosphere of consensus on this issue.

FURTHER READING

Anna Aluffi-Pentini and Walter Lorenz (1996) *Anti-Racist Work with Young People – European Experiences and Approaches,* Lyme Regis: Russell House Publishing Ltd.
David Morley and Kuan Hsing Chen (1996) *Stuart Hall – Critical Dialogues in Cultural Studies,* London and New York: Routledge.

5

Interculturalism in Europe

The relevance of intercultural education cannot be viewed as a consequence of those who have recently immigrated to Europe. The European continent has a long and complex legacy of a multicultural past. The implications for interculturalism and intercultural education have to take cognisance of the complexities represented both by its past as well as by the contemporary aspects of social diversity.

This chapter provides a view of Europe through slightly different lenses than is normally the case, in discussions about intercultural education. It argues that educators need to engage with the problems represented by Eurocentrism in Europe to enable them to engage meaningfully with the issue of what constitutes legitimate knowledge and a canon within the academic establishment.

Education systems which are able to engage with issues of xenophobia and racism need to be part of broader public policies to ensure that the belongingness of various groups is legitimised in the European context. Measured at the level of the European Union as well as at the local and city levels such policies need to be undertaken.

MULTICULTURAL EUROPE

European Diversities and Unities

One of the earliest personal memories I have of European societies came from a prominent Kenyan chief who visited Europe in the 1950s. My father asked him what struck him about his visit to Europe. There was prolonged laughter when he said that he was very surprised to find white people all over Europe engaged in menial work. Obviously, in the European colonies in Africa, Europeans only did the supervisory jobs, thus, as the functionaries of the European nation states, presenting a monolithic image of European societies. The visiting chief had, however, observed that this was not consistent with his experience in Europe. He was obviously struck by the class nature of the European countries which we in the colonies were not taught about.

When people move to Europe to stay or settle they are able to examine the layers of difference and divergence in the European nation states. What becomes clear to them is, on the one hand, the diversity of European societies, and, on the other, the powerful unitary structures which govern them. They note the presence of the Scots and Welsh in Britain, the Bretons in France, the Samish (or Lappish) people in Sweden, and the existence of different European languages and dialects, of religious conflicts as well as religious co-existence. Moreover the class divisions in contemporary European societies which the Kenyan chief observed have a major impact on the lives of those who have become settlers. So when they hear discussions asserting that diversity in society, or racism, or multiculturalism in education, are consequences of their presence, they are surprised. They feel that such questions relate not only to their own presence in Europe, but to fundamental questions about society, the nation, and the national minority questions.

For instance, they observe the problems faced by the Roma in Western Europe where, as Puxon pointedly observed as long ago as 1980:

> Roma are dumped as illiterate, or semi-literate, among the unskilled and unemployed, rendering them a disinherited and exploited race. The accumulative effects of their persecution are catastrophic.
>
> (Puxon 1980: 14)

They cannot help but identify with the plight of the Roma because they themselves have experienced the 'catastrophic' effects of colonialism, underdevelopment and racism. These effects are not dissimilar from the persecution of the national minorities, and are clearly indicative of the harsh nature of the state apparatuses in many European nations. Yet, once settled in homes of their own, they may well tend to identify with the norms of their settled neighbours and persecute the Roma.

Hence, the existence of authoritarian tendencies in governments, and the rise of xenophobia, can be related to the governments' long-standing fears of not being able to deal with these underlying dichotomies, schisms and diversities. So indigenous minorities like the Samish people look on the Swedes, or the Greenland Inuits on the Danes, as dominant groups which have undermined their society and assumed control over their own resources. Bretons and Corsicans have long-standing grievances against the government in Paris, while in Spain virtual war has been waged in the Basque country for years.

The continental European societies are, like Britain, historically multicultural and continue to be so. No more than Britain have they suddenly 'become multicultural'. European governments, however, tend to camouflage these dichotomies and the social diversities within Europe. To protect the national unities established in not too distant a past, they are presented by the national governments as being unitary, uniform, monocultural and monolingual. Yet if we examine maps of Europe and study its peripheries, we would observe the presence of the Samish peoples in Scandinavia, the Celtic in Britain and France, the Basque in Spain, and a Muslim presence in the Balkans, giving us an indication of only one element of diversity in European societies.

The tendency in Europe to homogenise and create uniformity out of diversity has a very long history. Robert Bartlett has shown vividly how Europe as we know it was the product of conquest and colonisation in the eleventh, twelfth and thirteenth centuries, not by kingly power but by knights, ecclesiastics and merchants. The English colonised the Celtic world, the Germans moved into Eastern Europe and the *reconquista* of the Iberian Peninsula began, all entailing cultural assimilation.

> The world of the early Middle Ages was one of diverse, rich local cultures and societies. The story of the eleventh, twelfth and thirteenth centuries is of how that diversity was, in many ways, superseded by a uniformity.
>
> (Bartlett 1993: 311)

Far from having 'introduced multiculturalism' into Europe, the new immigrants have contributed to its long-standing history of multicultural diversity.

Redefining Nationalities

As immigrants have settled in Europe, the European governments have been concerned to define their legal and political position. They are customarily designated 'ethnic minorities' – a definition which, as we have already shown in the British context, implies that the host peoples are somehow *not* 'ethnic'. Moreover the new settlers, by and large, have backgrounds of nationality and citizenship which are unrelated to ethnicity. Most of them come from nation states which have themselves diverse 'ethnic' populations. They are, therefore, either nationals of the country of origin, or of the country of settlement. Similarly, as and when they resist racism in European countries, they do so not on the basis of 'ethnic' solidarity, but as, say, Turkish nationals in Germany, or, more generally, as people persecuted on grounds of race. And the legislation which defines, and continually undermines, their legal and political status is racist in its intent, and not directed against their 'ethnicity'.

The use of this term by social anthropologists has certainly not helped to clarify this complex issue. Until recently they have been unwilling to apply the methods and concepts deemed suitable for analysing 'primitive' societies and their 'ethnicities' to analysing those of Europe (Delamont 1995; Godard, Llobera and Shere 1994). It is therefore necessary to undertake a more systematic social science analysis of the basis of the European nation states in historical as well as contemporary terms, so that a clear definition of issues may emerge.

What, for instance, are the differences between the national minorities and the 'ethnic' minorities? How do the national minorities of Europe – in Scotland and Wales, in Brittany and Corsica, in the Basque country and in Catalonia – accept the nation states as defined by the dominant ruling class? We need to define the nature of European societies, and their relationship to the centralised structures of the nation state, which exclude groups on their peripheries. We must also define them in terms of citizenship of the European Union.

Since the national minorities necessarily occupy different positions within the different European nations, the settlers are similarly faced with differing definitions. Differing status is accorded them based on different national contexts. The national minorities generally have a territorial basis, and are constitutionally recognised within the state. However, the newly settled communities also occupy urban spaces, not constitutionally recognised by the nation states, but nevertheless representing the birth of new communities. In Paris, Marseille, Berlin and other European cities, they live, as they do in Britain, in their own areas, a sanctuary against the racism they experience, a rudimentary 'territorial basis'.

Hence, though Europeans may deny the multifaceted and multifocal origins of the modern nation states, their overwhelmingly centralised and dominant ethnicities need to bring a clearer focus on their historical basis and contemporary nature. Nation states ought to recognise the complex societies in which they function. Complex societies require complex national machinery which is finely tuned, able to function precisely because it is in harmony, so that its different parts are able to function harmoniously within a framework, as in complex modern technologies.

Instead, these ancient dichotomies and diversities within Europe tend to be camouflaged. For instance, the very viability of Belgian society depends upon the Flemish and Walloon people cooperating on matters of bi-lingualism to make Belgium a viable nation. Yet there is an attempt to sidetrack from these fundamental questions and to scapegoat the immigrant community in Belgium as the cause of malaise in Belgian society. This can be illustrated by a speech of the Belgian Minister for the Interior, Joseph Michel, in October 1987:

> We risk being like the Roman people, being invaded by barbarians who are the Arabs, Moroccans, Yugoslavs and Turks. People who have come from far away and have nothing in common with our civilisation.
>
> (*New York Times* 22 November 1987)

This statement reflects the 'commonsense racism' and xenophobia of large numbers of Europeans, normally attributed to the presence of the new immigrants in Europe. But, as we have shown, and Michel's Belgian context illustrates, there are historical and contemporary diversities in European societies which are being camouflaged by labelling the immigrants as the only divergent group, and by declaring that society has only recently '*become* multicultural'.

We must therefore explore two salient issues. The first is the whole issue of migration and settlement in the post-World War II period and the need to contextualise its position within the comity of European nation states. The second is that Joseph Michel's statement, while reflecting a narrow definition of a nation, does not rest on ignorance of European nationhood. It is a construction which is consciously created, recreated, manipulated, obscured and mystified to enhance or ensure the continuity of established nationalisms. Groups can be excluded, pathologised, dominated, marginalised or distanced by being referred to as 'barbarians', 'ethnics', 'migrants' or 'immigrants'. It is, therefore, important to explore the notion of 'our civilisation' and its distance or connection with those considered to be 'barbarians'.

The New Settlers

The enormous post-war economic growth of Europe has been directly related to the ready availability of labour, partly through 'natural' increase, but overwhelmingly through migration. There have been various types of immigration to Western Europe since World War II, involving a movement of over thirty million people, of whom about ten million have stayed on in Europe. The first consisted of European colonists who returned to Europe. They included the British from India, Kenya and Zimbabwe, French *pieds noirs* from Algeria, the Dutch from Indonesia, and the Portuguese from Angola and Mozambique. The second consisted of refugees, at first particularly from Eastern Europe, but from the 1970s increasingly from the southern hemisphere. The third consisted of manual labour recruited within Europe, for instance, from Italy to Northern Europe, from Ireland into England and from Finland into Sweden.

The fourth type of migration, from the 1950s, included migrants from other southern European countries to northern Europe while Britain, France and the Netherlands also received large numbers of immigrants from Africa, the Caribbean and Asia, many of whom were citizens of the receiving countries. Many were brought by recruiting agencies like the European Voluntary Worker Scheme in Britain, the Belgian contingent-system, the French *Office National d'Immigration*, and the West German Federal Labour Office recruiting scheme. West Germany recruited a large number of workers from 1956 onwards, in attempting to catch up with the other European countries; these particularly included Turks, since many southern Europeans had returned home. Britain, France and West Germany are the largest immigration countries; over forty per cent of the immigrants originating in the southern hemisphere (Cohen 1994: 161–91).

Most of the European countries wanted labour to come and work in the country of immigration – but not settle. This was done through systematic institutionalised discrimination. As Sivanandan puts it:

> The crux of the problem, therefore, was not migration but settlement – and not discrimination but racial discrimination. For the purposes of exploitation, it was labour and not colour that had to be discriminated against – and that could be done on the basis of citizenship, of nationality, rather than of race. And since nationality laws by definition distinguished between citizens and alien, foreign or migrant labour would be automatically subject to discrimination.
>
> (Sivanandan 1982: 107)

Institutionalised controls were even applied to those who came from ex-colonies to settle in France and the Netherlands. And though the German Guest Worker system was different from the settlement of nationals from the former colonies (see below), as were the regulations enforced in Sweden and Switzerland, all these systems of migration, while taking place in the context of different policies, laws and bureaucratic rules, led to a single and similar consequence: settlement.

Eventually France and the Netherlands, like Britain, enacted legislation to stop the migration of their citizens from their former colonies. This discriminatory nationality legislation has caused an enormous amount of hardship to the dis-enfranchised citizens because it was enacted with the express purpose of con-trolling their immigration and settlement. Yet the stricter the rules against immigration and citizenship became, the faster the transition from one of tem-porary stay to a process of permanent settlement.

One of the greatest myths, particularly for immigrants who move for economic reasons, is that they will save money and return to their country of origin. The following conversation quoted by John Berger makes the point:

> Then, full of excitement of arrival, he said, 'Here you can find gold on the ground. I am going to start looking for it.' The friend, who had been in the city for two years, answered him, 'That is true. But the gold fell from high in the sky, and so when it hit the earth, it went down very deep.'
>
> (Berger and Moore 1975: 68)

As immigrants attempt to accumulate capital the vast majority find they have no chance of doing so. They have to accept a life of exceedingly hard work, frugal living and also loneliness because of social discrimination. As Castles and Kosack describe the process:

> Immigrants and their descendants form groups characterised by nationality, certain physical traits, language, culture and lifestyle, distinct from the indigenous populations. These minorities are to a certain extent isolated from the rest of the population, and they are discriminated against. They form their own institutions and identities.
>
> (Castles and Kosack 1973: 4)

The only option which has seemed open to them is to invite their families to join them in Europe, so that family members could help in the process of accumu-lating capital and ease problems of social isolation.

Yet while their loneliness has become less of a problem, their class position as unskilled or semi-skilled has ensured that the new family units still find it diffi-cult to save much money. In fact, single workers are probably more able to do so. Once children have joined their parents, or been born in the metropolis, the process of life in Europe begins to develop with its own internal dynamic. Their increasing peripheralisation in their countries of origin lessens their mobility, adding to the problems of reintegrating themselves there. Moreover these countries will have been further marginalised through political and economic exploitation. The Moluccans, for instance, who were brought to the Netherlands with promises of return to Indonesia, still want to return, but the second gener-ation has grown up amidst massive discrimination and uncertainty about their future.

Hence, throughout Europe there are settled, mainly working-class communi-ties who not only highlight but also reinforce the diversities in European societies. Teachers, and those working in other social policy areas, receive con-tradictory messages about their rights, contributions and problems. For, once they began to settle, racism in various forms began to increase, and they were made scapegoats, because of the alleged social costs they incurred. The newly settled communities have as a nucleus a young working population who were nevertheless accused of being 'scroungers', or adding to the social cost of running the state.

Yet this working population was providing taxation which subsidises the welfare and retirement benefits of the older populations. Those who have migrated alongside the European working-class have made immense contributions to the economic growth of Europe. It is also important for those who receive these messages on the social cost of immigrant labour to know that this movement of workers is one form of a 'hidden transfer of value from the periphery to the centre since the periphery has borne the cost of education and training of this labour power' (Amin 1974: 27).

The Manual Worker in Europe

While in the 1960s Europe 'never had it so good' (to quote Harold Macmillan, later Earl of Stockton) many of those who came to help in this process never had it so bad. Most of them were manual, semi-skilled or skilled workers, often involved in shift work especially at night, and paid for piece work. But as the nature of technology changed towards automation and process production they became increasingly deskilled. Many have paid a double price. During the initial process of migration and settlement their qualifications and skills were not recognised. Subsequently, when the technologies in European industries changed they became unskilled once again.

In Germany and Britain this has happened particularly to workers engaged in textile production. The French building industry, comprised of one third non-French labour, has suffered the same fate, resulting in massive unemployment. Thus, immigrant labourers live in 'bidonvilles' which must be some of the worst housing in Europe. John Berger, early in the period of migration into what was then West Germany, described the process of becoming a so-called *Gastarbeiter*, a 'Guest Worker' – a genial euphemism which absolved the receiving country from all responsibility for its 'guests' beyond those connected with the workplace.

> They are coming to offer their labour. Their labour power is ready made. The industrialised country, whose production is going to benefit from it, has not borne any of the cost of creating it; any more than it could bear the cost of supporting a seriously sick migrant worker, or one who has grown too old to work. So far as the economy of the metropolitan country is concerned, migrant workers are immortal; immortal because continually interchangeable. They are not born: they are not brought up: they do not age: they do not get tired: they do not die. They have a single function – to work. All other functions of their lives are the responsibility of the country they come from.
>
> (Berger and Moore 1975: 64)

Now with rising German unemployment their position has become even more precarious. Those who are unemployed are in danger of losing their work permits, so many do not register their unemployment. Many a worker has felt that the more inequitable the laws, the more precarious his position, and cursed the ruthlessness of such laws and systems. In the former East Germany in particular they face open and aggressive anti-immigrant nationalism, often acted out on a frightening, even life-threatening, scale (Fijalkowski 1996; *The Guardian* 21 January 1998).

The presence of the now settled immigrant communities who came from countries which were either colonies, or peripheralised through the larger phenomenon of imperialism, are part and parcel of a larger process of domination and control. Britain, France and the Netherlands have seen a vast influx from the territories of the old exploited empires. In Germany workers from Turkey who, as *Gastarbeiter*, are foreigners (*Ausländer*) are an example of a national group who have been historically exploited by a European power. For by 1914 Germany, having directly colonised Tanganyika, Namibia, Cameroon and Togo, was involved in turning the Ottoman Empire (Turkey) into a neo-colonial dependent country.

This Turkish presence in Germany has long term implications. As long ago as 1979 Heinz Kuhn, one time premier of North Rhine/Westphalia and Ombudsman for Foreigners, one of the few politicians who has shown some concern, stated:

> Future policy towards foreign employees and their families living in the [then] Federal Republic must be based on the assumption that a development has taken place which can no longer be reversed, and that the majority of those concerned are no longer guest workers but immigrants, for whom a return to their countries of origin is for various reasons no longer a viable option.
>
> (Quoted in Castles, Booth and Wallace 1984)

Yet while they remain *ausländische Mitbürger*, 'foreign fellow citizens', they cannot enjoy the civil rights of citizens. For the German government to end the *Ausländerpolitik* and adopt a policy of settled immigration would require a fundamental shift – a shift which the Social Democratic government elected in 1998 has, however, undertaken to consider.

The European working class, apart from the skilled workers, has never been very mobile, but this immobility has been compounded in the case of the new settlers in Europe. They have been used as a reserve army of labour which has not been given any systematic continuing education. Their language learning has not been considered in the context of linguistic diversity and of a broader educational policy, or of education for citizenship, but only as work-related language training.

During the 1990s the concept of 'Fortress Europe' became increasingly entrenched, particularly after 1993 when the planned but postponed political unification of Europe was shelved and with it the possibility of a larger Europe without borders, where citizens as well as goods and capital could freely circulate. Of the estimated 320 million in Europe about 8 million are non-EU nationals, the biggest groups being Algerians, Tunisians, former Yugoslavs and West Africans – whose rights are very different from those 'protected by wealth and privilege', like Swiss or US business executives (Cohen, R. 1994: 182).

In Europe, 'as borders go down, walls go up' (*The Guardian* 15 February 1995). The TREVI (1986) and Schengen and Dublin (1990) Agreements have tightened rules about migration, asylum seekers and refugees. Border controls have not gone down but been reinforced. Moreover, in France and Britain in the relics of the old colonial empires, the formerly inclusive definitions of citizenship have been made even more exclusive, the *Département d'Outre-mer* notwithstanding. In Britain the Nationality Act 1982 took away the British citizenship rights of British citizens of Hong Kong and replaced them with a dependent territory travel document.

These various categories of non-citizens in Europe live vulnerable lives in twilight zones. And as central EU controls grow to exclude them they become only more vulnerable to xenophobia and racism.

The New Racism

These new settlers belong to the working class because of their relationship to the means of production. However, their relationship to the European working classes is marred by racism, which may in turn be nurtured by the state. European governments had expected that with the deepening economic crisis of the 1970s many of the new settlers would return to their countries of origin, and that they would be able to export any accruing social costs. But this did not happen, nor has it happened in the economic crisis of the late 1990s.

In addition, expenditures on housing, schools, health and social services have been cut throughout Europe since the 1970s. This has led to an increase of tensions in many cities. The obvious response of the state is to seek a scapegoat: the 'visually' different communities, because of their vulnerability, provide this facade, and a political culture of racism in European societies sustains and nurtures it. Thus the very workers whose exploited labour had assisted in the creation of the post-war expansion are blamed as a threat to public order and safety, and as the cause of urban decline.

Politicians like Dregger (Germany), Schwarzenbach (Switzerland), Powell (England), Le Pen (France) whipped up racism by stressing foreign swamping – as did Thatcher as head of government in Britain. Le Pen, as the Chairman of the group of the European Right, attempted to suspend the work of the European Parliament's Committee of Inquiry into the Rise of Fascism and Racism in Europe in 1984 and 1985. Since then, however, the European Union has established a Monitoring Centre for Racism and Xenophobia in Vienna. Moreover the Amsterdam Treaty under Articles 13 and 29 gives competence to member states to deal with racist issues.

Yet few, if indeed any, of the European governments have provided any of the newly settled communities with confidence in their place in European society. The discussions about combating racism are not reflected in actual policies. Instead the communities of settlers across Europe regularly experience and, where they can, resist the growth of this 'new racism'. They have documented and registered growing threats in the media, at political rallies, in the housing estates, workplaces, schools, and the street, in the legal statutes and the courts of law, in parks, cafés, festivals and celebrations. There is no area of life which is immune from this malaise because it takes many forms, from bombing and physical attacks to blatant or sophisticated discrimination in civil codes and commercial practices. Neither women nor children are spared. (For a well-informed account of the rise of Fascism during the economic crises of the 1970s and 1980s, especially right-wing terrorism in Italy and France, see Harris 1990.)

The new settlers have also adopted defensive measures. However, when they have attempted to defend their families and homes by adopting a 'siege mentality', they have been criticised for being patriarchal, conservative or traditional. They reject the blame that is attached to them for purportedly having created social problems and having deficient family backgrounds. The young similarly are aware that their teachers are inadequately educated or trained to deal in the classroom with the fascist propaganda of the National Front in Britain or the French *Front Nationale*, or the Young Nationalists in Germany. Yet few progressive forces have attempted to overturn this growth of fascism and create spaces for dynamic change.

In some of the countries where immigrant workers have settled there have been splits between them and other members of the working class, exacerbated by racist and colonial attitudes, linguistic and religious differences, and differential rates of payment. As Sivanandan has pointed out, discriminatory nationality laws and contract labour have had a political function – 'they have prevented the integration of migrant labour into the indigenous proletariat and thereby mediated class conflict' (Sivanandan 1982: 106).

The workers' organisations and movements have had to deal with divergent issues. Because employers have used immigrant labour as 'buffers', the unions have opposed the use of immigrants and have not tried to include them. Thus they have failed to represent the concerns and interests of the whole working class and uphold internationalist principles based on solidarity. While the Trade Union Congress (TUC) in Britain has theoretically opposed racial discrimination, it has in practice tended merely to deny the widespread existence of racism and taken few steps to combat it. It never opposed the racially discriminatory Commonwealth Immigration Acts of 1968 and 1971 which were primarily directed against the Black community. The *Deutsche Gewerkschaftsbund* (DGB) has on the whole supported state policies on labour and not done much to fight discrimination and exploitation. Above all, it has not fought for the permanent settlement of workers which would entitle them to civil and political rights. The *Confederation Générale de Travail* (CGT) in France has been involved in playing the middle-ground which means in effect that they have ignored the interests of the newly settled workers.

For their part, the settled workers have taken a major part in some trade union activities. For example, they played a major role in the 1973 Ford strike in Cologne – but it was broken by the employers and police with the active co-operation of the German union leaders. There are in many parts of Europe emergent alliances between workers and new settlers. However, on the whole, with the deepening of the crisis in Europe, the trade union movement faces exacerbated problems of a racially divided working class. In those EU states where immigrants have citizenship rights the unions tackle issues of discrimination, though with varying levels of commitment. Elsewhere there can be no question of their attaining equality when they lack even legal status. Nevertheless the unions are taking issues of exclusion more seriously and anti-racist strategies are emerging (TUC 1996).

The Youth Question

As the permanent settlement of the new settlers and nationals has grown, youth has been seen to be a threat to the existing national order. This seems to be the inevitable response of the inherently rigid and oppressive nation states. Instead of recognising their oppressions, they tend to blame young people as a threat to 'law and order'. In some European countries, namely Belgium, France, Germany, Sweden and Switzerland, xenophobia of this sort has meant that almost four million under twenty-five year olds have yet to gain citizenship of the host country. It is argued that the portrayal of these people by the media does not help the situation and in many cases attempts are made to undervalue the cultures emanating from formerly colonised countries (Gundara 1991).

At the beginning of the new millennium their position is little different, indeed has worsened through the massive loss of jobs through new technologies. Most of these young people live in terrible urban housing and face chronic unemployment. They are also simultaneously subjected to social control by highly mobilised social structures. These elements of social control include the school, 'vocational training', the police, courts and prisons.

In Germany, where they have been described as 'the social time bomb', and in Switzerland, such young people, despite their birth in these countries, never acquire the country's nationality. This contrasts with Sweden where 422,000 remain foreign nationals, while those who have settled number over a million. In France over 2.2 million people up to the age of twenty-five have parents who are foreign nationals. Of these over three-quarters have been born in France while only one-third have acquired French nationality.

While those who acquire nationality do surmount one obstacle of institutional discrimination, other forms of discrimination still persist. For while the legal, social and economic structures help to marginalise and criminalise youth, the state blames the victims of the situation as the cause of the problem. Educational provision for them varies within and across Europe. While, as has been shown, the British mainstream education system fails them, the German system fails them by means of separate national classes with teaching in mother tongues, introduced to facilitate repatriation to the countries of 'origin'. Meanwhile, in the UK, the demand by the Black community for community language teaching is based on pedagogic (though in practice often more political) issues. These differences notwithstanding, both communities have large numbers of semi-lingual children.

Yet when the parents, on arrival in Europe, accepted low level jobs, they had at least expected that their children would have a choice of employment through the educational route. These parents have now experienced a calamity of major proportions in terms of their children's future. Not only have these families seen their dreams evaporate, but also they have become embittered and angered by callous neglect and overt discrimination.

The parents originally accepted low paid jobs with hopes of things improving. The young, however, only have metropolitan experiences and therefore have a consciousness which has been conditioned by these experiences. Although their specific consciousnesses differ across the many European states, the basis for political militancy is clearly visible across the horizon.

The Eurocentric Model

Anthropologists have used concepts of social and cultural pluralism to describe post-colonial nations. Similar analysis needs to be developed to suit the study of nation states in the metropolis. The assumption that the 'mega-societies' of the West are beyond the goalposts may be premature, because concepts of 'national integration' and 'nation building' are dynamic concepts and ought to apply to all nations at all times. They cannot be used merely to apply to 'developing' countries and then prove redundant for 'developed' countries – as the devolution policies in the United Kingdom illustrate. Indeed it is encouraging to see the present trend towards democratically evolved devolution in some of the states of Europe.

As we have stressed, the citizens of the European Community originate from many diverse cultures. Yet the educational systems of the member states are still devised as if they were meant for citizens with one national culture. Education remains tied to a hegemonic canon, shut up in a cultural prison which recognises only its own Eurocentred tradition or, if it does recognise those outside it, interprets them according to its own values. Opening the prison demands an intercultural curriculum, a multifaceted and multifocal curriculum, which redefines the Eurocentred canon and presents the traditions of the world within their own standards and not those of the Eurocentred tradition.

We confront a Eurocentric tradition informed by the imperialism of Europe. As Edward Said writes:

> Without significant exception the universalising discourses of modern Europe and the United States assume the silence, willing or otherwise, of the non-European world. There is incorporation; there is inclusion; there is direct rule; there is coercion. But there is only infrequently an acknowledgement that the colonised people should be heard from, their ideas known.
>
> (Said 1993: 581)

As a result of the imperial enterprise not only is Europe in the world but the world is in Europe. Ostensibly this has profound implications for the transfer of knowledge. Yet, discourses from the periphery are still treated as being marginal in contemporary Europe.

The issue of Eurocentrism is not, however, simply an issue of prejudices and errors which heighten xenophobia and chauvinism. Eurocentrism, according to Samir Amin:

> has replaced rational explanations of history with partial pseudo-theories, patched together and even self-contradictory at times . . . The Eurocentric distortion that makes the dominant capitalist culture negates the universalist ambition on which that culture claims to be founded.

> (Amin 1989: 104)

The Enlightenment, for instance, came not as a universal phenomenon, but as a narrowly defined European response to the obscurantism of Christianity.

Martin Bernal has indicated how in the eighteenth and nineteenth centuries Europeans developed a historiography which denied the earlier understanding that the Greeks in the Classical and Hellenistic periods had learnt as a result of colonisation and interaction between Egyptians, Phoenicians and Greeks. As intellectuals during the period came increasingly to adopt racial interpretations of the course of history and society, including the persistent Christian tradition of anti-semitism, Greece was distanced from the Egyptians and Phoenicians and constructed as the pure childhood of Europe. It became impossible to accept that Europeans could have developed any learning and understandings from Africans or Semites.

This historiographical shift has major implications for how European history is constructed, and particularly for how knowledge and linguistic systems from civilisations constructed as inferior are excluded from the European academe. As Bernal puts it, the paradigm of 'progress' was used to put the Greeks to the fore and to cast aside the Egyptians who were governed by priests (Bernal 1987).

The geographic unities constituting Europe, Africa and Asia have no significance in the history of civilisation. The notion of a European culture separated from the world south and east of the Mediterranean is a mythical construction. The contributions to knowledge in the ancient period from this immediate region include Mesopotamian astronomy, the Egyptian calendar and the Arab enrichment of Greek mathematics, notably with the Arabic numerals. The opposition set up between a Greek-derived 'West' and an Egyptian, Mesopotamian, Persian 'East' is an artificial construct of Eurocentrism. Christianity and Islam derive from an identical Judaic tradition and are both heirs of syncretic Hellenistic culture (Gundara 1990).

After 1492, with the continual Europeanisation of the globe, Eurocentrism became crystallised as a global project. This Europeanisation of the globe bears within it a deuniversalisation of knowledge, expressing itself as European, nationalist and secular with a worldwide scope. Moreover, it had to construct, arbitrarily and mythically, its counterpart in 'the other' and 'the Oriental'. The so-called 'Western' thought and philosophy was presented as having emerged from Greece, and as being based on 'rational principles' while the 'Orient' does not move beyond 'Metaphysics'.

Africa and its peoples were also constructed as 'the other', not only within Africa but also in the New World. From the early sixteenth century Africans were shipped as slaves across the Atlantic: every single European colony in the Americas and their offshore islands had its population of African slaves. Everywhere it became accepted that African descent denoted slave origin, and that even those who were freed, and their descendants, retained the irrevocable stigma of an inferior race. When in the late nineteenth century the European states conquered and partitioned Africa the conquered African populations were assigned the same racial stigma. Race became a rigid barrier separating Europeans who ruled from Africans who obeyed (Fyfe 1994).

Elsewhere in the world, in the territories ruled by Europeans or their descendants, in Asia, Australia and the Pacific, it was the same. Europeans constituted themselves as a superior white race and assumed the right to control those not so constituted. Race became a symbol of authority. And with the unquestioning (and by the subject peoples unquestionable) assumption of European racial superiority went the assumption that the culture of Europe was equally superior.

The Challenge to Europe

These are critical issues for the whole of Europe. Teachers have a vital role to play. But action in education and other areas of social policy cannot solely be based on exhortations about the reasonableness of the European citizenry. There is need for rigorous analysis of causes. Strategies will fail if they do not take into account the deep features of racism and how they have been transmitted to various levels of consciousness in the operations of the body politic.

None of the continental cultural systems is frozen or has a fixed status. Teachers need to challenge the muteness that has been imposed upon the knowledge and images of oppressed civilisations. The first process to consider is to 'unlearn', as Raymond Williams says, 'the inherent dominative mode' (Williams 1958: 376). This unlearning, and letting 'the other' speak for itself, is an ethical question for Western culture. It would entail avoiding the depiction or the containment of those outside the dominative framework – be they Blacks, women or 'Orientals'. This would require the development of what Said has called an 'oppositional critical consciousness', so that the 'seductive degradation of knowledge can be avoided' (Said 1978: 328). Ultimately cultures in transition are themselves a reflection of the societies in transition, something which the state apparatuses would do well to recognise.

THE POLITICAL CONTEXT

The Need for Political Action

The need for political action has become the more critical because as we begin the twenty-first century many of the gains of the modern state in the nineteenth century are being reversed – the abolition of slavery and serfdom, the institutions of democracy and the enfranchisement of peoples, the laws to regulate labour and protect children, and the constitutional frameworks which guarantee people's rights. These hard won rights and developments are being increasingly over-ridden by the recent rise of narrow ethnicisms and nationalisms. In most parts of the world seemingly normal national political forces have unleashed violence at many levels – neighbourhoods, communities, localities, regions and nations. Civilised and educated polities have turned into Hobbesian jungles. Ethnicised violence has arisen from within what were considered stable, national, educated and civilised states. For conflict and violence in the past few decades has not been between nation states but within them. Hence, the importance of action at a European parliamentary level.

Parliamentarians must not only develop their own agendas; they should establish a Europe-wide parliamentary group, which cuts across all political divides. Issues of racism and xenophobia are too deep in their intensity for intercultural relations to be made the prerogative of any particular political perspective or any one political party. This obviously requires parliamentarians to work together across party political divides to enhance notions of multicultural Europe. The 1997 European 'Year against Racism' initiated the process, but one 'year' is not enough. Only long-term strategies can deal with this malaise. There is a need to form coherent political principles to recognise and legitimise societal diversity. There is as yet no evidence that this process is taking place coherently across the European Union.

The need is urgent because reactionary, racist and fascistic groups are already mobilised in Europe. The abominable phenomenon of 'ethnic cleansing' has again reared its ugly head only fifty years after it was defeated. Unless the formulation and enforcement of prophylactic intercultural policies is taken seriously the threat to European multicultural democratic policies could undermine European stability.

Not only parliamentarians but also state and regional agencies ought to develop instruments to deal with intercultural issues at local (urban and rural), national and supernational (European Union, Council of Europe) levels. At European Union level it is essential that racism is not only monitored, as it now is in the Vienna Monitoring Centre, but also effectively dealt with. The member states of the Union ought to provide treaty competence in the renegotiated treaty to ensure that measures which are more effective in negating racism and xenophobia can be devised. Articles 13 and 29 of the Maastricht Treaty have already started this process and the Starting Line proposals would take this process further.

Terms like 'multiculturalism' and 'social diversity' are used in contemporary discourse descriptively, to highlight the presence of the 'non-European other'. But if issues of intercultural relations and equitable intercultural public and social policy are to become a reality, then this 'other' has to be treated as being central rather than marginal to European societies.

As we have stressed, all European societies have been historically as well as contemporaneously diverse. Hence European Union member states need inclusive policies to ensure that in legal and legislative terms all groups who reside in a polity have citizenship rights. It is moreover vital that such instruments seek to negate what Balibar refers to as 'the internal decomposition of the community created by racism' (Balibar and Wallerstein 1991). Any development of intercultural measures must start with negating racism, xenophobia, narrow nationalisms and ethnicisms.

What must above all be addressed is the institutionalised exclusion and racism within educational systems. Intercultural learning can only be meaningful if it can help resolve the practice of 'exclusionary power and powers of exclusionary institutions' (Goldberg 1993: 235–6). Hence, the task is one of developing a critical interculturalism, based on sound intellectual foundations and firmly grounded in the core functioning of institutions.

Public Policies

Exclusions in socially and culturally diverse societies and nations breed in turn mentalities of exclusivity – mentalities that have led to ethnic Armageddon in many parts of the world. States ought, therefore, to safeguard the citizenship rights of all groups not only to ensure an equitable resolution of conflicts but to establish public and social policies which strengthen democratic ideas. Such national policies ought to bridge ethnic, religious, linguistic and racial differences to counter the rise of narrow nationalism and xenophobia. Civil and political rights need to be validated in order to sustain the validity of the civil state. As it is, the marginalised – the immigrant minorities, indigenous minorities, refugees, travellers and Roma – become increasingly vulnerable, and the stability of the state is endangered by inter-group tensions.

Intercultural policies would seek to provide safeguards against the job losses and de-skilling brought about by rapid technological change. They would also seek to minimise social inequalities and prevent the growth of a vast European underclass – what Castells has called the 'globalisation of power flows and the tribalisation of local communities' (1989: 350). Provision of equal access, equal opportunity and equality of outcomes is still not a feature of European societies. Harshness and inequalities in the market economy are more manifest than equality of social and educational provision. Provision is not enough. All groups should have a 'voice'. The European education systems have so far not been effective in providing this 'voice' to young people and the marginalised communities they come from.

Belongingness

I return to the notion of 'belongingness' reflected on in the Introduction. Societies embody notions of belongingness as well as of alienation. They have features of a universalistic nature as well as particularisms and local differences – thick and textured layers of political, social and economic contexts which intersect with their histories, cultures and languages. European societies need not be lonely and confining. They provide possibilities and prospects of an infinite nature, whereas non-confederal localisms can become parochial, racist, insular, stagnant and authoritarian.

Our intercultural approach would link individual groups and localities, giving them a sense of belongingness. The challenge for the political and educational systems is to develop a shared and common value system in which inclusive rights and responsibilities would be developed as an outcome of the work of schools, and of social and political institutions (a theme I shall be developing in Chapter 7).

Here, however, we are confronted by the obstinacy of those members of the dominant nationalities who see society as 'theirs', and as encroached on by 'others' who are aliens and are therefore not seen to belong. Nevertheless in a modern democratic society the dominant and the subordinate, the coloniser and the colonised, the rich and the poor, come together in politics to make it function, in all its complexity. This complexity includes the way in which material and social goods are produced and distributed and includes political, economic, literary, cultural as well as media output.

At this point the 'other' is no longer out there, but is here, and, as Chambers puts it, there is an intersection of 'histories, memories and experiences' (1994: 6). It is therefore important to develop an agenda for public and social policy and to create spaces where we can negotiate the complexity of our societies, urban and rural, inclusive of all who live in them, overcoming past and current exclusions.

Here the silent 'voice' would be heard, and would initiate and participate in a dialogue among the various groups. Their interaction would enable the construction of a more realistic understanding of the pasts of the European and other societies with all their issues of antipathy, conflict or cooperation. It would also better inform their present, and in turn construct a less biased and more meaningful future – for instance, the teaching of Spanish history would include the contributions of Islam and of the Basque, Galician or Catalan nationalities to Spanish culture and history. It would also show the members of the dominant nationalities that their own culture, by ceasing to be privileged, had become more dynamic.

THE INTERCULTURAL CHALLENGE

The Intercultural Approach

The 'Eurospeak' phrase for pluralistic initiatives in relation to education, 'intercultural education' (Batelaan 1983), has enabled educationists across Europe to exchange concepts, contexts and practice within a common frame of reference. This potential for development and change extends beyond educationists. Minorities, for example Roma, have made new groupings that transcend national boundaries, giving the potential to make more effective interventions both at the national and European levels. It also has the potential to enable minorities to gain a platform in their own right, avoiding, if they wish, the device of using the nation state of origin as their sponsor.

Nevertheless the dilemmas for intercultural education in Europe have increased dramatically in the recent period. Despite unification in the European Union, narrow national identities are increasingly being asserted, bringing a rise of xenophobia and racism, and the exclusion of immigrants, refugees and asylum seekers. Rising unemployment, and the de-industrialisation and de-skilling of large numbers of people, is leaving whole areas of urban and rural Europe impoverished and demoralised. Previously stable communities have become fragmented and isolated, and the former solidarity of groups and communities eroded, creating uncertainties about the present and the future. High youth unemployment, deprivation, racial disadvantage and political exclusion all lead to disaffected communities and schools.

Racism and xenophobia in education have, however, been marginalised by most governments in the European Union. Political parties tend to identify them as non-vote-winning issues. But their negative dimensions, as well as the positive aspects of anti-racism and intercultural work, are important for the whole community and ought not to be viewed as minority concerns. The health and well-being of the state depend on serious attempts by all governments to eliminate racism and xenophobia, as well as requiring substantive measures to bring about greater levels of equity in the European Union societies.

EU member states need inclusive modalities to ensure that in legal and legislative terms all groups who reside legally in a polity have citizenship rights. Much is made of the heritage of the Renaissance, the Scientific Revolution and the Enlightenment, but if it is to have a reality, then the rational principles on which the states are governed have to be reflected in public and social policy.

If immigrants are represented in a discourse portraying a relationship between them and crime, drugs and terrorism, they are made to seem part of a chain of equivalence. But seen in the historical context we have indicated, they are only highlighting what are the underlying features of any community marginalised on linguistic, religious and social class diversity.

The Intercultural City

Peter Hall wrote in 1990:

> Here then is the final irony: in the mid 1980s the problem of the urban underclass was still as stubbornly rooted in the world's cities, and in the consciousness of its more sensitive citizens, as in the mid-1880s, when it provided the vital stimulus of the birth of modern city planning.
>
> (Hall P. 1990: 399)

A decade later there has been no change. While the cities have generated sophisticated knowledge, complex physical landscapes, as well as socio-economic and political innovations of great splendour, they still remain sites of squalid human failure.

Nevertheless cities, for all their squalor, do embody notions of belonging-ness as well as alienation. They can be lonely and confining. Yet despite the par-ticularisms and local differences which may make them parochial, racist, insular and xenophobic, they still provide far-reaching possibilities and prospects. They offer inspiring dreams as well as nightmares.

We must, of course, beware of constructing a singular identity for cities, not only in Europe but also in other parts of the world. Not many people, apart from a few isolated communities, can claim that they are firmly located within pure city communities. As Murray Bookchin states:

> the city is the historic arena in which – and as a result of which – biological affinities are transformed to social affinities. It constituted the single most important factor which changed an ethnic folk into a universal civitas where in time the 'stranger' or 'outsider' could become a member of the community without having to satisfy any requirement of real or mythic blood ties to a common ancestor.
>
> (Bookchin 1992: xvi)

Urban culture can, therefore, be seen, as it has been historically, as a welcoming intercultural melting pot which accepts diversity and offers opportunity. What the education and other social systems can do is to seek to develop an inclusive culture and with it a sense of corporate belongingness, but once city communi-ties break down into ghettos and *bidonvilles* with their single nationalities and marginalised groups, it becomes difficult to enact inclusive public policies. And when these communities become the focus of policy it can only lead, as the Archbishop of Canterbury's Commission (1985) put it, to 'separate territories outside mainstream life' which reinforce the separation and obstruct the sense of belongingness. The dominant majorities will then go on seeing the city as something that is 'theirs' which is being encroached on by 'others', by aliens who cannot belong there.

But these fears that the culture of the European cities is being swamped by alien minorities are grounded on a notion of the city as something static and timeless, perhaps quaintly archaic. In fact the vibrancy of being the citizen of a Spanish, French, Dutch or English city has a greater chance of being actualised, if it is seen as being multicultured, vivacious and interactive. Such interactiveness, welcoming the 'other' as a creative force, allows for dynamic change and the creation of an inclusive sense of citizenship and belongingness. The education system has an important role to play in developing such an approach.

Intercultural Education

I have already outlined issues confronting intercultural education in Britain in Chapters 2, 3 and 4. Seen in the context of Europe the main issues are similar. A fundamental issue is the need for an intercultural curriculum. Nation-centred or Eurocentred curricula can only reinforce the sense of exclusion and disadvantage and, as in Britain, lead to a demand for separate schools, to the 'politics of recognition' with its own 'curriculum of recognition' – the system already followed in Germany.

It is an issue that must be taken seriously and not just rejected out of hand as an issue of 'political correctness' (Gundara 1993). Here the United States gives a warning. In order not to slip into the acrimonious debates which have raged there, the curriculum must be critically examined before it is too late. If some education authorities were to take the lead in this field it would have international reverberations.

Language diversity must also be taken seriously – not as a problem to be surmounted by rigidly teaching in a European 'first' language, but as a means of cultural enrichment for school and community. Recognising their potential would ensure that those with other first languages would acquire a second more systematically.

A strategy at the European Union level needs to be developed which ensures that there are strong school–community links in major European cities. The use of the concept of lifelong learning by young adults, within the framework of community education, ought to ensure that xenophobic adults are not able to negate the good intercultural work being done by the school. It should also be seen as a way of valuing education in its own right and, through partnerships with training institutions and employers, of providing appropriate skills and training as well as jobs.

Schools should use these school–community links to ensure their staff do not construct the differences in communities as social and educational deficits. Hence school policies should quantitatively and qualitatively monitor whether there are excessive levels of exclusion from certain communities, and take measures to rectify the problems they cause. Together, schools and teachers should be enabled to reform mechanisms which are dysfunctional in the school. This is primarily an issue of school management, which requires coordination with youth workers and social and psychological services.

Formulating appropriate policies is only a start. Their success depends on the teachers who are going to implement them. A European-wide network of good intercultural school practices ought to include a consideration of good intercultural teacher education. Unless there are good interculturally educated teachers, the process of exclusions will continue to alienate children and lead to greater inequalities and low educational outcomes.

Good intercultural teacher education (not training) is one of the greater challenges we face in the European Union. This ought to ensure as a bare minimum requirement that, as a professional matter, teachers are not overtly or covertly racist (Gilborn 1995). Secondly, teachers should be educated to work in complex schools to ensure that they can deal professionally with xenophobic and racist behaviour, and to organise classrooms in such a manner that children with different competencies and different levels of cultural distance can learn from each other rather than disrupt the learning process.

They must also be aware of the varying cultural endowments their students bring to the classroom, be willing to welcome unfamiliar interpretations, and be ready to question their own. In this way the teaching can become a cooperative pedagogical exercise which may generate new insights and give both teachers and students an enriched understanding of the society they live in.

The issues presented here are of the gravest importance for the future of Europe. Introducing them requires pedagogical patience and persistence. There has to be a constant reappraisal of the histories and national identities into which we have been inducted with such care. But above all there must be the political will which sees that these issues are not peripheral to our societies but fundamental.

INTERCULTURAL POLICY IN EUROPE

The Legacy of 1993

The question of immigration is at the heart of the difficulties raised by the planned but postponed political unification of Europe in 1993. That year will be remembered as the year in which one dream vanished – that of a larger Europe without borders, ensuring the free circulation not only of goods and capital but also of citizens. The reason why this dream was abandoned has partly to do with the growth in numbers of unemployed people, but it is also connected with the question of immigration. The flows of immigrants and refugees across the European borders from Eastern Europe, and fears of refugees from the southern hemisphere, have led to policies of strict immigration control. The notions of a free market and the freedom of internal movement envisioned by the Schengen group in 1985 belonged to the days when there was no migratory pressure from Eastern Europe and no Yugoslavian war, and the flow of refugees from the southern hemisphere was not seen as a major problem.

The meeting of European heads of state in Copenhagen in June 1993 led to the first steps to stop illegal immigration into Europe. The ministers of the interior of the twelve states approved a 'recommendation' which states the position of national authorities in response to illegal (clandestine) immigrants, refugees and workers without permit. The proposal is to improve methods of detecting and expelling citizens of 'third' countries who are not considered to be legal residents. The decisions of this meeting were similar to the immigration policies of Britain and Germany, and of France where the French Minister of the Interior, Charles Pasqua, declared that France, formerly a country of immigration, did not intend to continue to be so.

This policy of closing borders to stop the kinds of immigration which are seen as a threat to Europe contradicts the broad idea of an open multicultural society where the mutual exchanges among the dominant groups, immigrant minorities and territorial minorities not only allow understanding and tolerance, but also the flourishing of democracy. The policy of closing borders also contrasts with the present reality of transnational 'diasporas' which have established commercial empires across European countries as well as between the European countries and the rest of the world.

Decisions to close the borders necessitated a move towards integration policies for the settled immigrants. Racism and xenophobia can only be countered
if agreement is reached between immigrants and governments to create an inclusive society – a society within which education must play an important role in
ensuring equity at all levels.

But simplistic notions of assimilation and integration are problematic in a continent where covert and overt racism and xenophobia not only persist but
increase, threatening the minority communities with violence. The fearful 'ethnic
cleansing' in what was Yugoslavia has now become a threat in the countries of
the European Union.

Moreover, in the past twenty years southern Europe, after a long spell as a
source of migrants, has emerged as a new immigration area. Spain, Portugal,
Italy and Greece had previously taken part, as sending countries, in the Council
of Europe's programmes to assist in the improvement of their children's education in the northern European countries. They now face the arrival of immigrants from the southern hemisphere and Eastern Europe, and are themselves
trying to formulate policies about immigration and intercultural education.

As Fritz Wittek, Marianne Nijdam and Piet Kroeger have noted,

> as the distinction between countries of emigration and countries of immigration is
> losing its relevance, there is a growing awareness in the new immigration countries
> that the challenges arising are not fundamentally different in nature from those which
> the older immigration countries have had to face during the past twenty or thirty years.
> (Wittek, Nijdam and Kroeger 1993: 8)

Discussions about intercultural education have taken place for over a decade in
the north European context. Southern European countries have only initiated
work in this field in recent years. It is now important to establish a dialogue on
intercultural education between the southern and northern member states of the
European Union, as also within the Mediterranean region with its long history
of conflict and cooperation.

The challenges, which are posed to parliamentarians at local, national and
European levels, are of critical importance in addressing these questions, success
in which would ensure citizenship rights of all groups. Such a political initiative
needs to establish broadly based educational policies, measures, strategies,
actions and institutional changes. Such initiatives need also to be undertaken in
other regions of the world. Without the development of these strategies, and
analysis of the negative aspects of those educational systems which promote
ethnic conflict, the initiatives would remain sterile. Positive policies and actions
to counter ethnic conflicts and genuinely intercultural relations would then be
indefinitely postponed.

There is an urgent need to form a network of institutions and structures to
initiate further work: development of Internet and other informational networks,
disseminating findings, establishing educational and political strategies for different contexts. The International Association of Intercultural Education and the
European Parliamentary Group can act as enablers in activating these initiatives.

The Future of Intercultural Policy in Europe

The success or failure of intercultural education in Europe will depend on facing and tackling the following:

1. No concerted effort to eliminate racism in the wider context, nor any systematic approach to implement intercultural education, exists in any single European country, nor within the European Union, nor in the area covered by the Council of Europe.
2. Intercultural education has become an issue of theoretical debate and analysis amongst academics, but changes within the school system or higher education remain in their infancy.
3. There is no uniform model of intercultural education across the European Union. This is despite a theoretical agreement that intercultural education is not only an immigration issue, but is a more general social diversity issue, and a recognition of the need to develop a model of a future European society in which intercultural education plays a prominent role. Legislators take different stances and measures, whether these are on bilinguialism, experimental projects or teacher education.
4. International recommendations from the European Union or Council of Europe have exercised only a marginal influence on national policies, because the educational systems are still strongly controlled by the mechanisms of the various nation-states. The differences among the school systems, whether centralised or decentralised, have resulted in differing ways of implementing or ignoring policy issues. At the present time the changes in the European school systems are supposed to provide flexibility and autonomy for the schools, to promote competition amongst schools, and to improve participation of teachers, families and communities. Yet important recommendations from the Council of Europe for intercultural preparation for newly qualified teachers still remain to be implemented. The ongoing marginalisation of intercultural discourses within higher education retards their implementation, and hence even these haphazard and half-hearted measures are only feebly reflected in schools through the inadequately qualified teaching force.

FURTHER READING

Tom Nairn (1997) *Faces of Nationalism: Janus Revisited*, London: Verso.

Gertjan Dijkurk (1996) *National Identity and Geopolitical Visions*, London and New York: Routledge.

Mark Mazower (1998) *Dark Continent: Europe's Twentieth Century*, London: Allen Lane.

Tore Bjorgo and Rob Witte (eds) (1993) *Racist Violence in Europe*, Basingstoke: St Martins Press (Macmillan).

Richard Caplan and John Fetter (1996) *Europe's New Nationalism: States and Minorities in Conflict*, Oxford: Oxford University Press.

6

The Role of the State

The state in most parts of the world confronts complex challenges to deal with social diversity. The notions of blood and soil which form a local community or a nation are too one-dimensional. The other dimension is the way in which diverse groups in a society have legitimacy in terms of belongingness which accrues from the rights and responsibilities which are conferred on citizens by constitutions. Modern states are also negotiators with various international instruments which confirm the inviolability of citizens.

The exclusions and problems of belongingness at local levels in most societies have become a serious issue within the last few decades of the twentieth century. The need to develop confederal communities which derive their basis of emerging shared and common values is one focus of intercultural policies. However, the triumphalist histories as well as other aspects of knowledge need to be tackled to allow for the nurturing of confederal localities and inclusive polities. This chapter draws on issues from various contexts to examine the developments which are needed to reverse the onset of civil strife, violence and war.

NATIONAL AND LOCAL PERSPECTIVES

The State and Identities

Within the state there is an issue which Edward Said refers to as 'the idea of a nation, of a national-cultural community as a sovereign entity and place, set against other places', which separates 'us' from 'them' through boundaries. He suggests that this idea of place does not cover nuances which constitute a cultural issue. 'It is in culture', he writes, 'that we can seek out the range of meanings and ideas conveyed by the phrases belonging to, or in, a place, being at home in a place' (Said 1983: 8).

Interculturalism raises issues for the state in articulating policies at national level to ensure that the multicultural nature of their societies is recognised. This involves a state-craft which ensures that all citizens, immigrants and refugees have legal rights and responsibilities. To avoid ethnic Armageddon it is necessary that the state at central level ensures national resolution of conflict and inequity in all areas of public and social life. However, as we have indicated, many conflictual and chauvinistic aspects of education remain largely intact at national levels. Issues of teaching history and languages will be discussed as aspects of educational policy requiring consideration and action at local and national state level.

National policies should ensure that democratic solutions in complex societies are based on inclusive, non-violent value systems and on shared and common understandings in the public domain. National policies to bridge ethnic, religious, linguistic and racial cleavages can invite extreme forms of xenophobia. Indeed it is partly the failure of state-craft that is responsible for the rise of caste-based identity, xenophobia and racism because such phenomena are not natural to groups in society, and preventative policies are preferable to reactive strategies.

The stress on *jus sanguinis* (based on blood) rather than *jus soli* (on soil) notions of citizenship (Kristeva 1991: 95–104), and the privileging of the ties of blood and soil, undermine not only the civic concept of national societies but exacerbate tensions in local areas, particularly when local territories become contestable spaces because the non-belongingness of certain groups is emphasised. Notions of public safety and policies to defend human rights and plural social environments are of fundamental importance to the civil state (*état de droit*). The school, as an educational institution, has a formative role in developing a peace-oriented and inclusive ethos amongst all young people, and in ensuring that all young people in a state stand together as they grow together. Yet our survey has shown that many current education systems continue to stratify groups rather than develop a framework of inclusiveness and similarity.

The transnationalisation of the economic process raises further questions of governance and regulatory process. It is necessary to ensure that the polity retains enough control over its political economy to obviate inequity – breakdown of communities, high levels of unemployment and the development of a disaffected and disenfranchised underclass. As Castells states, the 'globalisation of power flows and the tribalisation of local communities' become increasingly juxtaposed (Castells 1989: 350). At a national level, the doctrinal hegemony of the market has fragmented groups and increased tensions in mixed communities. Refugees and asylum seekers created by political and economic devastation are caught in 'Catch 22' situations both in countries of origin and in receiving countries. Neither provides a safe haven, yet paradoxically borders remain permeable. In a climate of scarce resources the refugees become the new victims of exclusion and violence at the lower strata of local life. Even more vulnerable are the older and nomadic traditional Roma and traveller communities who survive in twilight zones.

The basic issue of political representation and active participation in national and local politics is to ensure that rights, responsibilities and civic values are indispensable and that all voices are heard. There is the question of how to devise integrative public policies. For instance, to provide access to social institutions, should the underlying policy be based on social class or on the presumed 'racial' identity of excluded groups to avoid them being labelled as special beneficiaries?

Policies to bring about equity in education ought not to privilege one group against another, and as yet no optimum ways of equalising equity within education systems have been developed.

There are no hard and fast rules of how diverse communities come about. So, for instance, it is not true that communities are necessarily sedentary and that society is a static organism. Certain factors (economic, persecution etc) may 'push' a community, or members of a community, into migrating, and they may then be 'pulled' into another community. From time immemorial people have continued to move and settle – it is a universal and human phenomenon – for hunting and gathering, for economic, political, spiritual or climatic reasons, to go freely as travellers or on pilgrimage, or enforced as slaves. Hence, the development of communities as diverse entities is itself part of this larger process of the human dynamic of movement and settlement. Yet there is little educational analysis on the major import of this phenomenon with a view to creating the appropriate optimum educational policies, strategies and initiatives.

Then there is another issue – that of belongingness of all groups in local communities. This presents the problem that certain dominant groups may see the locality as 'theirs', encroached upon by 'others' who are aliens and seem not to belong. There are obviously specificities of different localities, communities, families and groups which provide a different colour, texture and hue to the different parts of a country. There are also the differences of local politics, economies and histories, and how they interact with regional, national and global contexts. Hence, for instance, an urban school in one country may have more in common with an urban school in another country than with schools in smaller towns or rural areas in the country in which it is located. Local initiatives need to be collated to draw repertories of 'good practice'. Travellers or Roma, because of their different lifestyle, are seen as marginalised with little notice being taken of their needs.

Local Communities and Identities

While attention to diverse communities tends to focus on immigrant groups or so-called 'ethnic' groups, the realities of these presences are more complex. Such complex existences require the education systems to develop appropriate policies based on an inclusiveness of all groups who live in the localities. The possibility of interaction and intersection between histories, cultures and languages enables the construction of a more realistic understanding of the locality's past and present which may in turn enable us to construct a less biased and more meaningful future.

Communities are not only situated within their localities but have other identities at both national and supra-national levels, which lends an enormous range of heterogeneity to a locality and its life. The complexity of all this activity defies a simplistic definition by either a dominant or a subordinate culture.

Hence, the sense of a mainstream, imposed by the dominant group, does not hold sway because the marginalised subaltern culture no longer accepts a subordinate status or its place in the triumphalist narratives (see, for instance, Guha and Spivak 1988). A reappraisal of the various narratives within the community is necessary. This requires a reunderstanding of its collated histories, one which is more inclusive of 'other' histories, languages and knowledge, and is not merely reflecting the dominant understanding.

One aspect of this reunderstanding is to examine the cultural production of the minority communities (in literature, films, dance, theatre, music, visual arts). It then becomes clear that the minority presence cannot be stereotyped on a simplistic 'ethnic' basis. The 'ethnicisation' of cultures as commodities militates against their genuine and syncretic development. As Michael Bracewell writes about one area of London:

> Notting Hill, along with Camden Town, has become a retail base for alternative lifestyles. There have probably been more self-satisfied articles about the exotic life of Notting Hill over the past five years than about any other district of London. Here, for instance, is the home of the 'trustafarians' – the rich white kids who subscribe to west London Bohemia – and here for the older generation, is the politically correct mix of creeds, colours and ideologies . . . areas like Notting Hill have come to resemble a cross between a zoo and a cultural supermarket.
>
> (*The Guardian* 8 January 1994)

The creation of stereotypes and caricatures is perpetuated by the mass-marketing of 'ethnicities'. But the real lives of the various groups and communities are very distant from the world of fashionable 'ethnicity'. The realities of the lives, struggles and the substantive concerns of those involved lose their meaning through this commodification. Those who are citizens face racial discrimination and devaluation of many aspects of their culture. Those who are refugees or asylum seekers, or do not have citizenship rights, face even greater privations and are continually undermined by oppressed lives here, as well as concerns about a dismembered home, whether it is in Somalia, a Kurdish village or Bosnia. There is also the loneliness of women who are disadvantaged and powerless, and often have appallingly deprived lives. Escape from political tyranny and war at home does not improve their quality of life in many of the poor parts or places they migrate to. A better and safer life remains a chimera, not least because the education systems in the contexts of settlement may continue to replicate difference, conflict and 'otherness'.

Such communities are trapped between the imagined pasts of home and the alienation experienced as a result of the dominant groups asserting notions of the 'imagined ownership' of 'their nations', thus reinforcing their exclusion as already marginalised groups.

Many of the migrants live as siege communities. Whether it is women or young children who are harassed, or whether it is young men and women and the elderly who are beaten up and even murdered, these victims become symbols of the need to retrieve what Phil Cohen has called their 'lost inheritance' (Cohen 1991).

The differences between neighbourhoods and parts of a locality mask the many ways in which there are crisscrossings making distinctions between localities quite bewildering. While for some this presents immense possibilities, for others it means a foreclosing of options. For some new identities are formed and syncretism is the order of the day. For others there is an activation of 'siege mentalities' within siege communities which can reinforce patriarchies and allow fundamentalisms to take root.

While identities of adults are already formed, those of children are in the process of being formed. Hence the issues of belongingness and exclusion should be part of educational concern and practice. Such educational practice should enable students to transcend narrow definitions of identity and develop intercultural understandings.

Children are able to construct a broader understanding of life based on their own personal concerns and experiences. These understandings underpin what may emerge as multidimensional identities. Children grow up and develop different identities as they begin to get involved in different types of collectivities, ranging from family, peer group, school and other socialising influences, including the media. Yet unless parents and adults are also part of the educational process, racism and narrow ethnicised identities are likely to be reinforced. This is true for both dominant and subordinate groups. Chauvinistic parents and adults can undo the work of school, and unless the schools have strong community links, negative spillovers can undermine their work.

In the journey from childhood to adulthood the symbols of what is important change from early to later life. The important issue to explore may be what the educational system can do in the early years of school, adult education and in higher education, to broaden the choice of identities to which young people have access.

Such questions become critical in modern urban contexts where young people from a diverse range of backgrounds inhabit the same territory. Those from one particular rooted neighbourhood may feel that 'outsiders' are occupying what they see as their locality. This feeling of displacement in their neighbourhood may be heightened because of the lack of secure identity, skills, knowledge and an ability to see the world in complex ways.

The nature of local areas and their complex populations, which include the skilled working class and those working in trades and industries, has changed dramatically. Not only have many trades disappeared but the movements of many industries to other parts of the world have removed the practices which apprenticed young men to masculine skills and cultures. As Phil Cohen states:

> The disintegration of this material apparatus and its replacement by 'post-fordist' systems of training and work has not had the effect of dismantling its symbolic structures, these continue to reproduce racism and ageism in working class cultures; but it has altered their modes of operation and anchored them to racist practice in a new way.
>
> (Cohen 1991: 11)

The consequent rise of local or neighbourhood nationalisms can be seen as defensive attempts at ownership of local communities. Yet while such groups might feel that they belong to certain neighbourhoods, these neighbourhoods may themselves belong to a totally different set of agencies.

The major problem facing the younger generation in poorer areas is their lack of educational attainments and skills. The lack of any certainty about the future may further mar their ability to operate in complex societies. It is obviously the case that children do have a range of survival and street skills that are not recognised by formal institutions like the school, and only have currency as a subculture. One question is how can the school build constructively on the knowledge about survival and street cultures which are part of the lives of modern youth.

While many adults from rural backgrounds had skills related to rural areas, the younger generation, who are mainly products of the urban and industrial civilisation, belong to neither, largely because of the failure of schooling to take both the educational, as well as the work and skill, aspects of their lives seriously. Hence there are now many young adults who have little security, education or technical skills to function as fully fledged citizens (Gundara 1983: 43–50).

We must always be on our guard against the danger of constructing a singular identity for each country, ignoring its diversities, and recall that local culture is not merely a way of life but a realised signifying system. To develop such an understanding requires a rational mind based on a rational system. Yet an insecure national or local elite which has not had the courage and openness to deal with this critical issue has made things worse. It may also be a result of blinkered political vision – because politicians have ignored the positive dimensions of social diversity in their countries. Through a sleight of hand, the deep social changes and inequalities which affect the belongingness of the various groups are ignored, and problems are instead blamed on market forces, or on the alienness and otherness of other groups, based on real or perceived differences.

As uncertainties in the polity grow and the industrial economy declines, conurbations encroach and the rural becomes a haven, particularly for middle-class patriots and refuge seekers. The construction of this safe ruralism by those who are themselves thoroughly urban harks back to the purities and certainties of the past. The values of being English in England or Hindu in India are not dissimilar from those of the German *Volk* and emanate from the close perceived connections between blood and soil. The village and rural area is not therefore just a haven, it is also a construction born out of English or Hindu identity which excludes 'the other'.

The construction of a viable state polity lies in reinventing a notion of the urban, as well as of a countryside which is non-exclusive. In areas where there is urban and rural poverty, obviously the construction of a secure national haven raises greater integrative problems.

AN INTERCULTURAL APPROACH

Education systems have an important role to play in developing understanding and shared values, and in cultivating a more inclusive notion of citizenship with a sense of belonging within society. This is a challenge which, as I have shown, has failed throughout the European Union. Issues of intercultural education in a multi-cultural society are merely seen to be relevant because of the presence of the immigrant 'other'.

The dominant bias in the curricula obviously has to be corrected to meet the needs of a range of very diverse societies. But it should not be a way of imposing curricula which are not commonly and democratically negotiated with all the constituent groups. To quote the OECD/CERI (1989) Report:

> What one would like to point out here is the fact that most of the multicultural curricula offered in schools (particularly in the European countries) are targeted at the 'others' and only concern pupils from the ethnic minority communities instead of the whole school population.

The Report goes on to recommend the intercultural approach as a way out of this perspective:

> Its aim is ambitious: to form a new open cultural identity which is neither Euro-centric nor ethno-centric, nor passionately tied to its own beliefs and values.
>
> (OECD/CERI 1989: 7–9)

Part of the problem in actualising this aim is that different cultures have different views of knowledge. Intercultural education cannot be restricted solely to studies of cultures, since it would distort cultural imaginations and symbol systems and ignore substantive issues about knowledge.

Strategic Plans and Priorities

National governments ought therefore to develop citizenship and inclusive rights for all. The issue of educational rights and equity in education is one such right.

In the development of educational provision, a community education approach, where parents, adults and children all learn together (as outlined in Chapter 3), may help to obviate the development of segregated and separate schools on a racial, linguistic and religious basis. In this sense, good intercultural education should be seen as equality and quality in education, to enhance educational outcomes and life chances for all children.

A multi-agency approach is needed within the context of broad social and public policy. There is a need to build a repertoire of good practices, at school, local and national levels, which are transferable from one state to another and can be used to develop cooperation.

A collation of experiences in intercultural initiatives can enable educationalists to analyse what has worked in different contexts and what has failed. Such information could be used to develop strategic plans which can help prioritise action on a long-term basis to ensure that measures undertaken at different educational levels are effective. Conversely, policies based on vacuous rhetoric which are not implemented by skilled school and local management systems have the opposite effect. Therefore, effective monitoring and evaluation of all measures are needed to provide quality education for all.

To be effective, improving quality and equality in education not only requires priorities of action and a strategic plan, but also calls for resources to be made available so that significant shifts in educational experiences in local areas can be made.

Triumphalist History and Distortion

History at local and national level plays an important role in shaping identities of communities and nationalities. These identities can be exclusive of certain groups or inclusive of diverse elements in society.

All children have a right to know their own personal 'story'. When children do not have access to their parents, family or community history they become obsessed with it. Young people need not only access to their stories, but to be able to read them critically. They should be able to analyse historical information, facts and documents critically. These historiographic skills would be invaluable to them in evaluating 'stories' and 'histories'. Members of societies generally think that their understanding of the history of their own and other societies corresponds to the reality of events. Yet the norm is that we generally have notions based on falsified histories. Part of the problem lies in the way in which descriptions of events, even by participants, is by definition partial. As historians become more removed from historical events or periods, their narrative becomes more removed from historical realities. It is, however, possible to devise certain narratives that are more accurate than others and to remove the excessive levels of ethnocentrism.

But since societies are located in time and place their members' experiences have socially centred views of the world. At a group level they have notions of centrism based on their ethnic community, or as a group defined by its culture. At a supra-national or regional level such cultural entities may traverse over a number of states (for example, Pan-Kurdism and Pan-Slavism). At a macro-continental level such ethnocentrism can include diasporic notions of being a Black African, or an encompassing identity as Chinese. Individuals and groups may therefore have access to competing versions of history from personal, familial, community, national and even supra-national levels.

While ethnocentrism may focus on culture it can be distinguished from racism which depends on the attribution to biological heredity of the cultural peculiarities of a group with highly distinctive physical features (Preiswerk and Perrot 1978: 11–29; Fry, Mawe and Simmons 1991). Ethnocentrism as a phenomenon may have an older history, and have preceded racism, because racism became more pronounced in the eighteenth century. The subsequent rise of nationalism has complicated matters further. Political organisations and the use of force have provided the ultimate sanction, especially if the nation has been able to define its territory and those who belong to it, or are excluded from it. At the level of internationalism and international relations it is the nation (however defined) which is the accepted player.

The nation uses political and educational institutions to normalise internal group relations. This process of normalisation is capable of being used very narrowly as the Nazi German State was able to demonstrate. Ordinary Germans and those who worked in state institutions internalised rules of exclusion of groups like Jews and Roma. Education systems legitimised the most appalling events as normal, and ordinary people accepted these authoritarian rules. The role of the educational processes to legitimise these actions and to accept gossip as fact should not be underestimated. Authoritarian systems can generally bypass the critical functions of education. The best defence for an educational process with a critical edge is within democratic schools and systems where people do not have to obey rules unquestioningly.

Omissions and distortions of history play a major role in allowing gossip or stereotypes to become crystallised. The presentation of African history by its absence, especially the absence of its pre-colonial past, has helped to construct Africans as a people without a history or a past. Dominant African groups have used similar exclusions against non-dominant communities while subjugated groups like the Dalits, or tribal people, of India, and other subordinated peoples in other parts of the world, are also seen as having no past or history.

Additionally, heroes in history are largely warriors and victors of dominant groups. The heroes of peace and their victories are far more rarely included. They need to be recorded so that history can be used to disarm and not to re-arm.

Understanding History

To develop more universalised understandings of history, the underlying hypotheses and implicit theories of writers need to be unpicked. An epistemological and methodological break could add to developing more widely acceptable histories which include not only written sources but oral understandings. Since school level understandings of history vary so vastly, not only between but within countries, one cannot provide abstract solutions. Nevertheless, in general, they should include: notions of civilisations, the evolutionist schema, the impact of stereotypes, and the re-voicing and re-imaging of invisible and subordinated groups.

The use of terms like 'tradition' or 'modernisation' as applied to the study of history have their own parochialism and linearity. Non-western civilisations get constructed as traditional while the west is seen as the acme of modernity. Such notions detract from the development of a more universalised or global approach to understanding history. Liberating the notions of the modern from the Eurocentric straitjacket can help to revalue the notion of modernity. The works of Samir Amin, Immanuel Wallerstein and Eric Wolf have explored western 'dominance' through the development of capitalism (Amin 1989; Wallerstein 1974, 1980; Wolf 1982). These provide grounds for reappraising the writing of newer historical texts and tackling other historical 'centrisms'.

For instance, the complex and conflictual encounters of the local and the global in economic and cultural terms provide further clues to notions of the development of markets, as well as the resistance, retrenchment and development of siege communities. The undemocratic features of globalised and global economies have led to erosion of good local values, and stable and sustainable communities, as well as of local skills and economies with consequent ethnic conflicts and tensions.

Nevertheless, as Raymond Grew writes, the development of global history can be a product of our own time which:

> offers some historical insight into contemporary concerns and therefore into the past as well. And it will do so while substituting multicultural, global analysis for the heroic, national narratives on which our discipline was founded.
>
> (Grew 1983: 245)

Teachers and schools also need to explore the viabilities of syncretic understandings and histories which may exist at local levels to help bring about intercultural learnings and understandings.

However, at an inter-state level we see only too clearly the threat of the education system being used to construct curricular fictions which reinvent the past with notions of an imagined and glorious history which excludes their neighbours and disregards their common foundations. The inter-state conflicts between Greece and Turkey, or India and Pakistan, which have the potential to destabilise not only the states in question, but also the Mediterranean or South Asian regions, ignore the over-arching historical links, based on shared histories of the Ottoman Empire, or of pre-independence India, and replace them with an antithetical view of the neighbouring state.

In the case of Turkey, the modernising ideas of Ziya Gokalp and the Tanzimat Reforms (1839–76) were given new force by the modernised Republican Turkey of Attaturk – Turkey comes from the East and marches towards the West (Kazamias 1997; Sayyid 1997). While the Greeks build on the classical past, the Turksreject it and subscribe to notions of modernity – despite the modernising process being itself Hellenocentric, and based on a narcissistic conception of European modernity. Both states construct notions of the barbarians, 'within' as well as 'without'.

On the sub-continent modernisers like Jinnah and Nehru also used complex historical legacies to propel notions of modernity. Both raised the wrath of traditionalists. Hindu and Muslim fundamentalists rear their heads, using the modern state apparatuses and education systems not only to exacerbate inter-state tensions, but also to raise tensions within the state. The ancient mythical past represents powerful cultural symbols which resonate through informal educational channels to reinforce received wisdom. The neofascist BJP government of India totally miscalculated the power of these ancient symbols by exploding a nuclear weapon and were put in their place when Pakistan did the same. Meanwhile the Mohajar, Shia and Sunni conflicts in Pakistan, and Hindu/Muslim relations in India, are like tinder boxes. On the slightest pretext there is an ethnic explosion.

In neither Greece nor Turkey, India nor Pakistan have the modernisers coped adequately with these inter-ethnic tensions. Textbooks, religious schools, mosques and temples are mobilised by traditional elites, using new technologies to propound ancient and exclusivist myths and glories. While modernisers hark to secular state ideals the traditionalists hark to certainties of the past in Greece and India. Turkey and Pakistan seek the Islamic route while Greece chooses Eurocentrism to reinforce the classical past.

Textbooks, Maps and Monuments

The development of teachers' critical understandings demands the development of appropriate teaching materials and textbooks, based on new research. Preiswerk and Perrot have carried out a critical analysis of thirty textbooks and conclude:

> In short, it is not enough to recognise in eurocentrism a factor which distorts images on the level of social knowledge, but to see on the level of the specialists' knowledge, the fundamental epistemological problems of plausibility of the epistemic subject.
>
> (Preiswerk and Perrot 1978: 371)

Their work can be used as a basis to develop other initiatives which critically analyse historical texts.

However, vested political interests make it very difficult to correct historical misrepresentations in textbooks. The Japanese atrocities during World War II have been illegally deleted from Japanese textbooks, despite campaigns against such censorship by academics like Professor Ienaga. There is no reference to the biological experiments against 30,000 people in North-West China which were committed by Unit 731 of the Japanese army (*The Guardian* 30 August1997). This has aroused concern on the part of South Koreans and Chinese who have alleged that Japanese children are prevented from learning about the wartime cruelties of their country.

This is additionally difficult because governments or dominant groups tend to stress national identities. Yet most people have more than one identity which does not detract from their national loyalties. Education has an important role in legitimising these notions of multiple identity as being normal, and not a reflection of aberration or disloyalty to the state.

Educationalists need to explore ways of giving force to these heterogeneous identities. In India, religious extremists like the Hindu revivalists tend to ignore the non-religious and complex identities, not just of individuals, but of social groups – yet the Indian nation, far from being a Hindu country, contains not only the third largest number of Muslims in the world (over 100 million), but also adherents of many other faiths, including Sikhs, Christians, Parsees, Jews, Jains and Buddhists (not to mention atheists and agnostics). Yet the Delhi government has tried to ban the Christian churches as places of worship because

Hindu fundamentalists objected to the use of wine in the Christian services.

For example, in 1992, Vidya Bhavvati prepared a new set of history textbooks which were to be used in schools in states controlled by the BJP. In their textbooks,

> The revivalists depict the Mughals as foreigners and oppressors, and interpret Indians' achievement of freedom from English rule as but the latest episode in a long ongoing struggle to free India from foreign influences. Muslims are, by this interpretation, the contemporary incarnation of the Mughal pattern of dominance.
>
> (Kumar 1993: 555; see also Kothari 1993)

The challenge posed to historical textbooks and to the Indian secular policy by Hindu revivalism is great, and their hegemonic views require a concerted effort, including curricular initiatives, to re-legitimate the broad social diversities of India. While schools stress the uses of literacy, its abuses also need focusing on.

Even maps can be used, in the teaching of geography, to exacerbate ethnic and racial conflicts. In the United States map names like Nigger Lake in New York State, Chinks Peak in Idaho, and Jap Valley in Utah, illustrate the potentially derogatory nature of naming places – though, given the sensitivities of all groups in the United States, some are being changed. Military conquest and political revolutions have led new occupiers to change names. In Israel old Palestinian place names have been replaced by Hebrew ones. In partitioned Cyprus, Turkish and Greek place names have been changed, as they have been in the Balkans with 'ethnic cleansing'.

The appropriation of heroes, even in activities like mountain climbing, is reflected in the way Hillary and Tensing were claimed by Nepal, India, New Zealand and Britain. While the climbers themselves did not divulge who climbed Mount Everest first, pressures for them to do so, for nationalistic reasons, persisted. An event which could have been used historically to bring East and West together was used, despite the wishes of the climbers, to try to advance national aggrandisement and supremacy. Most of our monuments are based on the victories of one nationality over another in war. There ought to be better ways of celebrating historical events than the norm of displaying triumphalism in public spaces.

The Emperor Ashoka (272–232 BC) built an Indian Empire across the length and breadth of India. His message on the victory column that he had built was very different from that of other conquerors. It was a declaration of non-violence and adherence to the teachings of Buddha. On one column it was stated that he had been moved to remorse, and that he felt 'profound sorrow and regret because the conquest of a people previously unconquered involved slaughter, death and deportation'. He had learnt from Buddha that 'moral conquest was the only true conquest'. So, while the Hellenistic Empire had been established through military conquest, 'Ashoka sent missionaries to all the Hellenistic rulers in the west to preach Buddha's pacific doctrine – to where the Greek king Antiochus dwells and beyond the Antiochus to where dwell the four kings severally named Ptolemy, Antigonus, Magas and Alexander' (Smith 1901: 131).

Hence, the route of trade and conquest also became the means of disseminating peaceful doctrines which could prove a less aggressive way to determine the course of history.

Instead, the modern state educational systems generally fail to reconcile territorial, religious and linguistically based diversities, and project a coherent and cohesive scenario which the whole society is supposed to accept. Educators in ministries and state sponsored projects are propelled by national elites to construct educational systems, curricula and textbooks which homogenise and centralise these diversities for fear that the state system would fragment. Yet the real danger is that this homogenisation and centralisation can lead to greater levels of disintegrative tendencies.

Obviously the situation varies in different contexts, but the educators and political forces have to try to deal with these questions more rationally. Modern secular and complex educational systems are failing to address the needs of local identities, modernisation and progressive national needs. New global and marketisation forces complicate their role and no easy solutions can be offered. However, concerted and prophylactic educational initiatives led by UNICEF, UNESCO and other stabilising international agencies can be called upon to provide expertise.

A MULTILINGAL APPROACH

Linguistic Domination and Conflict

Language is a basic curriculum issue. For much of the modern period languages have been disappearing at a seemingly ever increasing rate. For example, the colonisation of Australia has resulted in the demise of the majority of the Aboriginal languages. Even today, when many accept the importance of maintaining them, the decision has had to be taken, on grounds of cost if nothing else, to remove governmental support from those with only a very small number of speakers and/or only adult users.

The pattern of language loss found in Australia is not unique. All over the globe small language user groups are disappearing, particularly if they are economically or politically powerless groups. At the same time other languages are rapidly growing in terms of numbers of speakers, particularly Chinese and English, the latter mainly as a second language. This language loss is not, of course, new. Languages have been disappearing for as long as records of them have been kept. Even the linguistic landscape of Europe, which to an extent escaped the colonising linguistic power of European colonialism, is spotted with the memories of dead languages. Latin is the most famous, but even countries so seemingly linguistically homogeneous as England have Cornish and Manx as dead, or nearly dead, languages.

If language history shows languages constantly disappearing it also shows others growing, in terms of numbers, and in terms of adequately dealing with the vast explosion of knowledge that has characterised the last few centuries. A key example is the way English dominates scientific discourse: scientists who wish to be at the forefront of their area have to have access to scientific journals, some eighty per cent of which are published in English – while monolingual English speakers have no access to the other twenty per cent. An even more alarming example is that eighty per cent of messages on the Internet are in English.

This linguistic domination raises the question that, apart from sentimentality, why should languages that fail to compete linguistically survive? Do they not follow a path of linguistic Darwinism leading to the survival of the fittest?

These questions are harsh, but they need to be addressed. To start with, one can assert that languages are a part of humanity's heritage that should be cherished. Over 200 years ago, in 1773, Dr Johnson told James Boswell that he was 'always sorry when any language is lost, because languages are the pedigrees of nations'. More recently the Indian scholar Professor D. P. Pattanayak put it equally elegantly:

> Many languages form a national mosaic. If some petals on the lotus wither and fall off, or some chips are displaced from the mosaic, then the lotus and the mosaic look ugly. With the death of languages, the country will be poorer.
>
> (Pattanayak 1988, in Skuttnab-Kangas and Cummins 1988)

Such views are powerful and of long standing nature, and are increasingly being accepted by state governments, as the adoption, in 1992, of the Council of Europe's European Charter for Regional or Minority Languages indicates. If loss of a language is a diminution of our common humanity a further answer to the linguistic Darwinists is that languages are not commodities. Moreover smaller linguistic communities whose languages are not in common usage are more likely to have their human rights diminished.

We must also remember that many of the languages spoken in Asia, Africa and parts of Latin America are unwritten. Here languages not only express the group's own culture but their social identity. They reflect the way in which its members perceive nature, universe and society. The Inuit language has many different words for the colour white which is important for life in the Arctic, while in the tropical forests the languages have different words for their forest environment. The designation of such languages as 'dialects' is a travesty.

> In the predominant statist view of national unity, assimilation and development, the languages of indigenous and tribal peoples, particularly when only spoken by small minorities, have usually been destined to disappear.
>
> (Stevenhagen 1990)

These political decisions by governments therefore annihilate not only languages and linguistic systems, but identities, ways of life and knowledge. Indeed prohibiting the use of a language as a means of destroying a political entity has been a regular tool of oppressive governments – for instance, when the British government outlawed the use of Gaelic in Scotland after the 1745 rebellion, or Kemal Atatürk outlawed the Kurdish language in Turkey. And today the Algerian government's attempts to marginalise the Berber language have resulted in violence.

Fragmentation of immigrant and indigenous families, because of the different levels of linguistic understandings, knowledge and skill levels, is an increasing problem. The men tend to become bilingual, and operate within different skill and knowledge levels. But in many underclass communities women and girls remain monolingual, unskilled, and only able to do traditional tasks. As the children grow up they learn different languages and skills, and operate in different knowledge systems. This leads to underperformance by children in schools, and total isolation for women, with ensuing social and psychological problems.

The school curricula ought to ensure that such groups can remain within their communities, if they choose to do so, rather than being totally propelled as marginalised, fragmented peoples on the twilight zones of their societies. Here the role of the dominant 'other' is not to make minority communities de-culturalised, but to ensure that they remain viable entities, able to operate on their own without becoming anomised and peripheral.

Linguistic and school curricula which allow groups to lose their culture by denying civil and political rights, as well as discriminating against them on educational grounds, violate Article 27 of the International Covenant of Civil and Political Rights, and Article 13 of the International Covenant on Economic, Social and Cultural Rights. The role of colonialism has been allowed to continue after independence by national governments undermining the education of such groups through Christian missionaries, who paid scant interest to local knowledge systems, or even destroyed them. The role of the Summer Institute of Linguistics, a Protestant American Church operating in Mexico, is an example.

Though missionaries have played an enormous role in studying indigenous languages, as Professor Stevenhagen has pointed out, the missionary Summer Institute of Linguistics has been involved in transitional bilingual programmes whose function is to phase out first languages (Stevenhagen 1990, 1994). He points out that in Peru in the 1980s, the right wing government intervened, with the involvement of the Summer Institute, to phase out the Quechua language while converting these communities to Christianity.

Correcting these manipulative or short-sighted policies poses major problems of appropriate educational provision and planning, including curriculum development, and provision of textbook and audiovisual materials. The urgency of this issue – which involves the destruction of religions, social relationships, spiritual values, names, dress and sites, as well as artistic and sacred properties – cannot be ignored. It demands the highest priority at regional, national and international levels in the interests of the most oppressed groups in the 'third world'.

Intercultural Bilingual Education

Intercultural Bilingual Education (IBE) is not only of importance for academic reasons. It may also prevent tensions between linguistic communities.

IBE has relevance for most societies, but especially for threatened indigenous peoples – firstly to equip them to participate as citizens of the country in which they live, and secondly to support them in their right to empower their own communities. Their belongingness to the state should be on their own terms, and not subject to political vagaries, or to exploitation by national and transnational corporations, or to racial and cultural oppression. IBE presents them with the knowledge and means to defend their interests against wider encroaching forces, as well as revitalising and strengthening their own cultures.

IBE, however, is not about destroying but about developing and enhancing linguistic diversity and repertoires. For loss of a language means a loss of the perception of the world, a way of life and a knowledge system. A meaningful bilingual education places the learners and their beliefs, values, customs, socio-economic and cultural situations at the centre of the education process.

If IBE is the basic structure and content of the formal education process, it gradually brings in thematic areas from the dominant culture in a non-conflictual and non-substitutive way. This can assist the process of interculturalising. More importantly, in the context of majority/minority, dominant/subordinate relations, it is the majority and the dominant who require intercultural bilingual education (Aikman 1997: 79–89).

National policies vary from being hostile, through assimilatory to accepting. The international NGOs and some aid agencies can help in the process of acceptance. This is necessary because generalised IBE, centralised from a national level, can be anti-democratic and may only deal with differences superficially. For instance, if the minority people perceive the world holistically, and therefore knowledge is seen in similar terms, then subject-based divisions of the curriculum may not be suitable.

IBE is important, not only in countries where there are indigenous minority languages, but in the urban milieu of the European cities where diasporas have brought in small and vulnerable languages. These necessarily require educational support.

The state's response that the national language must be taught to the exclusion of minority or subordinate languages, on the grounds that to do otherwise would lead to less political separation, does, of course, require examination. The enormous resources or skills required to teach other languages may also constitute an impediment. But the following rationale is worth considering: (a) IBE prevents language loss; (b) the first (minority) language provides the child with the best medium to learn at early stages – hence literacy in the first language precedes literacy in the second; (c) the acquisition and development of the first language assists in the successful acquisition of the second – it advances, not detracts from it.

Moreover, IBE enhances the sense of belongingness of a group, its knowledge and values in a school. The use of the first language is useful in developing an inclusive ethos. Children with other languages, cultures and histories from those of the school and its curriculum are less likely to be marginalised, if their languages are used in the school.

Transitional bilingualism, where the first language is used as a vehicle for learning the second or dominant language, is one form of bilingual learning. Other forms include shelter or maintenance programmes (akin to Finnish language in Sweden) and immersion programmes; for example, where English-speaking children from Canada learn French. Here, high-status-language users voluntarily learn the curriculum and the language through French.

Where linguistic predominance prevails and is a source of ethnic tensions among those whose languages are excluded from the educational process, an international collation and replication of good IBE practices could help minimise conflicts.

FURTHER READING

Bill Ashcroft and Paul Ahluwalia (1999) in Edward Said: *The Paradox of Identity*, London: Routledge.
Norbetto Bobbio (1996) *The Age of Rights*, Cambridge: Polity Press.
Manuel Castells (1996, 1997, 1998) *The Information Age: Economy, Society and Culture*, Volumes 1–3, Oxford: Blackwells.
Phil Cohen (1997) *Rethinking the Youth Question: Education, Labour and Cultural Studies*, Basingstoke: Macmillan Press.
William Kymlicka (1995) *Multicultural Citizenship*, Oxford: Clarendon Press.
Michael Walzer (1997) *On Toleration* New Haven: Yale University Press.

7

Building a Common and Shared Value System

SHARED VALUES

Diversity and Democracy

Amy Gutmann, of Princeton University, speaking at the Jerusalem Conference on Education for Democracy in a Multicultural Society in June 1993, suggested that three underlying values are necessary in diverse societies – 'non-discrimination, non-repression and democratic deliberation'. But these values do not exist in a vacuum. They are given meaning by the culture and society in which they are expressed. Values can be universal but they are applied in particular situations. Even if we were able to agree on which universals were to be considered as values to be protected and taught, we would still have to appreciate that their absorption into the social fabric would be influenced by the diversities which exist in any community.

Theoretically, the democratic process should keep these diversities in tension. Social diversities have a historical pattern of leading to or exacerbating conflicts, and the vast majority of conflicts have ethnic or religious roots, so the degree of protection from discrimination and oppression afforded to cultural or religious minorities can be taken to be an expression of democratic stability. Agreed upon standards upholding the values embodied in international and regional human rights instruments offer a pedagogical tool for understanding and dealing with these diversities. The school should have a basic role in teaching principles which are opposed to any form of racism, fascism and restrictive fundamentalisms.

But such teaching will have little effect if students are marginalised outside the school by state sanctions and religious pressures. Ethnic and religious minorities, women and blacks, the young and the ageing, all demand recognition because they know and feel that they are unequally treated. For if democratic societies are to be open and are striving genuinely to achieve greater levels of equality, education for democracy must be based not only on the legal features of citizenship but on the way the notions of equality are exhibited in *all* sectors of society. Hence the need to develop educational strategies to acknowledge and protect these diverse identities. In the pursuit of toleration, acceptance and an appreciation of human dignity, we have to discover a common base in which diversity can be faced.

Universally accepted human rights standards, as set out in the Universal Declaration of Human Rights, may be difficult to implement, but they constitute a valid model for renewed thinking and a challenge for a world ethic of values in socially diverse communities. The sobering realities of the protracted ethnic/religious atrocities in the former Yugoslavia, and the racist and fundamentalist atrocities elsewhere in the world, do not invalidate the standards, but indicate the length of the educational journey needed to implement them.

Living in a society in which equality is the main component of being a part of the public domain, regardless of cultural, religious, linguistic, racial or sexual identities, brings a price – the 'impersonality of institutions' with which, in the absence of particularisation, some may feel it impossible to identify. Are there particular identities which can claim exclusion from the broad social demand for equality? An assertion of liberal discourse says that neutrality of the *public sphere* which protects our equality and freedom is essential, and that there must be no recognition of private identities in the public domain (Taylor 1992).

On the other hand, as we have seen in Chapter 1, there are groups preaching a 'politics of recognition' – the special recognition of their own uniqueness and identifiable contribution and hence of their separate identities, rights and participation levels. Their demands hold in tension the need to balance a search for values within a democratic society. They can only be resisted if notions of the national or universal are made inclusive, accepting of diversities, not excluding them. Otherwise there is conflict – in the nation, in the community, and above all in the schools where young people acquire a sense of their own identity.

Common Basic Values

Is there a clear concept of the values requiring transmission or 'negotiation' through education – are there any *basic values* in a multicultural, multifaith society? Many polities would claim that there are.

Governments have agreed to implement the provisions of existing human rights instruments, as well as to modify their own domestic legislative provisions accordingly, applying to substantive and basic values. But they are slow to enforce them. There is a paucity of concern in introducing effective remedies for violations, in the adoption of conciliation procedures through interfaith dialogue, and in using the educational process and communications media to promote common basic values.

Common values based on a political culture assume an educational process which ensures that all groups and citizens are knowledgeable about the complexity of modern societies. This aspect itself requires serious consideration within the educational process.

Individual attitudes and behaviour are a result of interaction with the social environment. The school is only a small part of it. Common basic values deal with the relations between people, between people and culture (which includes science and technology), and between people and nature. They are marred by the inequalities, domination and subordination which exist in society which can lead to the rise of counterforces which violate these common values – ethnocentrism, racism and fascism, violence and vandalism, and rampant consumerism and pollution.

The effect of educational activities is therefore highly dependent on the experienced attitudes of society. If, for instance, the teacher teaches values like 'solidarity' and 'equality' but they are marginalised outside the school, positive results cannot be expected. It also would be hypocritical to 'teach' individuals how to behave in society if they were not taught about the structure, the mechanisms and the effects of society and its institutions, including the nation state. Schools should also adopt a critical approach towards the 'values' which regulate the state itself.

An educational model based on integrating the different purposes of education would, for example, foster the development of values and the promotion of positive human behaviour. Such an integrative approach would enhance the utility of education. But integration can only be achieved when there is a clear understanding of the constituent elements within the educational process. Is there a clear concept of values requiring transmission or 'negotiation' through education? Are there any basic values in a multicultural and multifaith society where there are minority communities?

An awareness of common basic values is necessary in a society characterised by interdependency and pluralism. Interdependency requires mutual respect, including openness to criticism, when these values prove incompatible with other belief systems. There is, therefore, a need to build a framework for a set of common basic values and a curriculum relevant for education in a diverse society.

Such a framework demands, first of all, respect for human dignity and human rights. The opening phrase of the Universal Declaration of Human Rights recognises the *inherent dignity* of all members of the human family. The now widespread use of the elastically defined concept *human dignity* serves as the cornerstone for this, the most broadly accepted document in human history.

A second prerequisite for a set of common basic values is respect for culture and cultural diversity. Respect for cultural diversity must be taken as a common basic value which intercultural education has a significant role in maintaining. The Christian-humanistic-liberal traditions of Western society accept cultural diversity. Since, however, they also have a strong commercial and industrial tradition, they do not stretch to include broader social needs and positive attitudes towards nature as do many other civilisations. Nature itself is seen as something to be used and consumed. The industrial system nurtures consumerism, and constitutes a direct threat to the environment and to the existence of the planet. The earth has been used as a capital good, like an industrial plant in which it was not necessary to write anything off. Concerns about pollution seem to be directed by economic considerations, and not to arise out of reflection about nature as something which has value in itself.

A third prerequisite is reverence to the earth. Here we can learn from the Native American and Hindu philosophies which have a very different approach to, and concern for, nature which are of deep significance and relevance in the context of modern industrial systems. What Native Americans refer to as 'reverence to the earth' could be taught in schools. It is already formulated in Article 29e of the Convention on the Rights of the Child as 'the development of respect for the natural environment'.

Ethical and Values Education

Values are part of the identity of an individual, a group or the state, including the secular state. They are part of what Habermas (1991: 11) refers to as 'the political culture'. Examples of multicultural societies like Switzerland and the United States demonstrate that a political culture, in the seedbed of which constitutional principles are rooted, by no means has to be based on all citizens sharing the same language or the same ethnic and cultural origins. Rather the political culture must serve as the common denominator for a constitutional patriotism which simultaneously sharpens an awareness of the multiplicity and integrity of the different forms of life which coexist in a multicultural society.

The educative process should have to rely on enabling students to confront 'moral dilemmas' which would encourage them to develop a shared value system with others, based on the process of reasoning. It is, however, a more difficult process than it might seem, because it needs to encompass various cultural traditions. Teachers additionally have to build on students' own value cognition, and the value distinctions children are able to make.

The use of narrative, particularly folk tales, provides teachers with powerful teaching materials because they are able to make distinctions between good and evil. As children use their own experimental knowledge to make these basic distinctions, the school can build on more nuanced value implications, based on imaginative and subtle possibilities.

In multilingual classrooms, where children bring a range of cultural frameworks, the development of bridges across different cultural and linguistic patterns poses a real challenge. Promoting genuinely democratic values in a pluralistic context requires a sophisticated and rich vocabulary. As Puolmatka states:

> The beginning of value education includes teaching a rich vocabulary of values and helping the child to gradually relate his (her) own value cognition to value terms and in this way making him more conscious of his ability to recognise values and to state them in words.
>
> (Puolmatka 1990: 11)

If children are to understand such value systems they must understand and respect them. This access to values can only become part of children's consciousness if it is structured within linguistic and cultural contexts. If they are based on dependence or authority they will lack authenticity.

Yet children, like adults, may adhere to values that are no more than prejudices. Such unreflected values, or even values based on reason or deep beliefs, require both teachers and students to question the assumptions on which they are based. The teachers in such classrooms obviously have the much bigger task of understanding, articulating and presenting alternative, viable values to children which will allow them to make sense of the society they live in.

The underlying question is: how can the school build upon these complex realities and solidarities for teaching purposes in developing an acceptable inclusive ethos? The notion of transmitting values is not sufficient in attempting to develop a shared value system. A more complex relationship between schools and communities must also exist. Schools must not be impenetrable. In a strong education system, the partnership between schools and their communities should enable them to deal with the value dilemmas within our society. The learning process takes place not only in the classroom but also in the playground where the more complex values and identities of the locality permeate the school (Cohen 1997). It is only through the wider partnership of the school and the diverse communities that a common civic culture to which all children can subscribe can develop. Such a shared civic culture, drawing on the strengths of a diverse society, could assist the growth of a genuinely participatory democracy.

The Younger Generation's Own Values

Human rights principles, from politics to economics to ecology, are no longer the preserve of professorial predictions. They belong, most of all, to the value goals of young people. Yet all young people, rich or poor, are subject to uncertainty and change and may act in irrational, erratic and violent ways. There are numerous examples of wealthy young people being involved in ethnic or football violence.

As Hans Enzensberger writes:

Youth is the vanguard of civil war. The reasons for this lie not only in the normal pent-up physical and emotional energies of adolescence, but in the incomprehensible legacy young people inherit: the irreconcilable problem of wealth that brings no joy. But everything they get up to has its origins, albeit in latent form, in their parents, a destructive mania that dares not express itself in socially tolerated forms – an obsession with cars, with work and with gluttony, alcoholism, greed, litigiousness, racism and violence in the home.

(Enzensberger 1994: 42–3)

And where communities are poor and, out of despair, have little hope for the future there is self-destructive despondency and resistance to the status quo.

The modern value dilemmas for the younger generation in what Saul Bellow describes as the 'moral inferno' are dangerously manifested in the rise of religious fundamentalism, narrow nationalism, neo-fascism, racism and sexism. This rise is not restricted to the United States and Europe. It poses even graver threats in many other countries. Experience of injustice and marginalisation and being denied a voice, coupled with the continued stereotyping of victims as the cause of social problems, turns young people towards vandalism, violence and crime.

At the school level it may be the practical manifestation of being denied 'voice' in the classroom – an issue teachers can deal with by developing suitable curricula and teaching strategies. But in a period when alienation and cynicism are rife, the role of formal education as instrumentalist is not enough. David Plunkett argues for a spiritual education in which the mind, the heart and the spirit would engage with reason, intuition and faith. In moving away from an instrumentalist approach to education of the child, Plunkett advocates looking at a child holistically. 'Xenophobia', he writes, 'can be finally rooted out only when xenophobes undergo moral and spiritual change' – although he does not say how (Plunkett 1990). Here a collective school approach to the value issue may allow the school to develop a strategy to deal with these complex matters.

The net result of teaching is what children end up learning. But what we teach is not the same as what they learn. Education goes through the interaction between the educational system – which itself is part of the 'political culture' – as represented by the teacher, and the students who are developing their own individual identity, and have their own images of reality, highly influenced by cultural and social traditions.

This interaction should not be seen as in principle problematic. As Ogbu and Mature-Branchi find,

> Immigrant children generally learn to switch back and forth between the school and ethnic cultural frames of reference, i.e. they learn to cross cultural boundaries. This ability to alternate between the two cultural frames of reference *without affective dissonance* enhances their ability to transcend barriers of language and culture and perform well at school.
>
> (Ogbu and Mature-Branchi 1986)

The interaction will only lead to the desired outcomes if the children find that their cultural interests are safeguarded, that their cultural vibrancy is represented in the curriculum, and that dimensions of their knowledge and skills are valued.

If we want to develop an ethical system which the younger generation adheres to, we cannot draw from one cultural tradition without taking into account the different contexts in which teachers are interacting with students. Francine Best refers to 'the ethical significance of knowledge' as:

> a significance which is lacking nowadays in a world where the supremacy of technology and economics overshadows the question of the meaning of human activity.

She goes on to argue that 'an end should be put to the fallacious contrast between instruction and education, between knowledge and attitudes, and between knowledge and ethics' (Best 1993: 4).

This can be taken further, not only from the philosophical perspective, but also in the interactive process. How do educators engage with the imaginations of young people? There has been a continual stress on universalistic and rational value development at a time when children find themselves in anomic situations. Therefore there is a need to explore the imagined values which children construct on the basis of 'imagined communities'.

These imaginations may have extremely diverse elements. The question is how teachers should harness the positive, creative, constructive dimensions of the imagination to develop social and meaningful values. Another real issue is how schools should deal with subliminal attitudes which are narrow and particularistic, but which the schools need to build upon to develop a shared value system. Regressive imaginations also thrive in children's minds and cannot be dealt with merely by disciplining behaviour.

Many young people find themselves disempowered. They have no control over their own lives. They have lost confidence in the 'democratic state'. There is a lack of involvement in any democratic process, especially in the inner-city areas, where working class communities, and in particular the racial minorities, experience discrimination and domination. The same applies to those marginalised rural communities which are classified as indigenous or national minorities.

The role of the school should be teaching civic or political education to ensure that all children are able to participate within the civic culture. As we have stressed in Chapter 4, this requires initial teacher education and subsequent staff development to ensure that this is an open-ended and not a narrowly doctrinal educational process.

THE ROLE OF RELIGION

Religious Education in Secular Societies

Given the religious, as well as sectarian, diversity in societies, we must have clear definitions about their secular aspect, and the religious rights and obligations of their citizens. Otherwise it may not only lead to antagonism towards other religions, but, because this question is bound up with history, become dangerously conflated with xenophobia and narrow exclusive nationalism.

This raises issues at two levels. One is how the different states ensure that within modern secular contexts others of different faith communities and nonbelievers receive equal treatment and freedom of speech, accompanied by their duties and obligations as citizens. The second entails a much more serious issue for educators, namely, an accretion of feelings, ways of seeing and understanding the rights of those citizens who are classified as the 'other' and whose voices are ignored.

The notions of secularism therefore throw into much sharper focus our own understanding of the issues which teachers and teacher educators need to confront – in intellectual terms, and in their implications for schools in diverse societies. Religious and values education merits a new sensitivity in schools and requires new knowledge and skills in teacher education.

In most states around the world the 'church' and the 'state' are divided. In

Britain, although the society is largely secular, the connection between the Crown and the Anglican Church still exists. A 1992 DES White Paper emphasises spiritual and moral development and states: 'Proper regard should continue to be paid to the nation's Christian heritage and traditions in the context of both religious education and collective worship in schools'.

It is not sufficient to treat the issues of a multifaith society in this manner. The mere provision for children of other faiths either to worship or else withdraw suggests that only Christianity has a recognised status. In children's minds other faiths remain second-class and exotic. This detracts from the understanding of other faiths and is in itself divisive. Such divisiveness may in turn lead to conflict, with faiths like Islam being equated with fundamentalism *per se*. Furthermore, all Asians may get constructed not only as Muslims but as 'Muslim fundamentalists' and notions of religious equality be thrown to the winds.

This privileging of Christianity raises serious issues for the multi-faith nature of British society, and has implications for the secular nation state. Historically, within the British/European context, 'freedom of religion' meant freedom to belong, or not to belong, to any religious group which originated from the Jewish and Christian traditions. The 'non-believers', such as humanists, had to fight longer to obtain the same rights as the religious, but in general terms the *de facto* separation of church and state came to be accepted.

Hence fundamentalist belief systems which reject the separation of 'church' and 'state' may seem to be threatening the freedom of religion of all other religious groups. The notion of an Islamic polity where there are no divisions between the public and the private, and no civic culture, poses a new challenge to the modern, secular society.

However, dividing the public from the private is not only a feature of a representative democratic framework. It may also be seen as leading to a creative dialectical relationship between what are essentially different but enhancing social spheres. In this context, the private domain should not be seen as offering a licence to leave mainstream society, or a sanction for alienation, withdrawal and moral aloneness. Indeed the public, secular framework has a vital role in nurturing the viability of the various religious communities. At the same time, we broaden our understanding of the development of secular societies by embracing the learning and understandings of other cultures.

The Fundamentalist Challenge

Intercultural education cannot ignore the challenges posed not just by religious communities but by fundamentalists who challenge diverse secular polities. Their general opposition to the modern condition in all civil societies needs to be examined, in order to improve public policies, and introduce educational innovations to strengthen the capacity of secular societies to protect all groups. Education systems have an important role in deconstructing the mythical pasts of societies, historical legacies and notions of identity. The failure to establish critical engagement with such issues can lead to the capture of state power by theocratic groups, with grave consequences for diverse polities. It is, however, critical to acknowledge at the outset that such discussions cannot be undertaken without serious consideration of children's rights to accept, modulate or reject views and belief systems inherited from parents.

The present rise in theocracy cannot be ignored. The rise, even in overtly defined secular states like the United States, of massive religious broadcasting and electronic churches is a pointer to the type of fundamentalism which may need to be faced in considering the multifaith nature of society. In times of uncertainty, the symbol systems of religion strike a stronger chord, even amongst those who are non-believers, than the diffuse systems of secularism. Educators, together with social scientists, need to appraise the nature of secular education, and its role in strengthening the legitimacy of all citizens in currently narrowly defined nation states (Batelaan and Gundara 1993). At a societal level, fundamentalist beliefs about the market economy can have similar exclusive effects and can give rise to fundamentalisms in other domains.

The problem for the secular polity is that while its messages have failed, the simplicity of these messages from religiously based groups touches a chord. As Gilles Kepel suggests:

> Movements for the reformation of religious identity have undergone a considerable change between 1975 and 1990. In fifteen years they have succeeded in transforming the confused reaction of their adherents to the crisis of modernity into plans for rebuilding the world, and in those plans their holy scriptures provide the basis for tomorrow's society.
>
> (Kepel 1994)

Hence the failures of secular ideologies to address many of the conditions of humanity may activate a longing for religious fervour.

Moreover disillusionment with the lack of political and social solutions to many societal problems has created insecurity, so it is not surprising that defensive reactions emerge, particularly from marginalised groups. For example, in many of the ex-colonised societies which have embraced a secular political form, the indigenous elites have failed to deliver promises made to the masses. As a result, many people have become disillusioned and reverted to imaginings of past glories, such as those of Islam or Hinduism. As Tehranian states:

> Culture has provided a last-ditch mechanism for the peripheries against the centres of power. Language, religion, ethnicity and cultural preferences as reflected in educational and media programmes have been thus politicized in a variety of contexts to an unprecedented degree.
>
> (Tehranian 1995)

Meanwhile the dominant group may respond to real or imagined fears of drugs, sex, violence, and a fall in discipline becoming more apparent in the secular schools, by sweeping aside the interests of the minority groups. They, in turn, suffering greater and greater levels of educational inequality, may make vocal demands for separate schools – 'the politics of recognition'. But neither separatist solutions to disadvantage, nor spiritual conversions, can correct serious inequality either in society as a whole or in the educational sphere.

Positive Secularism

The Standing Advisory Committee on Religious Education has drawn up many successful agreed syllabuses which reflect the diversity of values in local areas. However, this diversity of values cannot merely be taken to mean religious values. There are obviously within all the communities a large number of families who do not practise any religion. This poses questions, not just about a religious education, but about a broadly based values education. An analysis of the notion of secularism can extend our understanding of the intellectual issues educators need to confront to produce an adequate approach to values education in a diverse society.

Secularism provides by means of the law the necessary framework to nurture equality for all citizens at the public level, and to safeguard the sacred at the private level. It has taken root after long struggles. In some quarters there is a tendency to view secularism as modern paganism and conflate it with humanism. But humanism is a philosophical system in which humanity, not divinity, is central.

The secular collectivity is not necessarily theistic, atheistic or agnostic. Optimally it provides a 'nest' for all groups, and has a role to protect their citizenship rights. 'Positive secularism', or 'the nest', in this sense goes beyond merely the religious toleration of other groups. It entails an understanding by all citizens of our shared belongingness in a complex society of diverse groups and values.

Indeed it moves towards the notion of the 'belongingness' of all groups in society. The major issue is how the education system can legitimise that 'belongingness' for the diverse groups in society, particularly if the dominant groups reject it.

The modern state has a major interest in education since it is considered as a way of providing the labour market with skilled personnel. Education, however, also has a role in providing equity, and in transmitting humanistic, ethical and cultural values and for many groups and individuals these values have their roots in religion.

Hence, secular societies are being challenged by the demand for religious education, or an education system based on one religion. These demands contradict the notions of positive secularism. Problems arise immediately with the promotion, or the dominance, of one particular religion in public schools, or when certain behaviour, based on religious conviction, is denied in schools – for instance, the refusal in French schools to allow Muslim girls to wear headshawls.

However, the issue is not whether religious education should be implemented in all secular schools for the different religious groups, or whether pupils should be withdrawn for wearing a crucifix or a shawl. The issue is how to reconsider the consequences of secularism for education.

Secular education, as such, is not neutral education. It ought to form an important positive dimension within the cross-cultural theme of citizenship. More importantly for schools, moral values derived from Christianity or Islam are but one dimension of the great moral complex dilemmas confronting the younger generation. This is particularly the case since youth and peer group values themselves are an important feature of the culture of the school.

The school ought to respect the moral autonomy of students. It would be failing if it did not provide them with a critical edge to their thinking – which could in turn provide them with a solid foundation to defend their own belief systems. Indeed the critical negotiation of values between teachers and students may be a greater challenge for schools than the customary attempts merely to transmit them. At another level, this raises the wider issue of how to translate such understanding to living within complex social institutions, including workplaces.

An education which claims to be based on human rights, the democratic principles which claim to be opposed to domination, and which, at least officially, aims at mutual understanding, is not value free. But educators need to be aware of the pedagogical function of education, and the basic values on which secular education is based. Therefore, it is important to define the basic ethical and cultural values which should be negotiated through secular education. These are not values to be imposed on the students, but to be negotiated with them. This process of negotiation in itself ought to promote mutual understanding between students, parents and the communities in which the schools are located.

Since education in most contexts is provided by the state, institutionalised education belongs to the public domain, while religion in a secular state belongs to the private domain. This division itself is problematic in a multicultural and multifaith society, and needs to be negotiated and mediated, particularly when the state does not promote the notion of a 'nest' in which minority groups feel safe. The division between public and private should enhance everyone's well-being. One of its functions should be to counter the devaluing of subordinated groups. There is a problem here, since only certain religious communities have a right to establish their own schools within the state system, and these do not necessarily promote mutual interfaith understanding. More importantly, others are not permitted to do the same. This raises the important question of denominational voluntary-aided schools. Would the creation of Islamic denominational schools as demanded by the 'politics of recognition' merely lead to the creation of ghetto schools? Would they be seen at the bottom of the league and make the rhetoric of equality even emptier?

In principle, a critical negotiation of values by teachers and students should be limited to the values of the secular state within the public domain. The school in a plural society should by definition not interfere within the private and autonomous domain of the individual and the family, because the essence of pluralism is the recognition of, and respect for, diverse lifestyles and belief systems. However, as a social institution, the school ought to enable students to understand issues pertaining to the common good of all members of the school, and of the society of which it is a part. It should not ignore the religious knowledge and values that relate to the public values of a diverse and secular society.

Improving the Position of Minorities

Good values, ethical and moral considerations, should interpenetrate each domain in positive terms, so that the division of the private from the public becomes an enhancing distinction. One of its functions should be to improve the position of minorities and subordinated groups. This becomes a problem in those countries where different religious communities have a fundamental right to establish their own schools, but are not necessarily able to promote mutual understanding. Mutual understanding in diverse societies is more likely if there is a common and shared curriculum in a common school. Such a curriculum ought to be based on agreed and rational principles, rather than being imposed on the polity. A differential school system militates against the development of common understandings, and yet may paradoxically be necessary to empower marginalised groups. This is particularly true of remote tribal groups and marginalised indigenous communities, as well as travellers and Roma whose way of life is very different and under threat.

In a secular society one religion cannot dictate to heterogeneity of religions. A distinction needs to be drawn between private morality and law, as well as between sin and crime. It becomes incumbent on schools to nurture and inculcate a secular morality and value-system within public institutions. The ensuing distinction between metaphysical concerns and political ethics must be maintained, to impart an encompassing confidence in the polity as a whole.

The plurality of religious groups means that, since no dominant religion exists, and becomes morally corrupt because of its strength, it becomes incumbent upon the various groups and its members to struggle to maintain their faith. There cannot, however, be a prescriptive way in which schools can impose an across-the-board tenet since, given different features of commonality, and the weakness or strength of secular institutions, different action would have to be taken in different localities. Nevertheless, it is important for teachers to encourage in students the development of notions of a 'common good', or a broader 'public good'. In the final analysis this is a matter of public policy which needs to be considered by educational planners.

In principle the negotiation of values through public education should be limited to the values of the secular state within the public domain. The school in a plural society should by definition not interfere in the private, and the autonomous individual's, domain because the essence of pluralism is the recognition of, and respect for, diverse lifestyles and belief systems in the private domain of groups, families and individuals. However, the school as a social institution does have the right to foster and nurture the common good of all members of the school and the society which it is a part of. But the school may not wish to ignore religious knowledge. As far as values belong to the private domain, teachers should teach about values in such a way that the good values of all children are validated.

Religious instruction belongs to the private domain. But religious, spiritual and philosophical knowledge and values may form part of the public domain, and can be taught so as to achieve the aim of religious tolerance, a prerequisite for the maintenance of democracy. Teachers need to bring understandings of these complex issues to the school. To maintain the autonomy of believers and non-believers alike, the schools' role in religious instruction should be limited to providing facilities for prayers, for those who need them.

This is not, however, an issue for a single curriculum area, nor one that can be taught in isolation. It must be part of the context and content of all the subjects of the curriculum, and not relegated to its personal, social education. To uphold the values and future of a healthy secular state in our society, religious education must be seen as part of the wider values education which informs the planning and implementation of the whole curriculum.

While the religious school or curriculum teaches the Koran, Torah or Bible, the main issue in the secular educational domain is how to teach the 'profane' subjects like literature, history, geography and civic education in an intercultural manner, to broaden the understanding of children from different nationalities and religions. Educationalists working from infant to university levels need to understand how to teach the best religious values interculturally, but not allow secular humanist institutions, ideas and knowledge to be captured for narrowly religious or nationalistic purposes.

A HUMAN RIGHTS APPROACH

Interpreting Human Rights

The fiftieth anniversary of the Universal Declaration of Human Rights was celebrated on 10 December 1998. As Alex De Waal has noted, 'If there is a global religion today, it is human rights' (De Waal 1999). But the universality of Human Rights is still a goal and an ideal. One could argue that the notions of liberty, equality and fraternity, and of the Enlightenment project, faltered with the excesses of the French Revolution and that their universalisation was thwarted. And perhaps another value of importance was lost – that of solidarity which, combined with the other three, might have addressed some of the current crises differently.

The observance of these rights also varies across different cultures and over different time periods. The recent failures of East and Central European socialist/communist regimes, for instance, have their lessons about rights. With the faltering of the Enlightenment project, and the crises of human rights in late modernity, there is a need to reconsider whether there is a corpus of fundamental human rights values implicit in other cultures which need to be considered to make human rights more universal. If, for instance, human rights are perceived and constructed in

purely 'western' terms they are liable to be rejected by 'others' who assert oppositional Sinocentric or Islamocentric or other religious values.

Nevertheless the overwhelming diversities within the states which are members
of the United Nations system present an opportunity – to make use of the constitutional, democratic and modernising principles to which these states are signatory. For the issues raised in these diverse societies are relevant to all, whether
their own form of constitution is secular or theocratic. This involves a complex
sifting and careful examination of the genuine civilisational values with a view
to their more effective implementation. This requires evaluation of the relevant
values from all cultures to strengthen the legitimacy of democratised polities
(however constructed or defined).

One of the major obstacles to engaging with this project is the way in which
Eurocentrism and Orientalism are barriers to clarity about the contribution of
other civilizations. A second barrier is autocratic, reactionary and fundamentalist regimes which hark back to Afrocentric, Islamic and Asian values, which in
no way help in clarifying issues of 'individual' and 'group' rights. Such regimes,
with their articulation of particularistic and narrowly defined civilisational
values, only reinforce notions of East being East and West being West and never
the twain meeting (to use this overworked quotation which in fact contradicts
what Kipling was saying).

The 1993 Vienna World Congress highlighted the conflicts over human rights.
The conservative and reactionary regimes argued for cultural relativism. Hence
the Vienna Declaration and Programme of Action, having asserted that 'the universal nature of these rights and freedoms is beyond question', went on to inject
a note of ambiguity in the statement: 'the significance of national and regional
particularities and various historical, cultural and religious backgrounds must be
borne in mind' (Mayer 1995: 181).

China, and states as different from China as Iraq, Iran, Saudi Arabia and
Sudan, all required the addition of this ambiguity. And when Gasper Biro pre-
pared a report on the Sudan for the UN Human Rights Commission, criticising
it for violations of Human Rights and the Convention of Children's Rights, the
Sudanese Attorney-General Abd Al Aziz Shiddo denounced it as an 'enemy of
Islam' and 'Satanic', and compared Biro to Rushdie.

Moreover, some governments use problems of political stability and economic
development to excuse the denial of 'western-style' human rights. Educators
cannot fudge these issues. There have to be educational strategies which together
enhance democratisation, political stability and economic development. It is the
task of educational strategists to explore how best to enhance universal rights
by drawing from different cultural traditions, and demonstrating that universal
rights are often locally rooted. Such work must also take account of the rights
and needs of the marginalised, oppressed, indigenous and immigrant peoples in
most countries. Islamophobia, for instance, in many parts of the world is marginalising and excluding children of Muslim backgrounds.

We must take the overwhelming diversities within the states which are members of the United Nations system as an opportunity – how to make use of the constitutional, democratic and modernising principles to which these states are signatory. For the issues raised in diverse societies are relevant to all, whether they consider themselves secular or theocratic. And since values and belief systems, theistic and non-theistic, go hand in hand, human rights education can serve as the linchpin.

Human Rights Values in Education

Human rights are a rare and valuable resource in the struggle to correct the balance of power between society, the state and the individual. Unless their distinctive character is preserved and enhanced, including affirming their character as individual rights, their positive role in the struggle for human dignity will be seriously, perhaps even fatally, compromised.

But affirmation is not enough. They need also to be implemented. The rise of strong belief systems in modern secular societies may be partly attributable to strong assertions of human rights which are not accompanied by effective measures to ensure their implementation.

Nor must human rights education be perceived and constructed, as it so often is, in purely 'western' terms and therefore liable to be rejected by 'others' who assert oppositional Asian, Islamic or Afrocentric values. But western or Asian values may themselves be based on falsely constructed notions of an ethnically purer past which their advocates seek to activate in educational contexts. We have in this country the memory of the politically constructed so-called 'Victorian values' trumpeted during the Thatcher era. New Labour's 'family values' too have a backward-looking appeal.

Educational initiatives to teach human rights have to be developed which will take into account religious and cultural diversities within a conceptual framework. In the first instance this is an intellectual and academic matter, but secondarily it has pedagogic implications in translating them into practical school-based curricula, materials and effective teaching methods, including, for instance, whether subject-based or permeative models are most effective in teaching human rights.

Nor should these initiatives be limited to the classroom. It should not be forgotten that sports education can make an important contribution. Sports do encourage discipline, fair play and virtues of cooperation. The role of modern sports in developing solidarities amongst communities or national identities in many African and Asian countries ought to be explored as an avenue of human rights education.

Children and Human Rights

In 1989 the United Nations issued the Convention for the Rights of the Child. As the UNICEF representative in Argentina Emilio Garcia Mendez declared, 'It's a real revolution. It's as if the Declaration of the Rights of Man which gave birth to the French Revolution in 1789 had at last reached children. Two hundred years late' (quoted in *Le Monde Diplomatique* January 1999). But it is a revolution few have noticed.

From a survey conducted in Northern Ireland, India, Botswana and Zimbabwe for the Commonwealth Ministers of Education meeting in Botswana in July 1997, the researchers were able to establish the weak understanding most students have of human rights issues (Bourne and Gundara 1997). If human rights education is treated in a marginalised manner, or is not seen as being genuinely universalistic, then it loses its meaning for young people.

Interestingly this survey revealed that fewer of those surveyed in Northern Ireland are aware of children's rights than in India. The Indian children's better understanding of their rights is explicable because there is a wider understanding of the Indian constitution, and of the rights which accrue to Indian children as future citizens of India. Here, a basic part of human rights education had been made relevant to what they perceived as their own role in society, as it had not in Northern Ireland.

There is a need for more interfaith contacts between young people. Many of them still learn in religious schools while having to live later on as adults in complex, multifaith societies. Similarly, there is often a lack of educational initiatives to promote respect, and accept toleration of different cultures. And children should be made aware not only of their own rights as members of society but of the obligations that these rights confer.

Children's rights cannot, however, be seen merely as abstract concepts which schools teach through didactic instruction. The process of education, teaching and learning as well as the way schools function as institutions carry their own powerful messages in children's eyes and experiences. Democratic, participative and inclusive schools are an important part of children's experiences. They should be a child's right.

For in addition to its pedagogic role, the school has other institutional functions. It should provide a safe place for children where they feel accepted and not threatened, humiliated or exploited. It should be a place where real issues are addressed and made relevant to the children's lives. And it should be, to quote Edward Said again, 'a many windowed house' – a house where people are working according to the ethical principles taught there, and where all the children have equal opportunities to achieve academic success.

FURTHER READING

M. E. and R. S. Appleby (1993) (eds) *Fundamentalism and Society*, Chicago: University of Chicago.

J. Gundara and R. Bourne (1999) *Human Rights Issues for Secondary Teachers: A companion guide for Commonwealth teachers using the curricular framework for learning human rights in secondary schools* and *Human Rights Education: Learning Human Rights in Secondary Schools – Curricular Framework*, Human Rights Unit: Legal and Constitutional Affairs Division, Commonwealth Secretariat.

H. Küng (ed) (1996) *Yes to a Global Ethic*, New York: The Continuum Publishing Co.

G. Robertson (1999) *Crimes against Humanity: The Struggle for Global Justice*, London: Allen Lane, The Penguin Press.

8

Asian and Global Perspectives

MULTICULTURALISM IN ASIA

Issues of multiculturalism in society and the need for intercultural education are not peculiar to European societies but have relevance to most parts of the world. The Asian continent contains a vast proportion of the world's population. However, different parts of Asia represent a very different set of social realities. Most of the east Asian countries are highly developed, industrialised and urbanised. However, large numbers of people in south and south-east Asia are still engaged in the agricultural sector and live in under-developed rural areas.

The need for political understandings to ensure that societal values are not exclusive or excluding of the socially diverse presences are, however, needed right across the continent. All areas of the curriculum, including the history curriculum, need to be examined to ensure that good intercultural education is available to all students in schools. This chapter illustrates the problems confronted in diverse societies by using the example of the rise of a Hindu religious party within the Indian federal government. The necessity of a non-centric curricula require consideration in many of the Asian countries.

This chapter also explores the issues of the relationship between the local and global to ensure that the dark side represented by the economic global does not corrode positive societal values.

The Political Context

In many Asian states during the last few decades previously culturally peaceful polities have been marred by an upsurge of ethnic, religious and regional movements with historical as well as contemporary underpinnings. Throughout the region, the policies of national integration introduced by the centralised elitist governments have failed, to a greater or lesser degree, to integrate their ethnic, religious and cultural minorities.

In India the division of 1947, that 'colossal tragedy, a man-made catastrophe brought about by politicians' (Hassan 1997: 16), the Muslims represent the epitome of a castigated and marginalised community, threatened by the growing ascendancy of Hindu extremists. In Sri Lanka Singhala dominance has led to long standing Tamil resistance and civil war, as in Myanmar (Burma) where an oppressive government wages war on the Karens and other minorities. In

161

Malaysia the privileging of Bhumipatra policies has marginalised Chinese and other minorities. In Indonesia the devaluing of the rupiah led to anti-Chinese riots, an indication of the resilience of Chinese identity and of the failure of the national integration policies of the central Indonesian elite to develop an inclusive national identity for the 180 million people inhabiting the 6,000 Indonesian islands. And in Thailand too the core region tends to dominate the peripheries.

The failure of civil authority to govern minority peoples with policies acceptable to them leads only to government by violence. National authorities violate their own citizens' rights with impunity, and where UN forces have been deployed to stop conflict they have been largely ineffective. Authoritarian values and institutions have been allowed to prevail. Democratic values and institutions are forgotten and human rights questioned. Corruption and authoritarianisation of democratic polities, as has recently happened in Pakistan, divides already diverse Asian societies further. Such negative processes also negate the resolution of divisions, differences and divergencies in complex contexts. In societies where there are minorities the lack of recognition of civil society democratic institutions also leads to the weakening of educational initiatives and to the reduction of minorities' rights.

Add to this the role of structural poverty in Asia, particularly among the subordinated groups, which has a major effect on the life chances of vast numbers of people. Yet, as globalisation takes root economically, there is little guilt, anger or embarrassment about poverty. As Kothari puts it, 'joining the global march towards progress and affluence also involves forgetting the poor, the oppressed, the women and the aged' (1993: 16).

The Need for Political Education

We do not have to accept the rationale regularly offered for not engaging in political education – that ordinary people are not capable of understanding issues and are merely swayed by propaganda. Nor that Karma and heredity should govern Asian norms in public life and that political decisions are therefore unimportant. Political education is necessary for all sections of society, in Asia as elsewhere in the world. Politically uneducated or ill-educated people are dangerous because they can easily misrepresent the complexity of situations and opt for simplistic solutions based on populist politics or fundamentalist religious appeals which only inflame intergroup relations.

In most Asian societies education systems have been mobilised for modernisation and technological change, especially focusing on technology and mathematics. Yet these systems, and the universities they maintain, apart from a few islands of creative imagination, are not forums of originality in the arts, humanities, social science or scientific domains. Hence, they have limited capacities to educate the educators and research scholars needed to deal creatively with elements of social diversity. Rote learning without understanding is too often practised. Moreover, the days of the Confucian sage, the days when the scholar would emerge from seclusion to become a mandarin, have gone. The demise of such scholarly and virtuous public servants has led to a greater acceptance of injustice, diminution of social conscience and higher levels of ethnicised conflict.

Traditional sources of knowledge need to be syncretised with those of modernity to bring greater levels of rootedness, as well as imaginative and creative thinking. This has been attempted in some states where the uncritical adoption of the scientific, technological and vocational aspects of western education has been tempered by the assertion of Asian values as the mainspring of education for their young people. This is most starkly evident in Singapore (Wei-Miy Tu 1996).

In South Korea the legacy of Japanese colonialism has left an imprint on the Korean education system which cannot be described as American or Korean in orientation but is a complex interaction of western, Japanese, Confucian and Korean values and policies, and of reactions to them (Berger and Borrer 1997). Yet it can have its dangers. Prime Minister Mahatair of Malaysia has not only centralised and Islamicised the Malaysian polity but espoused East Asian values from overseas (Look East Policy) and the work ethos – yet at the same time discriminates internally against Malaysian Chinese citizens (Hashim 1996).

In a wider view, only broader based, critically appraised educational values which detract from national fortress mentalities can help to create counterbalances to the excesses of globalisation. As it is, nationalist and modernising pressures have led to education systems which, by stressing national unity, only provoke pressures towards fragmentation. Moreover, they militate against creating the broad prophylactic educational strategies which would introduce democratically derived and inclusive value systems.

The Intercultural Approach

The previous chapters have shown that what makes intercultural education so important in Europe is that the education systems have failed to deal with issues of diversity, in particular by their prevailing use of plural deficit and disadvantage models. As we have seen, those who use such models close their eyes to reality and refuse to admit that people are disadvantaged because of *present* forms of racism, *present* forms of structural inequalities and *present* barriers to choice. Hence, while old forms of inequality may be removed, new forms of inequality are continually being instituted. And until institutional forms of inequality are removed, the education of those considered to be disadvantaged will not improve.

It is, therefore, horrifying to find the old models acquiring a new lease of life in Singapore and China. In Singapore, an urban city state, the population is controlled by classification into purportedly national, but in fact racial, categories (Chinese, Malay, Indian (Tamil) and Eurasian) to provide discipline and uniformity in Singaporean society. False notions of meritocracy which relied on the socio-economic determinants of genetically based intelligence and IQ led to the legalisation of abortion, sterilisation and family planning policies organised through the Social Development Unit which matched couples on the basis of similar educational backgrounds. Poor women were given a financial incentive not to have children. The use of such pseudo-science was compounded by appealing to Asian cultural roots. Yet it used the English language to master superficially what was taken to be western science and technology, but ignored the deep civilisational Asian values which need to be activated (Kohin 1995).

Asian countries may proclaim policies of equality in education but in practice the choice of a good education is limited to the elite and middle class, excluding the children of the poor who are denied the good education all parents want for their children. Countries as different as India, Pakistan, Malaysia and Singapore practise an educational apartheid which condemns generations of young men and women from the poorer and subordinated nationalities and communities to a life as hewers of wood and drawers of water. Even though legally and constitutionally these countries are opposed to such separations the practice is different. Private education based on privilege continues to divide poorer from richer families. Moreover, those who control wealth use their old school ties to obtain the best education in elite universities for their children.

But it is not only children from the subordinated nationalities who suffer. Poor children from the dominant nationalities are similarly disadvantaged. Hence, neo-fascist and fundamentalist young people (Hindu, Muslim, Singhala) join forces not against the privileged of their own nationality or religion but against the 'otherised' subordinated nationalities or groups. In India after fifty years of independence and assertion of equity there is still no equality of opportunity. Egalitarian policies have been sabotaged by politico-economic forces of exclusion and inequality. Corruption within school and education systems further consigns deserving children to the margins of society. Unless serious attempts are made to demonstrate that changes of policy and practice can be introduced, the life chances and outcomes for the disadvantaged will remain unchanged. In Asia, as in Europe, the task is to inaugurate and practise interculturally conceived policies that take the issues of diversity seriously. The prerequisite is a serious political will.

An Indian Case Study

In India, the development of a complex value system incorporating the best of both secular and religious spheres presents a major challenge in political and educational terms. After India's independence from Britain in 1947, the Indian Constitution stressed the secular nature of India. Mahatma Gandhi supported it for philosophical reasons, while Nehru did so to create a liberal, democratic and progressive state. Secularity was seen as the only possible political solution to India's multi-faith society and was agreed on by consensus after discussion with minority groups.

Although notions of religious tolerance are historically not unusual in India, the development of secularism in the country has been by no means easy: extremist Hindu political groups in particular have increased in number and power in recent years. These do not accept such notions as tolerance and pluralism, nor that of a secular polity. However, as Amartya Sen comments:

> Secularism is, in fact, a part of a more comprehensive idea – that of India as an integrally pluralist country, made up of different religious beliefs, distinct language

groups, divergent social practices. Secularism is one aspect – a very important one – of the recognition of that larger idea of heterogeneous identity.

(Sen 1993)

The issue is, in fact, not only of heterogeneous identity but of plural identities. Religious extremists such as the Hindu revivalists tend to ignore the non-religious and complex identities, not just of individuals but of social groups. The other fallacy of this religious sectarianism is the assumption that there is one identity within each faith community. Yet there is an immense diversity amongst the Hindus, as amongst those of other faiths. Gandhi was not only a Hindu and a believer at a personal level, but also a secular Indian in terms of his role as a politician. Here we see the danger represented by the Bhartiya Janata Party (BJP) which is dedicated to the concept of a Hindu Indian nation. Though in its electoral campaigns it has had to modify its extremist views to gain votes, it remains a serious threat to the secular state.

Such narrow constructions by the Hindus not only twist historical and contemporary realities but are partially a result of the failures of the education system to address such questions. Partly because of low-level elementary education, educators, who have access to the long history of Indian tolerance of difference, are not propagating it. Rather, they are using literacy to misinform and to create bias – both of which can be dangerous. For example, in 1992 Vidya Bharati prepared a new set of history textbooks to be used in schools in states controlled by the BJP. In their textbooks:

> The revivalists depict the Mughals as foreigners and oppressors, and interpret Indians' achievement of freedom from English rule as but the latest in a long ongoing struggle to free India from foreign influences. Muslims are, by this interpretation, the contemporary incarnation of the Mughal pattern of dominance.

(Kumar 1993: 555)

The challenge posed to the secular schools and the Indian polity by Hindu revivalism is great, and their hegemonic views require a concerted effort, including educational initiatives, to re-legitimate the broad social diversities in India.

Unfortunately the educational and political elite are profoundly out of touch with the concerns of the masses. Any educational project enabling minorities in India to belong has to re-evaluate the role of religion in contemporary society. A re-examination of the public space in light of the re-emergence of the sacred can only take place if the educational and political concerns of the masses are met. Also, since in India secular and religious ideologies compete for the public space, a new balance of freedom and rights cannot be imposed from the top but needs to be made more locally relevant.

The failure of secularism in India is seen by Verma as emanating from a failure to implement 'positive secularism' which ensures that religion, as an institution, does not adversely affect the survival of the polity. 'In India the State should take over the total education system, along with training and other schemes of orientation, from secondary to university levels' (Verma 1986).

It is, however, doubtful if this is a feasible option under Articles 29 and 30 of

the Indian Constitution which allow linguistic and religious minorities to establish their own educational institutions. Also, even apart from the constitutional
problems, their abolition and replacement would create counterproductive reactive situations. Nevertheless the state ought to regulate the curricula and functioning of such institutions. A constructive way of resolving the issue could be
to rationalize and regulate those vocational and social aspects of education which
lead to greater equalities of outcome between majority and minority groups. This
could be done by the national curriculum planning agencies ensuring that the
social sciences, humanities, literary and arts curricula are not used to negate
notions of secularism or to foster caste-based identity or religious revivalism.

It is also important to ensure that neither dominant nor subordinate groups
use partisan and party political influences in education. State-funded schools not
following these guidelines should have their funds withdrawn. One of the dangers
to the secular polity is the presence of minimally regulated communal educational
institutions which foster narrowly based schooling and prevent critical thinking.

The educational process should enable the majorities and the minorities to
trust each other. This is particularly important if the rights of disadvantaged
minorities are to be protected. Hence, minorities as well as majorities should be
able to develop their mother tongues. Neither the minority groups nor their languages should be isolated, as Urdu, the language of the Muslim community in
India, certainly has been. The use of Sanskritised Hindi by Hindu revivalists
further alienates vast numbers of minority language speakers.

There is no doubt that the English-speaking Indian elite, which has capitu-
lated to Hindu revivalists in allowing media and educational institutions to give
a privileged position to Hindu discourses, has helped undermine the secular
polity in the last decade.

AN ASIAN CURRICULUM

Avoiding Centrism

Issues of knowledge and curriculum are critical to the way in which a state
constructs itself. Inclusions and exclusions of knowledge have grave implications
for ethnic peace or conflict. The challenges of societal diversity in the Asian
societies cannot be dealt with by imposing a 'centric' curriculum on the educational systems. To maintain safety and security within their diverse polities the
Asian states need to develop curricula which avoid centrisms. Devising the
necessary basis of knowledge, retextualised in the Asian context, presents curriculum planners with a difficult but unavoidable challenge.

A non-centric curriculum would enable teachers, students and other learners
to develop the inclusive and shared value systems which are so important for
democratic Asian societies. Particular attention needs to be given to the teaching of history from a non-triumphalist perspective. Nor need such curricular
developments be only part of mainstream education. They should also build on
basic education and acquisition of languages and literacies. Such an integrated
system would enhance the intercultural competencies of active Asian citizens

living in multicultural democracies. Subjects like history and social sciences, particularly, need to be appraised for their relevance to the contemporary needs of Asian societies.

There has to be a constant and fundamental reappraisal of the histories and national identities into which we have all been inducted with such care. The answer does not, however, lie in trying to establish either a liberal or a back-to-basics curriculum which remains founded in the centric, narrowly nationalist and empire-based intellectual milieu which has done so much to contribute to our present predicament.

Curriculum development should be engaging in democratic and inclusive processes of national integration, modernisation and development. Such issues ought therefore to include relevant consideration of participatory pedagogies. In marginalised communities learning and teaching ought to be seen as flexible processes which involve young and old in lifelong learning. Such participatory pedagogic situations would enliven the curriculum rather than deaden it. Hence, both formal and informal learning strategies are needed. Both should have the potential for lifelong learning.

Eurocentrism, as has already been shown in Chapter 5, is of particular significance in relation to knowledge, since it has an implicit theory of world history. It is also a global political project with universal ramifications. The curricular question is – how can the Asian education systems help to liberate universalism from the limits of Eurocentrism?

Current habits of thought within the educational systems tend to inhibit such questioning and reinforce notions of a fortress mentality – in relation not only to Eurocentrism, but to its equivalents in Sino-centrism and Indo-centrism. Similarly, despite its broad Asian context, Islam has come to be increasingly constructed as Arabo-centric, leading to violence in some states and the replacement of western corruption with clerical corruption. These substitutions of particularistic curricula only worsen ethnic tensions and activate siege mentalities. Moreover by continuing to perpetuate knowledge exclusion and dominance they allow Eurocentrism to dominate at the global and universal levels.

To install the 'voice' of the disenfranchised in the curriculum will require a great deal of delicacy, diplomacy, persistence and sophistication, particularly if the desired changes are not to be relegated to the margins of academic life. Reactive, rhetorical and rebellious responses in curricular terms are not only inadequate but also counter-productive. While action is needed across all Asian societies, those in the poorer parts of south-east Asia have greater levels of difficulties, and may require support from international agencies. Here, the more affluent and experienced educational agencies in north-east Asia can also be helpful and lend them support for educational developments.

The Role of Religion

A non-centric Asian curriculum cannot be created without understanding the role of religion within the Asian education systems. The Chicago Fundamentalist Project coordinated by M. Marty and R. Appleby has documented the role of religion on a range of issues, including education (Marty and Appleby 1993). Discussions have also been undertaken by UNRISID on issues arising from different types of religious groups (culturalist, syncretist, fundamentalist and community oriented) (Haynes 1995: 7). However, the impact of religion on education, and its educational policy implications, require a more detailed study to enable the development of inclusive policies and strategies.

The Islamic Umma has now emerged at a transnational level. So have the American Pentecostal churches which have followed the Roman Catholic Church into a global mission field. Hindu cultural chauvinism and the shift towards a purer Buddhist Sangha raise problems for the Indian, Thai and Sri Lankan states. The corruption of the secular state apparatus, notably in India, Indonesia, Malaysia, the Philippines and Pakistan, presents demands for 'pure', 'just' and 'xenophobic' states. Meanwhile, Christian and Islamic fundamentalism has permeated many Asian societies. The current backlash against Christians by Hindu fundamentalists in Gujerat has dangerous consequences for other religious communities and their schools – the more so when one recalls that Christianity and Judaism have been present in India for longer than they have in many so-called Christian countries, and are therefore part and parcel of Indian society. And now the impact of new aggressive missionaries of the Christian fundamentalist denominations attempting speedy mass conversions in Asia will only heighten the rise of reactions from Hinduism and Islam.

What is the role of religious educational institutions and curricula in the public domain, especially when they demand uncritical adherence to texts or to issues of religious justice? The issue is raised in acute form by an ex-philosophy lecturer at The International Islamic University in Kuala Lumpur (Akhtar 1997, 1998; for Christian views of contemporary Islam see Khuri 1998, and Hefner and Horvatich 1997). He suggests that the emphasis on rote learning, the reiteration of the revealed truth and message, and the curtailment of academic freedom are no way to resolve the problems of religion, education and state governance in diverse polities.

Akhtar's Malaysian critique applies as well to other faiths in other Asian schools and higher education institutions operating in the public domain. Nor are these issues only of import to the maintenance of critical inquiry and scepticism in educational institutions. They also raise the question of academic freedom – not a phenomenon to be considered peculiar to the western education system and university. Moreover they also have a bearing on inter-group and inter-ethnic relations inside educational systems and in the wider social fabric of societies.

The increased power of organised religions questions ideas of a non-centric curriculum. How then, in multicultural Asian institutions, can believers of one faith learn about other faiths, or non-believers learn about believers and vice versa? What is required is not merely religious instruction but a complex Kuhnian understanding of teaching about faiths and the knowledge derived from them. This can provide a way forward, out of the notion of a sterile, formal and strict division between secular and religious (western and Asian) intellectual discourse (Taylor 1991: 129–139). Inevitably it poses complex issues not just for educational policy but for curricular reform and teacher education. To replace obscurantism with rationality is not a simple or a linear path but a more complex strategy and journey. Others, like Inayatullah, argue for an alternative social science which is not based on the nation-state as a model of analysis but on new knowledge by 'creating layered sovereignty' (Inayatullah 1998: 27–43).

Tagore's Visva Bharati University near Calcutta, where a comprehensive vision of knowledge and understanding continues to exist since its founding in 1921, is perhaps a model worth exploring. Its connections with rural India also have implications for other Asian societies which need to educate a local peasantry – not only in literacy and basic education but against bigotry. As Brenda Gourley writes:

> Universities indeed had their conceptual origins in such fabled places as Alexandria, with its great library, the Greece of the academy and the lyceum, in the Persia of the Sassanids, and the Gondishapur, in India, of Das Guptas and the Nalanda, in the golden ages of Confucian China, in the Muslim worlds of Harun-al-Rashid and the House of Wisdom, in the late mediaeval Europe of Bologna, and many more.
>
> (Gourley 1998)

Education and university systems provide in Asia the potential to be intellectually open institutions which transcend narrow ethnic and nationalistic barriers. Many of them are already institutions which are not bigoted in narrow religious terms, which exist in a sea of corrupt materialism but are rich intellectually and spiritually. Such a shift may provide more grounds for integrated knowledge systems. It also bodes well for good inter-group and inter-ethnic relations.

Developing an Inclusive Asian Curriculum

Most post-colonial Asian states have not yet developed an optimum understanding of integrating the nation on an ethos based on including their various differing cultures. Many hark back to anti-colonial, dominant and majoritarian knowledge as legitimation of their polities. Knowledge systems and curricula for both formal and non-formal education are therefore excluding and ignoring the complex basis of knowledge and history that makes up their societies. For instance, the recounting of anti-colonial struggles, which exclude the contributions of minorities, cannot be equated with broadly based and inclusive national struggles.

The need to develop genuinely intercultural and inclusive curricula is urgent because of the spread of culturalist developments spearheaded by groups demanding a curriculum of recognition based on 'politics of recognition'. Marginalised groups, minorities and others who feel excluded by the twin processes of national exclusion and economic globalisation raise the stakes of exacerbating inter-group and ethnic conflict in a number of south and south-east Asian countries.

Representation of the national culture based merely on anti-colonial, economic development and class politics is not a sufficient basis to constitute a national culture in a city state like Singapore. The superficialities of multiracialism or 'Asian values' is no substitute for a serious consideration of the complex values and histories of its peoples. Arbitrary notions of colonially derived categories of racial identities are not enough basis for developing the curriculum.

In Malaysia and Indonesia the construction of the 'overseas Chinese' as 'othered' groups, even though they have historically been part of both the Malaysian and Indonesian societies and nations, raises important issues. The Bhumipatra Malays, whose aristocracy supported British colonialism, ignore the role of the Chinese as radical nationalists. The Suharto regime's casting the Chinese as communists has allowed them to be seen as non-belongers. Curriculum planners have the complex task of deconstructing the notion of 'the other', applied to those who are disenfranchised despite their having contributed extensively to the economic, social and cultural life of both countries. The demonisation of the Chinese in Indonesia and the destabilisation of the regime may then lead to its being subjected to a reactive and fundamentalist Islam wholly intolerant of diversities within society. Hence, the essentialisation of the Chinese minority would lead to the essentialisation of the complex Indonesian identity as patriarchal and Islamic.

Yet substantively, in knowledge terms, the issues of identities, whether those of the ethnic groups or others at local or national levels, are more diverse, layered, textured and complex. They are in other words not essentialist in nature and do not have the inevitability of being ethnic in the modern nation (Smith 1990), because they may have multiple identities within the imagined nation (Anderson 1983). In fact, both the cultural communities and the nations may be constructions of imagination, which result from the complex processes of political, economic, social, cultural and historical accidents and processes. The important issue on which Asian nations have to embark is how to construct and represent these complex features of their societies within the inclusive mainstream curriculum.

An inclusive curriculum by definition has to avoid demonisation of 'the other', whether it is 'the west', a caste group, or 'the Chinese', and reinstate certain archaic versions of the Islamic, Confucian or Asian particularisms.

This constitutes a major challenge in nation building, especially in the postcolonial states of south and south-east Asia where, for instance, there are complex and different issues pertaining to values like freedom. In terms of discussions about freedoms, rather than examine these in Orientalist or essentialist modes, is there not value in developing non-pejorative frameworks like 'Eurasian' which have specificities as well as cross-cutting of relationships (Kelly and Reid 1998)? On the issue of ethnicity, as Benedict Anderson states,

> the politics of ethnicity have their roots in modern times, not ancient history, and their shape has been largely determined by colonial policy. (It is no accident that uncolonised Siam has the least violently ethnicised politics in the region.)
>
> (Anderson 1998: 328)

The entwining of ethnicity with class and religion, as well as the differences between the 'alien' and the 'indigenous', make for complex curricular implications within the south and south-east Asian education systems.

In Malaysia and in Indonesia the 'alien' Chinese minorities are essential to the political and economic order. In both contexts, however, they face different futures. As for the 'indigenous', the demographically larger groups like Kachins or Ilocanos may have greater potential for being part of modern bilingual polities and being able to participate in the educational system. But the much smaller and geographically remote groups are more vulnerable not only to the nation state, but also to global exploitation because of mineral and forest resources coveted by the outside.

> The irony is that typically they are not ethnic groups; . . . often it means becoming Christian (in Siam or Indonesia) or Muslim (in Malaysia). Almost always it means the end of the kind of cultural autonomy and self-contained integrity they once enjoyed.
> (Anderson 1998: 330)

The state cannot ignore the complexities they present. Their equitable representation in the educational context could obviate the pessimistic scenario outlined above by Benedict Anderson.

Disarming Asian History

Those who plan history curricula face a very complicated task. On the one hand they need to engage with the identity of groups like the Burmans, the Hindus or the Bengalis. On the other hand, within the state educational systems, they need to develop a coherent and inclusive story of and for the whole nation. The question, therefore, for curriculum designers is (as indicated already in Chapter 6), what aspect of histories to select and on what principles to make that selection?

Here are two south-east Asian instances to exemplify the complex difficulties of selection. Hong Kong's history illustrates the problems of its historiography. Colonial powers normally granted a colony independence. In the case of Hong Kong it was handed back to China, control being assumed by one state from another. So neither in 1841, when Britain assumed control over Hong Kong, nor in 1997, were the residents of Hong Kong consulted about their wishes (Lowe 1991). Both Britain and China colluded in denying a voice to the people of Hong Kong, including those who fled from China as political refugees. Whose history of Hong Kong will represent its controversial pasts? Will it be a history of its land, its rulers, its institutions, or its peoples? How will its colonial past or its capitalist present be seen by Marxist historians? Moreover, from the point of view of intercultural and ethnic relations, there have been immense contributions by Indian Bohras, Parsees, Sikhs and Jews. But their histories have already been implicitly ignored and their citizenship rights undermined because only the Chinese can acquire rights as Chinese nationals (Bard 1993). Can a China-centred government ignore the history of a dynamic city-state?

Twenty years after genocide devastated Cambodian society there is still no agreement about how to structure the new history curriculum (*Times Educational*

Supplement 2 July 1999). How can the deaths of 1.7 million people between 1975 and 1979 be presented to children – how are they to react to this history, and what lessons are they to learn from it? These questions exemplify in an extreme way the dilemmas involved in terms of curriculum development, of choosing appropriate teaching materials and skilling teachers to teach the subject.

Disarming history therefore requires complicated measures, but they must be undertaken if the present is to be disarmed. Ehrenreich reminds us that the advance of the war-related enterprises of the twentieth century has also brought about resistance to war:

> The passions we bring to war can be brought just as well to struggle against war. There is a place for courage and solidarity and self-sacrifice other than in the service of this peculiarly bloody institution, this inhuman 'meme', a place for them in the struggle to shake our links free of it.
>
> (Ehrenreich 1997: 204–24)

Already a start is being made. In Taiwan an important development is the introduction of a democratically derived curriculum and the use of enquiry based learning. These initiatives take into account the students' different learning styles, an issue which is especially relevant to the children of the indigenous minority communities in Taiwan (Tsai and Bridges 1997: 36–47). And in Sri Lanka a UNICEF funded project on Education for Conflict Resolution (ECR) has developed an interactive and hands-on curriculum woven into the regular course of studies. Since 1993 it has been used in primary schools and in a few years will be taught in secondary schools and for teacher training. It is only unfortunate that such educational initiatives are not prophylactic and were put in place too long after conflict had been set in motion.

In New Delhi the National Institute of Educational Research and Training has an established record on teacher education, educational research and curriculum development. Its work in the Indian multicultural context is extremely impressive and could perhaps be replicated elsewhere in Asia.

The Japanese Ministry of Education, a centralised infrastructure with enormous potential for enabling curriculum development in the field of intercultural education, has seconded officers to London to the ICIS to learn about it. There are also Japanese civil society bodies like the Asia/Pacific Cultural Centre in Tokyo with resources to back up new educational policies.

In South Korea, the Korean Education Development Institute has already undertaken work on developing the Korean curriculum, as well as eliminating stereotypes in textbooks in other Asian countries. The Korean Broadcasting Service has also produced educational programmes for peak-time viewing which have positive intercultural and knowledge potential. And in China, as well as Japan, an enormous amount of cultural activity is done at a supplementary level. Such extracurricular work can be important in developing informal curricula to improve inter-group relations in countries where the formal curriculum is too rigid to be easily amenable to change.

EXTRA-CURRICULAR EDUCATION
An Islamic Model

In many countries an enormous amount of cultural activity is undertaken at a supplementary level. Extra-curricular work can be important in developing an informal curriculum to improve inter-group relations in countries where the formal curriculum is too rigid and not amenable to change. Hence, the role of non-formal and lifelong intercultural learning is important.

Asian societies are in general more positively inclined to improvement through education than some other contemporary societies. Consider the attitudes to knowledge in the Islamic civilisational system. The Muslim philosophy of education is a philosophy of lifetime learning based on literacy. All Muslims are required to study the scriptures and should go on studying them throughout their lives. Education is not only a requirement but a priority, so highly valued that 'an hour of learning is worth more than a year of prayer'.

Islamic knowledge draws on a wealth of cultures including Semitic, Hellenistic, Iranian and Indian. The *Ulema* (scholars) who have *ilm* (knowledge) have helped to clarify complex issues from the Koran in the Hadiths. In drawing from Hellenistic tradition, the role of Aristotelian philosophy, especially in the areas of reason, logic and the laws of nature, has been profound. The potential therefore of syncretic Islamic knowledge in progressively informing the curriculum is extensive. In many *madrasas* (schools) Aristotle was considered to be the first teacher, but the notion of reason was subsequently undermined by the faithful. To restore these very important aspects of Islamic knowledge and its earlier syncretism a constructive dialogue with the faithful is necessitated. The very powerful concept of knowledge is recognised by the notion that 'kings are rulers of peoples but scholars are rulers of kings' (Robinson 1996: 222).

The issue of negotiating with the faithful also applies to other Asian religious communities. However, some of the traditional systems which have not democratised elitist notions present problems for transforming education. The other aspect which requires consideration is the oral tradition. If knowledge survives through reiteration, as, for instance, transmitted by *Ulema*, then the developmental aspects of knowledge may be arrested.

The particular problem of why the sciences did not advance in many contexts is worth considering. However, even in Islam and across Asia there is no consistent support for rote learning. The Mahal family in Lucknow was involved in scientific learning, and one of their number, Mulla Nizam al Din, in the early eighteenth century stressed the need for comprehension of the rational sciences. More importantly, Asian civilisation has made very important contributions to mathematics, printing, gunpowder, medicine and sciences in general. These contributions need to be used in education systems to contextualise the important role of the sciences in Asian societies (Goontilake 1999). They have diverse origins and have potential for enhancing integrative learning of the sciences and encouraging original and fundamental research across cultural and national groups in Asia.

Active Citizenship

Ordinary Asian citizens who are either excluded or marginalised are not to be seen only as victims. Many groups have organised themselves and become active citizens.

Many women's groups and other mutual aid systems actively help communities to survive in inner cities or overstressed farmlands, and are playing an important role in nurturing groups at risk in diverse communities and building intergroup alliances. In India the Self-Employed Women's Association (SEWA) provides services needed by local communities, especially as a trade union of poor women which operates in Ahmedabad. Women's role is especially important in conflict resolution, and in Buddhist communities the use of the concepts of *Panch Shila* and *Panch Dharma* has an important role in educating the Asian inner spirit. This 'bending of the mind' in Buddhist and Hindu cultures has important educational implications. Asian educational systems can use these systems, non-patriarchal and non-violent strategies, as developed by Gandhi, to organise mass movements for social and political change.

The high-tech age is creating high levels of unemployment. In Japan, the charitable sector called *Koeki hojin* has developed enormously and provides essential services needed by communities, including private education and social welfare. This voluntary sector, much of it publicly funded, is becoming a powerful third sector in the economy in Japan. It uses notions of cooperation and harmonious relations derived from Confucian tradition.

In rural parts of Asia there is also an increase of this new third sector of the economy which helps the developmental process and helps resolve conflicts. In educational terms, the literacy programmes and early childhood education are particularly important, and many local needs are met by the voluntary sector. Asia boasts nearly 20,000 volunteer associations (see Fisher 1993). In Sri Lanka, the Sarvodaya Sharanadana Movement (SSM) claims to have 7,700 staff, and helps the local population in 8,000 villages. Likewise the Consumer Association of Penang (CAP) helps and protects vulnerable rural communities. In the Philippines, Pamalkaya as an NGO helps 50,000 fishermen and provides ongoing training and education for its members (Rifkind 1996: 281).

Many of these ventures turn into micro-enterprises and cooperatives and inter-village trading networks. In purely educational terms foundations like Nomura in Japan are involved in projects of lifelong learning and peace and conflict resolution which resonate with the interests of many education systems in Asia and with international organisations like UNESCO. These are examples, and small beginnings of engagement, as the global, millennial Third Industrial Revolution of the workerless world is on the doorstep of Asian polities.

Numerous other examples of active citizenship provide a powerful basis of people playing a democratic role in developing communities of hope.

A GLOBAL PERSPECTIVE

The Global and the Local

While the term 'global' is four hundred years old, 'globalisation' began to be used about 1960, and has been extensively used since the 1980s in academic discussions (Robertson 1992). Certain circles view it as a concept no less controversial than post-modernism (Waters 1995: 1). Here, it will only be used to give what is no more than a partial view of the issues it raises from an intercultural perspective. The aim is not to represent the details of multiple communication, informational and institutional manifestations, but to give a brief overview of the non-virtual global.

Part of the problem lies in the way in which the articulation of global visions is not democratic. Certain societal features are excluded by the way in which it is currently constituted. Just to give one example, in economic terms, because the transnationals and the World Trade Organisation determine capital flows and devise structural adjustment programmes, they do not necessarily take cognisance of local sovereignties. So rather than charting the glittering side of the global information and consumption patterns the attempt here shall be to describe its darker underbelly.

As in the case of the above example, the global macro economies do not necessarily work hand in hand with local micro economies, nor do the power structures largely located in the north deal equitably with the poorer south. The discussions at the 1998 G8 Birmingham Conference did not do much to alleviate the debt burdens of the poor states. A more democratic governance at organisational levels from local to global may be one way of legitimating global governance. However, the political economy of the global corporate order is based on integrating production/consumption patterns on a monocultural basis. In this process, relations and services between finance, as well as labour standards, are levelled out through centralised control and concentration of power.

These processes do not only have an economic impact on the local. Giddens refers to the global impact on the local as follows:

> Globalisation can thus be defined as the intensification of worldwide social relations which link localities in such a way that local happenings are shaped by events occurring many miles away and vice versa. This is a dialectical process because such local happenings may move in an obverse direction from the very distanciated relations that form them. Local transformation is as much part of globalisation as the lateral extension of social connections across time and space.

> (Giddens 1990: 64)

'Local transformations' include the rise of local nationalisms. Where these are conflictual in nature they can destabilise a locality, nation or region. They may even have wider reverberations. Globalisation therefore has many strands and does not have a single trajectory.

There is, as such, little international democratic accountability or any genuine international governance. Action by global financial institutions in the United

States can undermine the financial markets of certain nations or regions (e.g. Mexico and south-east Asia) as well as undermine the power of labour by employing cheap child and women labour. The liberalisation of economies underlying this has led to a lowering of terms and conditions of employment as well as creating insecurity at societal level. Local environments and local communities who have till recently lived in sustainable and stable conditions are being destroyed by conglomerate mining companies. National governments in many parts of the world have failed to protect national spaces, and the long-term livelihoods of many local communities have been eroded.

Many national governments are powerless in trying to reform the corporate powers – in fact, in many cases, past (Thatcher, Reagan, Bush) and present, leaders have played duplicitous roles with corporate structures in strengthening the undemocratic features of global control. One of the key elements in reforming this process is the democratisation of agencies like the World Trade Organisation, International Monetary Fund and OECD which manage global economies. This is of paramount importance because ordinary people, local ad hoc groups and civic groups are too weak to campaign effectively against globalised inequities.

Such global control affects intercultural relations negatively – and not just the fourth world peoples, the tribal and indigenous peoples in the southern hemisphere, but also those in the first world. The Samish peoples in Scandinavia, Aborigines in Australia, Roma and Travellers in Europe, the Inuits and Native American peoples of North America, are examples of marginalised groups in so-called developed polities. Increasingly, as Chomsky argues, the Galbraithian notion of private wealth and public squalor is also reflected in the third-worldisation of first world cities.

This enforced globalisation which respects no frontiers, and is allowed to function by national elites, wipes out differences and diversities within a society and can have serious consequences for social peace in a polity (Gray 1998; Hurst and Thompson 1996). Features of globalisation which are imposed on local communities without their consent lead to the wiping out of the skills and trades which maintain them, with consequent loss of security and certainties. The fragmenting of families and communities during the Conservative government in Britain took place while family values were being asserted, and ironically were presented by Norman Tebbit asking people to 'get on your bike'. Movement by workers to find jobs has eroded family unities and structures of local communities in many parts of the world, including Britain.

The Dark Side of Globalisation

There are obvious ways in which economic and social processes are subject to fewer geographical constraints than in the past, largely through capitalist developments emanating from the United States, the European Union and Japan. As a result of these developments, nation-state structures governing diverse societies are increasingly under stress, and at times have a limited role in controlling the impact of globalisation. The neo-liberalisation of economies has meant that many state systems have little control on the flows of capital, and most of their efforts to control their societies are accomplished through coercion and violence on their populations.

Most of the state systems in the southern hemisphere and east of the Elbe are peripheral or semi-peripheral to the dominant players. Their political, economic and cultural 'integration and development' does not result from a democratic process of consultation and engagement but is largely a result of dominant aggressive capitalist expansion. Corrupt and autocratic national regimes exacerbate the situation in which the poorer peoples find themselves.

Increasingly marginalised societies are also more vulnerable to global forces of terrorism, lawlessness and crime. The more authoritarian the societies, the greater the likelihood that forces of democratisation are curbed, as are those of legitimate and diverse market forces. The Asian economic crisis does not only represent a crisis of so-called 'Asian values'. It also represents aspects of the 'crony capitalism' of the Asian tiger economies which are autocratic, not democratic, conspiratorial not transparent, as well as embodying low levels of accountability and therefore reflective of bad governance. The darker side of undemocratic economic globalisation also entails a great deal of criminal activity which nets $750 billion to $1 trillion a year. (*The Independent* (London) 14–15 December 1998). In technological terms, the technocratic global cannot be equated with the democratic global.

Globalisation has currently taken shape in these worrying ways largely through the massive control of technological, financial and natural resources, media and communications, by transnationals. This massive harnessing of resources without any democratic constraints, and largely relying on market forces, is inimical to universal human needs. The negative features of globalisation do not liberate humanity from the menace of war, nor do they provide access to global resources for equitable sharing and distribution. The monopolies of financial and technological resources remain intact and there are no political institutions at a world level which would provide 'social interests on a global scale' (Amin 1997: 6). They, therefore, give rise to the negative features of xenophobia, chauvinism and fundamentalism. The assumption being made here is that unless globalisation processes are undertaken within the political realm, the alienations, inequalities and disadvantages felt by various groups, communities and nationalities will inevitably have negative consequences.

Achieving Resolution of Conflicts

Only in the context of a progressive political milieu can there be a resolution of conflicts between the universal and the local, or the particular and the general, and a possibility of bringing about social progress through democratic forces. In the absence of egalitarian goals to bring about equality and fraternity there can be no stability. Current economic forces have led to twenty per cent of the world's peoples controlling eighty per cent of its resources, so that tensions at local events in many parts of the world have been heightened. The problems in the Asian economies are just the beginning of a crisis which will affect ordinary people and

contain seeds of even graver consequences for inter-group and communal re
lations. The expansion of capitalism in global terms cannot be seen as being con-
ducive to development because it does not necessarily lead to full employment
or greater levels of equality in the distribution of income. Instead expansion is
guided by the search for profit by corporations. The consequences of their activities to local communities are seldom an important consideration, however much
transnationals may pay lip service to issues of equity, environment and ethics.

The post-World War II and post-independent movement of non-aligned
peoples set up in Bandung (1955) has received setbacks. The modernisation and
development which would have assisted the masses of peoples in non-aligned
countries has faltered because of the way in which the national states have been
undermined by current patterns of globalisation and their economies made stagnant. As Amin writes, 'For countries at the periphery, this stagnation leads to a
grave involution of which fourth worldisation of Africa is the most extreme
example' (1997: 38).

As a response to this phenomenon Amin suggests that national governments

> 'de-link' from globalisation processes in favour of internal national development.
> Countries which are peripheralised as a result of this de-linking may need to establish
> structures of solidarity to provide mutual support and create mechanisms of mutual
> adjustment, to replace the current unilateral adjustment of the weakest to the
> strongest. De-linking as such is a difficult process because corrupt national elites are
> the beneficiaries of the current 'links' and may not want to have to pay the personal
> and political price of reversing the situation. However solidarity is necessary for poorer
> nations, and also between groups at local levels to provide mutual support with others
> in similar situations. Such mechanisms of mutual adjustment necessitate deep political,
> institutional and democratic changes in every part of the world, so that the majority
> of people can benefit from 'interdependence with mutual respect for diversity'.
>
> (Amin 1997: 42; see also Mander and Goldsmith 1996)

Instead of the current globalisation imposed by capital, there is a need for
processes which take the social, economic, cultural and political needs of peoples
as their central focus. In the absence of such a complex process a disjuncture
between globalisation based on capital, and localisation based on xenophobia,
communalism, chauvinism, fundamentalism and racism is bound to increase.
This can be seen in parts of Africa and Asia which have become peripheralised
because of the differentiation between the semi-industrialised third world and
the unindustrialised fourth world. As segments of national production systems
have become part of the globalised productive system, the rest have not seen any
positive changes. In the African context this has led to 'Afro-pessimism' among
some sections of the population.

Halting the Trend Towards Disintegration

In those areas of Africa, Arabia and Asia which have become peripheralised, and
not become industrialised, there are vast reserve armies of labour with no
prospect of productive capacity or of migration (see *African Development
Review: Special Issue on Africa and the Future*, vol. 7, no. 2, African

Development Bank, December 1995). As the project of nation building and integration become remote for these socially diverse polities, the previous unifying tendencies turn sour. Forces become centrifugal and the state begins to disintegrate. 'The political crises are founded on this breakdown, on this disintegration of the state and the accompanying rise of ethnic movements and religious fundamentalism' (Amin 1997: 60).

Globalisation processes which are imposed on local communities result in resentment against 'the other', an issue which requires some analysis. The disintegration of many countries is a living example of the process whereby ethnic renewals take the place of the previous forces of modernisation and integrative nation building. The unification of nations as diverse as India and Mexico has been reversed, and there is rising religious fervour in the Arab and Islamic world (Naipaul 1998). In general, the weaker and more peripheral the state, the more vulnerable it is to global crises and especially to the negative aspects of market forces. Because economic globalisation is not as such based on equity and equitable principles, but on exploitation, it has led to greater levels of global polarisation. Globalisation as currently organised is not therefore based on rational principles, nor does it have a universalist character. Therein lies the real challenge of how to bring about inclusive global forces leading to the universalisation of equitable relations at an international level.

For while there are no frontiers for the transfer of capital, there is obviously no provision for the migration of labour so that labour can follow the flows of capital. The exacerbation of ethnic tensions within or across state boundaries is one result of the current economic crisis in Asia. The vulnerability of the three million or so South Asian migrant workers in the East Asian so-called 'tiger' economies, and the rough treatment meted out to Indonesian refugees in Malaysia by the Malaysian government, are a case in point. The fall of the Suharto regime in Indonesia results from the combination of the IMF's enforced economic medicine and the garnering of vast national resources by one corrupt and autocratic family. What is missing in current regional relations are ways in which collective regional bodies in Africa, the Arab world, Latin America or South Asia could consolidate the needs of diverse groups in the region. These needs are not just economic but are also for greater democratisation and the meeting of social policy needs. The trampling of the democratic voices in East Timor represents the tip of the iceberg of the need for regional security forces to preserve peace and stability, if states become destabilised.

One important issue is how to re-configure international relations to ensure that disaggregative tendencies of religious, linguistic, territorial and other diversities do not pull apart societies which have previously held together. At one level this poses a political and ideological issue, and at another calls for the implementation of social policies issues, including education, which can assist in reshaping diversity into unity. To turn diversity into unity can only work if democratic forces can plan towards unity. As Amin states, 'bourgeois revolution is not a viable solution, because it does not permit these societies to go beyond the boundaries of peripheral capitalism, while socialist revolution is not the order of the day, because the local social forces do not have sufficient maturity' (Amin 1997: 78).

Given this complexity, the solution does not lie solely within currently dominant financial globalising forces or with the local communities on their own. Given the Janus-headed notion of the nation, ties of blood and soil are likely to be reactivated. To reverse this process demands the political wisdom to strengthen and develop the other face of the monster, i.e. the notions of modern constitutional nations based on equality, fraternity and liberty. This presents a major challenge to educators and schools. For educators it poses a major problem. (Various aspects of these issues are analysed in King 1998; Axtman 1998.)

Developing Inclusive Globalism

Many national communities embody notions of particularism as well as those of universalism. There is an important function for academics, educators and other policy-makers to examine these complex notions and to analyse the myths, feelings, understandings and concepts surrounding them in order to develop rational ways of dealing with the resultant dilemmas. Education has normally been seen as secular or religious and the division caused by this separation has been very damaging. However, if civilisational knowledge can be pooled differently, to draw the best from each phase of human history, then a more syncretic understanding from across civilisations and periods of time could inform the educational process differently.

In the first phase, between the fifth century BC and the seventh century AD, universalist concepts of humanity were established by the great religions like Zoroastrianism, Buddhism, Christianity and Islam, and the Confucian and Hellenistic philosophies. However, as Amin states:

> This declaration of a universalistic vocation did not establish a real unification of humanity. The conditions of tributary society did not permit it, and humanity reformed itself into major tributary areas held together by their own particular universalist religion-philosophy (Christendom, Dar-es-Islam, the Hindu world and the Confucian world). It is still the case, however, that tributary revolution, like all great revolutionary movements in history, projected itself forwards and produced concepts ahead of its time.
>
> (Amin 1997: 80)

Although these earlier movements form an important part of the emergence of universalistic norms and values, they also continue to present unresolved dilemmas at a global level. Hans Küng, for one, outlines his major project for encouraging an ethical quest:

> No survival without a world ethic. No world peace without peace between the religions. No peace between the religions without dialogue between the religions.
>
> There can be no peace among nations without peace among the religions. There can be no peace among the religions without dialogue between the religions. There can be no dialogue between the religions without research into theological foundations.

His conclusion is:

> Therefore, the programme which guides us and which comes together as one may be summed up once again in three basic statements: no human life together without a world ethic for the nations; no peace among the nations without peace among the religions; no peace among the religions without dialogue among the religions.
>
> (Küng 1991: xv, 105)

The second phase, during the modern period, likewise has made a contribution to universalism through the philosophy of the Enlightenment. This vision of society was based on notions of a social contract, and the French Revolution which sought a nation based on ideas not of blood and ancestors but of free men. The abolition of slavery and ideas of secularism went beyond mere religious toleration. However, despite the fact that the nation was not an affirmation of the particular, but of the universal, such universalist objectives have not been achieved. In the American Revolution, in a nation largely based on immigration, the right to be 'different' was recognised. Nevertheless, there has been little defence of the right to be 'similar' within a constitutional state, especially of the descendants of slaves and the indigenous Americans. Hence, inclusive social and political frameworks have not been optimally developed.

Thirdly, the rise of socialism in the nineteenth century further contributed to notions of radical transformation especially through Soviet Bolshevism. The price paid by socialism in respecting difference and not building inclusive rights to be 'similar' has been very evident in the dissolution of Yugoslavia and the Soviet Union. These states did not develop inclusive citizenship with common and shared values.

Fourthly, the post-colonial states likewise faced great challenges of maintaining unity, with divisiveness being foisted on them by the colonisers. Most of them have tried to maintain national unity despite tendencies towards fragmentation.

Hopes for the genuine underpinning of globalisation therefore lie in the collective wisdom of the earlier religious epoch, and the Enlightenment philosophy, and their reinterpretation by the socialist movements, as well as from progressive elements from amongst the post-colonialist liberation movements. The educational and political challenge for democratic ideas is to hold notions of respecting difference, but at the same time ensuring the right to be similar. Such an approach could begin to break the polarisations between particularism and universalism.

Globalised capital does not necessarily provide nations with independence and dignity, but rather results in the opposite. Such globalised capitalism needs to be regulated by delimiting high levels of private profitability which are inimical to social good.

Civic movements attempting to create democratic governance need to use the global information systems to develop their capacities to establish more cooperative mechanisms for democratic and sustainable development. We have also to see what the sudden development of the Internet will bring. This version of the 'global village' still currently remains unrealised and in its infancy.

There are various forms and patterns of historical movements and shifts which lead towards progressive notions of inclusion. Many of the initiatives undertaken by the United Nations which have moved towards creating peace, stability, equity and tolerance are important developments.

The ways in which civil society has worked to create important instruments like the Convention of the Rights of the Child are an extremely important development in an age when children are the victims of poverty, exploitation, war, conflicts and abuse. But the global march of children to the International Labour Organisation's Geneva Conference illustrates the weakness of the United Nations system in general, and of legal measures against child abuse, labour and slavery. The various UN Summit Conferences like the Social Summit (Copenhagen), Environment (Rio de Janeiro), Women (Beijing), Population (Cairo) and Drugs (New York) have all helped in challenging the dominant paradigms of globalisation and providing civil society with a voice. Yet, they have remained unconnected and not coalesced or developed a momentum. Therefore, their effect has been minimal in implementation terms. At national levels single issue groups, or coalitions of groups, are in their infancy and are no match for well-established organisations like OECD or WTO. Nor do they have consistent voices at international gatherings like that at Davos, Switzerland. Human rights groups have cultural and regional problems and are seldom able to provide consistent support or make strategic interventions.

There have also been numerous globalised educational initiatives to meet the challenges of xenophobia, racism and communalism. Some of the major initiatives after World War II have been advocated by UNESCO, and initiatives like global, international, peace and intercultural education have been developed in many national and regional contexts. It is difficult to ascertain the impact of such initiatives. At the regional level the European Union has been slowly developing mechanisms to protect social rights and to counter xenophobia and racism. The Maastricht Treaty (Articles 18, 29) provides competence to initiate measures to improve intercultural relations in member states. Some national policies to develop and enact global education at national level, like those of the Republic of Korea, have been enacted but still remain to be implemented. What we must now ensure is that these international initiatives become part of the mainstream national education systems.

FURTHER READING

B. Anderson (1998) *The Spectre of Comparisons: Nationalism, Southeast Asia and the World*, London: Vergo.

Z. Bauman (1999) *In Search of Polities*, Cambridge: Polity Press.

B. Ehrenreich (1997) *Blood Rites: Origins and History of the Passions of War*, New York: Metropolitan Books.

M. Ignatief (1998) *The Warrior's Honor: Ethnic Wars and the Modern Conscience*, London: Chatto and Windus.

R. Kothari (1993) *Poverty: Human Consciousness and the Amnesia of Development*, London: Zed Press.

M. M. Sankhdher (1992) *Secularism in India: Dilemmas and Challenges*, New Delhi: Deep and Deep Publication.

9

Knowledge, Social Science and the Curriculum

Issues of the curriculum especially in higher education institutions have an enormous amount to say about what is taught and learnt in schools. Issues of societal complexity in the United States have had a very long airing. It is, however, unfortunate that this debate has not been as constructive as it should have been. It is obviously informed by the social structures and exclusions within the American polity with consequent demands for ethnicisation of the education systems and the curriculum. The critique of such demands and the labelling of any changes within the social sciences and the humanities has been referred to as 'politically correct'.

The American debate is, however, only one aspect of the types of changes and transformations which are needed as we move deeper into the twenty-first century In multicultural democratic societies, exclusions of knowledge from those civilisations, cultures, communities and groups cannot be simply represented as demands for political correctness. They represent substantive exclusions of knowledge from the curriculum. If multicultural democracies are to develop common and shared values they need to take these issues seriously and ensure that what constitutes legitimate knowledge in society has the democratic consent and is representative of diverse sources of knowledge.

This chapter, written from a vantage point in Europe, attempts to engage with these questions from a non-conflictual and non-partisan perspective. It is hoped that it will offer solutions from a more constructive, imaginative and creative perspective on issues of the curriculum.

SOCIAL SCIENCE AND INCLUSION

The North American Social Science Background

In the 1960s, social science in the United States was preoccupied by ideas of modernisation and development. As the 1996 Gulbenkian Commission *Report on the Restructuring of the Social Science* recalled,

> The key thesis was that there exists a common modernising path for all nations/ peoples/areas (hence they were all the same) but that the nations/peoples/areas find themselves in different stages on their path (hence they were not quite the same).
>
> (Gulbenkian 1996: 40)

Over the late 1960s and early 1970s the 'scientific and measurable' dimension became more and more suspect.

The challenge to the universal normatism of the social sciences came increasingly to the fore in the 1970s. In the post-Martin Luther King period the growth of a new autonomous voice for African-Americans had its counterpart in the development of a strong feminist movement. Both groups challenged the legitimacy of the dominant knowledge systems. The questioning of the theoretical reasoning of social science knowledge systems was based on a questioning of their presuppositions and demanded new modes of analysis. To quote the Gulbenkian Report,

> These new modes of analysis call for the use of scholarship, analysis and reasoning to engage in reflection concerning the place and weight in our theorising about differences of race, gender, sexuality and class.
>
> (Gulbenkian 1996: 87)

The Gulbenkian Commission suggested instead the development of a pluralistic universalism, akin to the Indian pantheon of past and present social realities. This represents an important recognition of the multicultural realities which have a bearing on both the historical study of the past and the social scientific study of the present.

The development of a more intercultural social science can re-engage with the complexity of different types of localisms, as well as those at the level of the state and, as they develop, into more global forms. Such a developmental notion of the social sciences, which does not leave out analysis at the level of the state, has the merit of carrying with it many of the disciplines whose focus is the state. It may also have the merit of developing a common social science which cuts across humanity. The key task, to return to the Gulbenkian Report,

> is to explode the hermetic language used to describe persons and groups that are 'others', who are merely objects of social science analysis, as opposed to those who are subjects, have full rights and legitimacy, among whom the analysts have placed themselves.
>
> (Gulbenkian 1996: 85–6)

The inclusion of these historical pasts and contemporaneous presents gives further possibilities of developing comprehensive knowledge systems.

In this study, starting from an autobiographical perspective, I have set out my own premises, directions and preoccupations. I have sought to demonstrate, among other things, how the subjectivity of a purpose can form a basis for developing more inter-subjective understanding and allow one to move from particularistic directions to more pluralistic and universalist notions.

The Politicisation of Social Science

One of the problems of studying the social sciences in the United States has been the use of them by the government as a super-power for its own specific state interests. Hence, systems analysis and input/output models were used in analysis of national, regional and international policies and the national interests of the state. When alternative voices were raised, the hegemonic official voice predominated and turned debate into contestation. This politicised contestation bypassed significant intellectual and academic issues and led to the overpoliticisation of these fields. Whether the features which have arisen in genderised and ethnicised studies can be reconstituted imaginatively into the dominant mainstream of the social sciences still remains unclear.

The contribution of knowledge to power politics has therefore had dangerous consequences. It has also affected the political role of the university as part of the state apparatus – and has led to a reactive 'hermeneutics of suspicion' (Hartmann 1997) which can be applied to everything. The issue is compounded because imperial adventures, two world wars and the Holocaust have led to the discrediting of instrumentalist reason. The question being asked is whether disinterested knowledge without linkage to power is good?

The right to be different, and acknowledgment of the study of difference, has now emerged among anthropologists and literary scholars. But in studying difference, all that cultural studies does is to study racial and ethnic knowledge and identities, and interminable cultural wars have ensued in which the conservatives support the dominant canon against those proposing to dislodge it.

Hartmann recognises how in the current academic battles, wars and discourses the role of multiculturalism has been under-theorised. But he recommends it because it

> has all the strength and weakness of utopian issues. Its main weakness is that it forgets what its strength comes from: that it was created in the wake of an older idea of culture, by the latter's heroic, historical struggles for land or against the land. Without these struggles, which are deeply secular even if involved in ideas of transcendence and religion, there would not be a plurality of cultural 'species'.
>
> (Hartmann 1997: 185)

The North American Curricular Debate

Curricular issues became increasingly polarised in the United States after the debate over political correctness was strengthened by the publication in 1987 of Alan Bloom's *Closing of the American Mind*. It was followed by a spate of similar books. They included *Illiberal Education* (1992) by Dinesh D'Souza, himself an immigrant from India (Goa) who considered himself more American than the Social Register Yankees of New England or Manhattan! As we have seen, this clarion call from across the Atlantic had strong resonances with the conservative ascendancy and regeneration in Britain.

One of this debate's most appalling features is the way in which issues have become polemicised and polarised. As Robert Hughes put it, 'We now have our conservatives promising "culture wars" while ignorant radicals orate about "separatism" ' (Hughes 1993: 13). The dispassionate and reflective judgments that debate over curriculum issues require have been denied, and substantive questions about curricula have been caricatured by lumping together a whole raft of single issue concerns such as the environment, gender and race.

This is not an issue of marginal concern. It bears on the core values of society.

Here, of course, we must remember that societal issues differ from one context to another and that the usages and terminology of Britain and the other European Union states differ from those of the United States. Nathan Glazer, for instance, uses 'multiculturalism' as a term to define the status of minorities and women, a usage not found on this side of the Atlantic. Nor is his equating issues of societal diversity with relevance to education as 'oppression studies' (Glazer 1997: 14).

Glazer formulates curriculum issues with reference to indices of disloyalty displayed by African-Americans, Puerto Ricans and Mexicans (ibid: 44) thus misreading the limitations of curriculum change. Issues like racism, inequality and exclusion cannot be resolved by curriculum changes. More importantly, in treating the minorities as the focus of disloyalty in the United States, he is shutting his eyes to the most anti-American activities to have emerged in recent years – those of the Christian Fundamentalist and other sectarian groups. Similarly the demonisation of Islam can only lead to the further alienation of the very complex community of American Muslims.

Multiculturalism as an issue in the United States demands more sustained consideration and, above all, research, to better inform the educational process and the devising of curricula. The educational professionals are, however, only too content to teach what is at hand and ignore new developments in theory and practice.

For without research and critical thinking, higher education institutions are reduced to being institutions of vocational training. The essential educational elements of reforming and redefining the issues for changing democratic society are lost. We really cannot take seriously the conservative assertion on both sides of the Atlantic that such critical edge thinking is ideological and propagandistic, a means of indoctrinating students. Educators are failing future generations of students if they are seen merely as purveyors of a received wisdom and common culture not subjected to scrutiny from a contemporary perspective. Exploring the possibilities and potentials of an intercultural curriculum has the prospect of revitalising higher education rather than reducing it to ritualistic modes.

Hence, a cosmetic focus on Afro-centrism for African-American students does not enhance their critical faculties, or improve their self-image and self-concept in a racist society. Nor does this type of curriculum of recognition lead to equality in a society where structural inequalities within the educational domain, as well as in society itself, continue to exist.

Instead, the first step towards refocusing the universal intellectual potential should be learning about the Asian, Chinese and African contributions, not only to the humanities and social sciences, but also to the physical sciences and mathematics. However, this is only a stage in re-engaging with the issues of how knowledge is suppressed, and how within learning situations across institutions, the important aspects of knowledge can be selected from across cultures for all students. This also means giving teachers the appropriate learning strategies to engage with a broadly based curriculum of this kind.

Reconciling Notions of Equality and Recognition

The fear of not offending the sensitivities of 'ethnic' groups detracts from the broad thrust of issues and questions needed for devising curricula. Stressing truth (Glazer 1997: 57–59) in knowledge, especially history, misrepresents what is required. Triumphalist historical narratives of the domination of one group or culture over others is not the appropriate strategy for devising history curricula, for with different modes of historical analysis, different truths would emerge.

Hence, the overarching political, economic, social and moral values and objectives that underlie the curriculum have to be clearly stated and understood – above all, how in a multicultural polity the notions of equality and of recognition of groups compete and should be reconciled.

These complex issues cannot be seen as Glazer casts them:

> I prefer what I got in high school, a full year of European history (Asia and Africa got in under the treatment of imperialism, colonialism and the causes of World War I).
>
> (Glazer 1997: 60)

Asian and African civilisations have a history outside that of imperialism, colonialism and World War I. Indeed it is the subsuming of these histories within a Eurocentric framework which has led to history becoming a battleground.

In the United States the crisis of confidence on how to deal with diversity within education is complicated by its position as a superpower. In Britain and other European Union countries it is a question of relating the representation of the nation and the state within the history curriculum. The added dimension of being a superpower is still not an issue in this context as in the United States – though, even there, the California curriculum on history and social science provides a statement in its framework which reads:

> From the first encounter between the indigenous peoples and exploring Europeans the inhabitants of the North American continent have represented a variety of races, religions, languages and ethnic and racial groups. With the passage of time, the United States has grown increasingly diverse in its social and cultural composition. Yet, even as our people have become increasingly diverse, there is a broad recognition that we are one people. Whatever our origins we are all Americans.
>
> (Quoted in Glazer 1997: 63)

The challenge obviously is how, in a democratic context, do the notions of oneness become manifest and strengthened? Taking the British immigrants as the informing fragment of American identity will not suffice. It continues to ignore, within the multicultural curricular debate, the fundamental position of the indigenous peoples within the articulation of Americanness. Moreover, assuming that it is the exclusion of African-Americans which lies at the heart of the multicultural debate distorts what is the fundamental issue – developing an inclusive policy through well thought out public policies.

The polarisation which we have seen both in the United States and in Britain between those who are seen as 'additive' or 'revisionist' multiculturalists and the more progressive 'transformative' multiculturalists must above all be rejected. It has already done immense harm, and has detracted from bringing about necessary beneficial changes in education and curricula for all American and British students. What has been particularly negative and counter-productive about this polarisation is the way in which it has raised strident and ethnicised voices in response to the dominant racisms. It has led to postures which have become intransigent, which do not help students, nor shift their lowered educational performances, nor increase their competencies.

Glazer's attempt to shift the focus to lifestyles is particularly unhelpful (ibid: 79). Lifestyles pertain to the private domain, to the lives of individuals and groups. However, he does go on to point out, rightly, that the issue is really about the substance of education:

> The issue in public education is rather, what shall be the content of required courses that all students must take and be tested in and that will make up their entire education in social studies and history and literature.
>
> (Glazer 1997: 84)

Yet this is still a very half-hearted attempt at changing the curriculum in a positive way, given the broadest needs in society as a whole.

This perspective is also reactive and not prophylactic enough. Hence, he suggests that the demands for change are not coming from Native American, Hispanic and Asian educators and that:

> we would not be seeing the present uproar over multiculturalism were it not for the frustration among blacks over widespread educational failures among their youth which leads them to cast about for alternatives, new departures, new approaches, anything that might help.
>
> (Glazer 1997: 95)

Here he has completely ignored the issues raised by Charles Taylor of recognition of cultures and the ascription of equal value to them. And he has sidetracked the societal diversity of the United States.

Acknowledging Diversity in the Public Domain

Admittedly it is difficult in any society to accord each ethnic or nationality group an equal value. But there can be a symbolic but substantive acknowledgment of diversity in the public domain which acknowledges the equality and parity of rights of all individuals and groups by powerfully asserting equity and inclusiveness. In other words, the notion of one dominant ethos determining the identity of the United States (as English), Canada (as French and/or English), Britain (as English) must disappear and be replaced by constitutional and democratic principles which can lead to the development of inclusive politics drawing on a more universal pool of knowledge and understanding.

Distinguishing the features of the different groups which have rights of belonging, a right to live the way they choose without undue hindrance, is an important first step. Here, the state protects the rights of these groups as autonomous agents but does not necessarily interfere if individuals or groups want to have their particular ethnic or cultural identities recognised. Ethnic and cultural identities are changing entities, not only in countries of origin but also in diasporas and countries of settlement. This is as true of the British who settled in Australia, the Africans in America, the French in Canada, as it is of the more recent Asian diasporas to many parts of the world.

Cultural distinctiveness and change as an autonomous group right needs to be safeguarded by law in the polity. However, within the public domain it is the issue of one 'equal citizenship' (Blum 1998: 73) and shared humanity which requires attention within multicultural polities. For instance, the negation of gender and racial inequalities must itself be negated. Hence, the complex balance within the polity has to deal with the tension between the distinctiveness of groups and the equality of citizens. Given the group subordinations pervading societies, including education, public policy-making must be concerned with access to equality. Issues are not about individual equality. But, as Blum states:

> The form of equality that is pertinent to multiculturalism as it is applied to groups then, is an acceptance of groups, as equal. But we have to be clear in what sense these groups are seen as equals. It can only be that they are the kind of groups who, having been denied full human equality, are demanding to be granted it. The groups in question that Taylor mentions are gender and racial groups.
>
> (Blum 1998: 88)

In postulating the issues in this manner, the recognition of difference is only one aspect that a polity needs to consider. The second, equally important, is that of the structural inequalities which need to be bridged in society. Theorists, therefore, must not 'supplant concerns for material equality with recognitional equality' (Blum 1998: 90).

Ethnic Studies for Ethnic Students?

The important question in terms of the curriculum is whether there need to be 'ethnic studies' for 'ethnic students'. Alternatively is there a need to develop a broader thrust of what is relevant from such curricular courses for the broadly based curriculum, depending on the nature of the subject (history, social science, science), or of an interdisciplinary nature, which are undertaken by all students?

This situation exists because the tensions between ethno-cultural identities and the rather incomplete notions of the Enlightenment remain, and are likely to remain, largely unresolved. While multiple identities may be a norm amongst societal groups of all backgrounds, they may still ascribe to one or other of the ethnicities. Alternately, where groups have been integrated or assimilated into dominant national norms, a more localised group identity may remain pervasive. The white Southerners in the United States, or Yorkshiremen in the north of England, provide territorial based or localised markers of identity.

Indeed the project of e pluribus unum is something which has not been taken up, even by Americans of European origin. The common pool of identity which constitutes, at least in symbolic terms, a sharedness of values and citizenship, just does not exist. What exists instead is a nation based on the norms and mores of the Anglo-American fragment which constitutes the norm for a core national identity.

To quote Lucius Outlaw, Jr.,

There were, however, always persons, white, red, black and otherwise who disagreed with the interpretations of founding principles and practices that provided for co-ercive assimilation, racialised enslavement, and gendered exclusion from citizenship, persons who fought unsuccessfully for full citizenship rights for those excluded and oppressed.

(Outlaw 1998: 390)

The struggles for justice by these excluded and oppressed groups, within a common and shared value system, or a public and civic culture, have still not taken place. Nor are they reflected in curricula which would integrate the multicultural American diversity into one nation. This becomes more of a problem for public and social policy, and especially educational provision, because the demographic and societal power relations are changing, and are likely to change further, making the Anglo-American fragment a minority. Here Will Kymlicka provides a challenging theory of group differentiated citizenship based on group differentiated rights for minorities in multicultural societies like the United States and Canada (Kymlicka 1995).

A positive role in education, especially in the creation of common and shared curricula, becomes of vital significance given that education is a major socialis-ing institution. As Outlaw writes, an educational experience based on critical reflection, reinterpretation and self-conscious efforts are needed to develop a political life

~ that allows for democratical, inclusive yet critical recognition and appreciation of cul-tural legacies of persons and people who together comprise our body politic.

(Outlaw 1998: 392)

Such an engagement, especially in educational terms, is therefore an epistemo-logical and pedagogic attempt to establish connections between the group and the local, the cultural and state, and the structural and national aspects and levels of education. Hence, the process of national identity(ies) becomes a dynamic process of being constructed and created.

Correcting the Distortions of the Past

The challenge therefore for the United States is not Glazer's reactive and assimi-lationist 'we are all multiculturalists now', but a forward looking and prophy-lactic perspective. The omissions and distortions of the past need to be corrected – and a transformation of the curricula is an essential feature of this shift.

It is true that, as Glazer rightly argues, African-Americans have long shared their difficult history with white Americans. But he then goes on:

The only possible comparison with Europe would be if the Saxons of England, or Gauls of France, had been held in a position of caste subservience for centuries. This kind of split, sunk deep in the history of societies, does not exist in Europe.

(Glazer 1997: 157)

Here he is obviously not right about the splits in European history. For instance, in Britain the Scots and Welsh have only just acquired the right to establish par-liaments in Edinburgh and Cardiff. In Spain the Basques and Catalans have long been fighting for their rights from the Madrid government. In France the Bretons and Corsicans still battle for their rights. What Europeans and Americans both have to face is a deeper understanding of the histories of their own societies, of how the past affects the present. A perspective of this kind is well outlined by Judith Green:

> That we are now, and increasingly, are becoming, what we have always been: a multicultural society whose component cultures have become hybridised and composite through our history of indivisible struggles, daily contacts and practical co-operation.
>
> (Green 1998a: 425)

The issues of devising appropriate educational curricula are not, of course, of recent vintage. Both the positive, interactive and the negative aspects of exclusivity have a long pedigree in the country. Given this experience, it is not enough just to add to a Eurocentric knowledge base a few tokenistic gestures, to include a few texts of the excluded groups. This would in no way meet the type of critical appraisal and rationale that would develop an intercultural curriculum.

Students need broadly based knowledge about the histories, and the content of life, of their own and other cultures, so that they can critically appraise the prospects and advantages as well as the problems raised in socially diverse polities. The polarities of the 'west' and the 'rest' need to be cast aside to establish a more broadly based understanding of knowledge. The American context does represent such a pool of the knowledge basis from its broad range of cultures, civilisations and regions. The Native American, Asian and African culture systems co-exist with those of the 'west'. More importantly, there are shared pasts, based on struggles as well as evolving common understandings, grounded in the society and its sometimes painful history. These experiences, however, need to be embedded in a more positive way in the lives of the peoples, so that the democratic functioning of society and its institutions can be optimised.

The development of a critically based intercultural democratic community requires at its core a sound curriculum drawing upon our multicultural pasts and presents. While recognising differences, it needs to develop commonalities and shared understandings of the complexities in which we live.

> Students nurtured within a curriculum, pedagogy and educational ethos guided by democratic multiculturalism would be equipped with self-understanding, confidence, and a sense of agency, to protect themselves against nihilism and their communities against erosion.
>
> (Green 1998a: 442)

Such competences would enhance and transform the democratic features not only of personal relations but also of institutions.

TIME TO STOCKTAKE

Avoiding Culture War

Two important issues fed the culture wars in the United States. First, it was the growing stridency, racism and fundamentalism of the public domain in the 1980s and 1990s which left a legacy of hatred, of winner and loser, white and black, Christian and 'others', patriots and aliens. The second was the response of the students whose expectations and dreams, heightened in the 1960s, were turned sour by the conservative backlash.

Now we are faced with prospects of culture wars in Europe. In the wake of the collapse of the communist regimes, and the consequent collapse of their social collectivity, as command economies were replaced by market principles, and public domains were privatised with lightning speed, there spread new racist, xenophobic and exclusive nationalisms, not only among eastern and central Europeans but also in the west. Such polarised reactions are obviously to be expected, given that in the last two decades, as has been demonstrated again and again in these pages, the minorities and their rights have not been seriously acknowledged. Obviously the higher the levels of exclusion from social and public policy, the more strident the oppositional voices have become. Cultural wars cannot therefore cause any surprise. But they can only have a disastrous effect on the educational outcomes of children from marginalised communities.

However, the situation is not totally negative, even in the polarised context of the United States. A range of institutions of higher education now focus on building self-esteem amongst children of the African-American community. The Afrocentrists too are focusing on a particularistic education for positive self-esteem, despite their low position in society. A distinguished team of scholars have been assembled by Harvard University to take on board issues raised for the academe by the African-American presence. Likewise at State University of New York in Buffalo there is a course on American pluralism taken by all students.

However, such liberal education courses have to increasingly compete with vocational studies. What is therefore needed is a broadly based defence of liberal education for all, rather than polarisation between the cultural and traditional conservatives and the radical academics. As Martha Nussbaum writes:

> Unlike all other nations, we ask a higher education to contribute a general preparation for citizenship, not just a specialised preparation for a career.
>
> (Nussbaum 1997: 299)

The purpose of this for her is to extend the benefits of citizenship across class, race, sex, ethnicity and religion and to develop mutual understanding and individual self-scrutiny within a reflective and deliberative democratic culture. This would move groups away from oppositional and collision-based positions which were not examined or privileged. It would enable students to know how to inquire about what they do not know, and to have a critical and inquiring mind. Institutions of higher education could introduce such an approach either within individual subject areas or within interdisciplinary courses, depending on how they operate and function. As Nussbaum warns, it would be a catastrophe

> to become a nation of technically competent people who have lost the ability to think critically, to examine themselves, and to respect the humanity and diversity of others.
>
> (Nussbaum 1997: 300)

This is a task for all academics, both in the sciences and in the humanities, here as well as in the United States. The task requires traditionalists, liberals and radicals to attempt to develop strategic interventions which can deal with the complexities of allowing students to develop their understanding not only of self, locality and tradition, but also of the broader, plural, conflict-ridden but also interdependent world. Nussbaum's call is to support Seneca's dictum to 'cultivate humanity'.

The cultivation of humanity is, however, not within the exclusive purview of any particular culture, social class, group of people or civilisation. The conservative assertion of cultivated elitist values is based on the incorrect assumption that only one civilisation represents the acme of cultivation and of civilised behaviour, and of standards in learning and academic life, and hence that accessi-bility to the masses leads to a populist education and a lowering of standards. This regular accusation by the conservative right, that any academic changes which become more inclusive become more demagogic and lead to a new barbarism, demands rebuttal if only because it is no more than an imaginary construction of the old curricula. It allegedly represents the best in the Arnoldian tradition, when it is no more than nostalgia for the methods of their own education.

The Opening Up of America

Reflecting on my own experience in the United States, the mind of America was more closed in the period I lived there. It has gradually needed to be opened up as the society has changed, as has the role of the country in the world. This opening up has obviously required an engagement with different cultures, groups and civilisations. One could ask Allan Bloom, Lynn Chenay and Dinesh D'Souza whether the democratisation of the educational system and of knowledge are not part of the American ideal. If this democratisation is a feature of American society and is to be equated with lowered standards then American standards in education have always been low! Why is it that at a time when other cultures are gaining increasing access to the mainstream education system all of a sudden there are accusations of lowering of standards?

The conservative response has come as if the knowledge of the 'Dead White European Males' has not merely been supplemented by new knowledge but has been excluded from higher education lock, stock and barrel. How is it that old knowledge is never seen as having resulted from advocacy, while new knowledge is seen as having merely resulted from it – an advocacy moreover which has degraded American academic life?

The conservative response represents another paradox and dilemma about knowledge. The older Anglo-American establishment was very suspicious of Europe and its influence in cultural and institutional terms. In 1825 John Adams warned Thomas Jefferson against the employment of European tutors and professors in the new University of Virginia because of their 'prejudices both ecclesiastical and temporal'. Jefferson himself did not look favourably on European immigrants because their influence would warp and bias the American system, and on another occasion wished that there was an ocean of fire between America and the Old World. Nor was he alone. Secretary of War, William Crawford, in 1816 wished that the freedoms could be shared with the indigenous natives and not the fugitives, whether as a result of their crimes or their virtues, of the Old World. In 1818 Secretary of State, John Quincy Adams, wanted immigrants to 'cast off their European skin never to resume it'. Henry Thoreau wanted them to 'walk towards Oregon, and not towards Europe', and Walt Whitman in 1871 was no less complimentary (this important discussion is from Levine 1996: 60–63).

The other part of the paradox is that in the period between the world wars this nineteenth-century preoccupation with the western American frontier got transformed into a conflict with the 'Western Civ' courses on issues of classical civilisation which had been dominant during the earlier period in the universities. Levine comments:

> The manner in which Western Civ declined and American Literature and American Studies emerged in the canon and the curriculum, teaches us once again that canons do not reside in some protected galaxy of universal truths beyond the reach of merely temporal events.
>
> (Levine 1996: 91)

Nevertheless Gertrude Himmelfarb, a conservative and elitist historian, can write:

> Multiculturalism is the obvious effect of politicising history. But its more pernicious effect is to demean and dehumanise the people who are subjects of history. To pluralise and particularise history to the point where people have no history in common is to deny the common humanity of all people, whatever their sex, race, class, religions. It is also to trivialise history by so fragmenting it that it lacks all coherence and focus, all sense of community – indeed, all meaning.
>
> (Himmelfarb 1995: 154)

Here, in common with other conservative historians in the academic establishment, she has allowed particularistic concerns to outweigh any broader implications, thus plunging the discipline of history into a crisis.

In Britain we have been spared the dreadful polarisation of the American academic community. It was refreshing to find Dr Nicholas Tate, then Chief Assessment Executive of the Qualifications Assessment Authority, opposed to sanitised 'heritage' history and, perceiving the dangers of 'pathological nationalism', seeking instead to develop a more democratic and sanguine understanding of English and British societies (Tate 1997). And to quote Richard Evans:

> History has become a multicultural domain where different groupings struggle for intellectual supremacy on the battleground of ideas, courses and university history syllabuses. It is surely not out of place in this situation to plead for a little intellectual tolerance, and to warn any one particular orientation against the arrogant assumption that its own methods and procedures are necessarily better than those of its rivals.
>
> (Evans 1997: 182)

Evans's sensible approach to history contrasts with Himmelfarb's vociferous demand to return to traditional political history, especially that of the nation state. We can today see how the contributions of Carr, Elton, Collingwood and Namier have been enhanced by the work of Zeldin or Braudel. Though the contributions of social scientists or of the *Annales* historians may not in themselves create better history, they do provide historians with enabling tools. Their work is not 'trivial, irrelevant or misguided' as Himmelfarb or Elton might suggest (Evans 1997: 182; see also Munslow 1997).

Uncovering 'Hidden History'

What is remarkable about these academic voices from across the Atlantic is that they pretend to speak for democratic peoples. Yet, as Levine tells us, Professor Vann Woodward of Yale in 1982 denounced the tendency to examine the lives of ordinary folk instead of the 'elites and powerful'. Likewise Gertrude Himmelfarb grumbled about the 'current prejudice against greatness' (both quoted in Levine 1996: 147). They claimed that the contributions of social and cultural history negate political history. Yet the political dimensions, contributions and resistances of ordinary people in democracies to oppressions, discrimination and inequalities can be ignored by academe only at the peril of society at large.

It is the previous focus on the significance of the powerful in society which has led to the impasse in societies at the present time. Ignoring the ways in which the masses, the excluded, the marginalised, have contributed to knowledge, and should therefore legitimately form part of the societal curriculum, is what is leading to fragmentation and fissures.

Historians who have followed the stories of the powerful and the elites have, for instance, ignored the people's contributions to the American society and polity, as Howard Zinn has demonstrated. William Katz's pioneering work on the hidden history of multicultural America, and on the hidden history of Black and Native American alliances, has been largely ignored by the academic historians (Katz 1986, 1993). Ignoring their histories as not being political is a perversion of the political domain. Their history, as Katz shows, represents a camaraderie amongst the oppressed American peoples who were fighting for liberty. They are part of the American frontier mentality. Yet they remain invisible. If this resistance to domination and slavery is not political what is?

Katz describes their story as:

Black/Indian participation in democratic movements, years, decades, or centuries before the American Revolution. It also demonstrates that dark people ignored the boundaries drawn by Europeans in their move from one 'country' to another in search of liberty, justice or a better life.

(Katz 1986: 6)

Given this broader historical frame why should the European fragment in the Americas define the so-called 'New World' – its politics and subsequent history, knowledge and canon?

To quote Levine again, there is a need to

find ways to give voice to peoples who have been rendered historically inarticulate by historians who concentrated on a relatively narrow spectrum of written sources and thus transformed the American people into what Ralph Ellison called 'the void of face-less faces, of soundless voices, lying outside history'.

(Levine 1996: 150)

It is a simplistic misunderstanding of the history of the Europeans in America to represent them as a unified whole. They are, as Levine puts it, 'a series of cultures, languages, religions, nationalities, worldviews, political systems, folkways' (Levine 1996: 159). Rather than being defined by the European Americans, it is the Native Americans and the Black Americans who have been, and continue to be, the definers of the American polity, the contributors to what are its parameters and defining frameworks.

Their cultures are not the simple stereotypes in which the dominant group would have us believe – they represent a complexity which, for instance, informs the history and structures of American working people and of the public domain as it pertains to employment, labour and industry. Understanding this complexity enables one to construct a new and more nuanced understanding of society. We can then see that it is the failure to understand it that has led to the enforcement of separate identities, and to the ethnic chauvinism which has been wrongfully branded as multiculturalism. But, as its 'hidden history' reveals, American society has always been multicultural.

Stocktaking of Curricular Change

Developments within the broad curriculum as well as specialist or discipline based studies cannot and should not start from scratch. Changes, reforms and transformations have already begun. What is now necessary is a stocktaking of these changes, and the critiques made of them, to develop a new paradigm. Here again American responses are illuminating.

Harold Bloom's notion that any questioning in this field constitutes the 'School of Resentment' (Bloom 1995: 4) is unnecessarily, if not ridiculously, defensive of the western canon. Similarly Bernard Knox writes:

In the intercultural curriculum that is the ideal of today's academic radicals there can be no valid objection to the inclusion of new material that gives the student a wider view. But that new material will have to compete with the old and if it is not up to the same high level it will sooner or later be rejected with disdain by the students themselves. Only a totalitarian regime can enforce the continued study of second rate so that greater levels of equality will prevail in society texts or outworn philosophies.

(Knox 1993: 21)

Knox's setting up a polarised argument is scarcely helpful in assisting 'the inclusion of new material'. The discussion should not be about replacing one set of the canon with another, but of developing broader and inclusive understandings of knowledge universally. Knox does, however, go on to express a very proper concern that the humanities do not lead to lucrative careers like studies in the sciences.

The modern disillusion with the humanities begins in the nineteenth century; it stems from the sudden simultaneous expansion of industry and the physical sciences and with large scale industrial employment and first steps towards universal education at fairly high levels.

(Knox 1993: 78)

At present the need to develop an inquisitive society is as important as it has ever been, and all students who enter higher education should take humanities subjects in higher education: literature, anthropology, history, social sciences. For democratic societies, liberal education and a study of the humanities which poses questions but gives no definite answers, remain important. To quote Knox again,

> The Greeks relegated practical skills, *techne*, to a lower sphere; the ideal of a free man was leisure, *schole* and the pursuits which permitted it. But the modern world has made *techne* into a prodigious instrument for scientific investigation and material progress – only to discover, not, we hope, too late, that it is also a monster which may destroy all life on the planet.

(Knox 1993: 104–5)

This privileging of the scientific subjects and the negating of classics, humanities and the arts because they are neither instrumental nor have a function, can only have negative consequences as Bernard Knox rightly points out. It is all part of the ongoing process through which schools and institutions of continuing and higher education are subjected to increasing scrutiny and control, ostensibly to enforce accountability. However, such controls, which do not necessarily even lead to higher levels of public accountability, undermine the autonomy of academic life and project education towards *techne* and not *schole*.

As academic autonomy is weakened, issues that raise complex questions for modern society – for instance, what we are concerned with in this chapter, integrating intercultural issues into curricula – are ignored. But, as I have stressed throughout this book, in the diverse polities in which we live, such issues are marginalised at our peril. Integrating broadly based notions of the humanities and the sciences into the educational system cannot be consigned to the periphery. It is a matter of core concern to a democratic polity.

The old curricular divide which entrenches the division of the sciences from the humanities must be reappraised. Imparting training which is largely based on *techne* to a large segment of the young population is insufficient to develop the inquisitive mind. Focus on subjects like commerce, business studies, technological and computer sciences is not a sufficient basis for successfully completing higher education. A broadly based liberal education is needed for most of those who attend institutions of higher education. The formation of a critical understanding and an inquisitive mind is bound to lead to more autonomous and educated minds. Hence, even those who are working in areas of *techne* ought to have an education (not training) which fosters the creativity, imagination and critical perspectives nurtured within thinking minds.

There is also the question of whether students in higher education institutions are treated as individuals or as part of a group, a question of great importance where there are inequalities in society. Students must not be treated as if they had no fixed identity beyond their ethnicity, and do not represent a much more complex set of multiple identities. It is inappropriate to provide them with simplistic, cosmetic and separatist, ethnically derived and based curricula. The higher education institutions do not have any obligation towards specific ethnically based identities. As public institutions they have a responsibility to reconstitute inclusive curricula suitable for all students in a diverse society. They also have an obligation to provide equal access to the curricula so that greater levels of equality will prevail in society. And while not necessarily validating the specificities of each ethnicity, they must recognise its right to particularism, to its own locality, religion or language.

In the final analysis societies have to re-evaluate the issue of social status and financial renumeration. If the dominant groups pursue careers in legal, medical or financial sectors because of their purchase in the social imagination, then those from minority, immigrant or marginalised communities will follow suit. The value of the educated and cultivated persons and communities will be lost. Academic and educational institutions will focus on training powerful elites and lose their broader perspective of educative critical democratic citizens within diverse polities.

Planning a History Curriculum

When the National Curriculum was discussed by government appointed working parties the teaching of history in schools in England created controversy. Since then the political configuration of Britain has changed dramatically. Scotland and Wales have their own assemblies and a new sense of Scottish, Welsh and English identities, informed by their different historical pasts, is bound to emerge. These histories could have a very narrow nationalistic interpretation, or a broader and inclusive one.

The archaeologist Simon James has been criticised for suggesting that Celtic identities are a 'recent invention' during the eighteenth century (James 1999). But how recent is the specific identity of being British (Colley 1992)? And who are the English (Paxman 1998; Hazell 1999)? Do Scots, Welsh and English constitute nationalities or ethnicities, or both? And what of those who get labelled as 'ethnic groups' – Indians, Pakistanis, Bangladeshis, Chinese, Nigerians and Jamaicans? They certainly represent nationalities because each one of the nations they migrated from has many ethnic groups. How are the histories of these peoples to be represented? Should each be taught only its own history? Or are there different and common, separate and shared, historical pasts which can be constituted in such a way that they will enable young people to understand the story of the peoples of these islands?

Plainly those who plan history curricula face a very complicated task. On the one hand they need to engage with the identities of all these different groups. On the other, working within the state education systems, they need to develop a coherent and inclusive story of and for the nation. The question is what aspect of these differing histories to select and on what principles to make that selection. This is an especially important issue for younger children and the teaching of history in primary schools.

In the now devolved polity the curriculum designers have to ask themselves what criteria are being used to decide which story needs to be told. They must also consider what constitutes a nation and how each devolved part of Britain would like to tell the story, so that friendships, intercultural understandings and inclusiveness rather than exclusiveness are stressed. To develop more universal understandings, the underlying historical hypotheses and the implicit theories of the writers need to be unpicked. Here, an epistemological and methodological breakthrough could lead to developing more widely acceptable histories which include not only written sources but the oral understandings of the different groups (Preiswerk and Perrot 1978: 11–29).

They must also consider the impact of stereotypes. They must try to re-voice and re-image, indeed to highlight, the subordinated groups, whether women or specific nationalities, whose struggles have been ignored. As we have stressed in our examination of American historiography, in a democracy it is not only the history of the great which needs to be studied but also the lives of the ordinary majority and their struggles to achieve equity and equality. These all children should learn. Nor should there be one single focus – women's history for women, ethnic history for ethnics!

The introduction of such a curriculum means developing teachers' critical understandings and appropriate teaching methods and textbooks based on new research.

The new history curriculum must therefore reconcile the territorial, religious and linguistically based diversities and project a coherent and cohesive picture acceptable to a complex and diverse society. Here, the danger arises that educators in central governments and curriculum planners in educational systems may produce curricula and textbooks which homogenise and centralise these diversities for fear that the state systems would fragment. But the far greater danger is that such centralisation and homogenisation would lead to greater levels of disintegrative tendencies. Obviously the situation differs in different contexts. But the politicians and educators responsible for our modern secular and complex education systems must deal with these questions rationally and address the needs of local identities in the contexts of modernisation and progressive national needs. The new global and marketisation forces complicate the task. No easy solutions can be offered.

COMMUNITIES OF DEVELOPMENT AND HOPE

Deep Democracy

Such developments necessitate the rebuilding of communities and establishing a connection with what Judith Green calls 'communities of development and hope' (1998: 431). The type of historical personal story I have recounted, and the historical analysis in the Introduction of an intellectual journey to engage with communities of memories, represent examples of the type of engagement which are needed. Such journeys give a sense of agency to the citizens of a democratic society which move beyond the merely institutional basis of its democratic features. It allows for what Green refers to as deeper democratic features of understandings which have critically based intercultural features. Moreover, rather than demonising 'the others', it opens a way in which complex interactions can be reappraised at individual and at community levels to form a sound basis for what Bookchin has called 'confederal communities' (Bookchin 1992).

Hence, deep democracy has dynamic and imaginative features which draw on one's own stories and those of the community. One's personal knowledge confers the confidence to deal with issues and to contribute to public life and public institutions with greater competence. Such a development of a collective critical consciousness would contribute to rebuilding the 'public square', as Cornel West puts it (West 1994). Schools and other civil institutions which have greater levels of autonomy need to be supported, as Green writes:

> for their effectiveness in facilitating public discussions, coalition development and multinational community building . . . fostering deeply democratic attitudes and by offering opportunities to develop skills and capacities that active democratic citizenship requires.
>
> (Green 1998: 437)

Small beginnings are one way of initiating involvement with deep democracies. An impressive recent British pioneer in this field, the Scarman Trust, sponsors small self-help projects in run-down communities. These projects are not just temples of democratic talk but are of the 'can-do' mentality which leads to practical action at local community level, using the community's own capacities and initiatives. They have included turning a derelict rubbish dump into a small park, re-opening and running a closed-down village shop on which the community depended, and enabling a group of jobless youngsters to acquire the house they were squatting in, renovate it as a hostel, and then go on to renovate other derelict properties.

Nevertheless there are numerous hurdles in developing such transformative institutions in the present context:

> persistent fundamentalism and differentiation in religious, ethnic and national identities, juxtaposed with increasingly interpenetrated cultures. It is a context of global economic competition along with global consciousness of disparities of wealth and well being.
>
> (March and Olsen 1995: 7)

What makes them particularly threatening to the prospects of deep democracy is the success of appeals to gender, racial and ethnic identities which undermine confidence in reason and enlightenment and, coupled with the pessimism engendered by *fin-de-siécle* introspection, have led to decline in confidence not only in democracy but in good governance.

Developing Notions of the Common Good

Institutions in society have an educative role – to foster sacrifices not selfishness, and a self-discipline which encourages civility rather than corrupting it (March and Olsen 1995: 49). Invoking the consciousness of the civic and the collective develops notions of the common good, and requires the shaping of a sense of inclusive solidarity based on a sense of security and belonging. Specific personal identities need to be shaped to that of being a citizen, so that the private self is confirmed in the public. This necessitates the state providing a framework within which the social and cultural pluralism of multiethnic and multicultural societies can establish a sense of inclusive and collective solidarity.

March and Olsen need to be quoted at length on this issue:

> Part of the craft of democratic governance is developing institutions that simul-
> taneously accommodate the ideals of pluralism and diversity, institutions that are
> capable of maintaining trust and mutual affection within a polity while simultaneously
> accommodating enduringly in constituent subgroups demands based on family ties,
> religion, ethnicity, language or personal affinity. That craft involves strengthening
> identities based on broad and long term conceptions of a community of citizens and
> a concern for others in that community, including future citizens and unborn genera-
> tions, and developing institutions that encourage both solidarity and civility.
>
> (March and Olsen 1995: 55)

The state-craft entailed in cultivating this community of citizens who are defined by a bundle of rights, duties and responsibilities should be an essential aspect of diverse polities where the ethos of civic virtue is absent. Nevertheless, intro-ducing a civic education which critically informs young students in diverse polities of their roles in society with skill and integrity is a complex task. It entails an involvement in critical public debate based on insights which accept the legit-imacy of pluralism and can accept both conflict and opposition – an aspect of the knowledge required to deal with the complexities of life in society.

Such a political life assumes the young citizens have a set of identities rather than one dominant identity. It also assumes that good governance will empower the positive experiences of the key political identities. It entails the management of conflicts as well as inconsistencies. Deep democracies, however, also embody the seeds of deep conflict, plus the simpler ones of self-interest and public interest which are in continual tension. Education for citizenship entails the learning of rules needed to negotiate reasonably in situations of conflict.

Establishing processes acceptable to young people necessitates having teachers who understand the difficulties of teaching in diverse polities, and of resolving conflicts and solving problems. Even agreeing about what is the common good is not easy. In a democratic context, teaching and learning demands accepting a commitment to democratic processes, even when differences and contradictions remain unresolved. The powerful rules governing democratic negotiation and civility are difficult not only to teach but to learn. Nevertheless knowledge and competencies can be acquired and sharpened through education and experience.

A social order which is highly differentiated and with high levels of in-equality presents greater challenges to the democratic process. Hence, greater levels of equity between rights, resources, competencies, knowledge and organisational capacities would help the chances of democratic accommodations and solutions being worked out.

> The objective may include not only education into the obligations and rights of the key identities of the polity, but also the establishment of widespread agreement on the main substantive purposes and ends of the polity, a sense of common good and common destiny. A key objective is to produce a political community within which citizens can discuss political issues in an atmosphere of mutual trust, tolerance and sympathy.
>
> (March and Olsen 1995: 244)

The absence of these measures and the inability to strengthen cohesive democratic cultures may lead to the fragmentation of such polities or to alternative models of authoritarian government (Dahl 1998: 145–65).

As it is, current societies embody complexities, paradoxes, contradictions and a deepening of differences. In the British and European contexts this is startlingly represented by the simultaneous phenomena of political devolution and the intensifying political and economic measures to consolidate the European Union. These contradictions need to be addressed in forthright ways in all areas of public, social and private lives to enable aspects of deep democracy to be forged. At a community level, there needs to be more of the interaction between enablers and can-doers which we already see being tackled on both sides of the Atlantic. Otherwise we shall see these contradictory developments becoming the dominant paradigm in British communities, and the linguistic, cultural, religious and nationality divides deepening and creating exclusive imaginations of difference.

The Role of the Universities

An important role for the universities is to uncover these hidden and ignored pasts to build a more inclusive notion of the polity. This task is, however, becoming marginalised now that academic research is increasingly governed by funded research contracts which pursue only projects which the funders find acceptable. These will tend to be directed towards maintaining the corporate system.

But the task of the universities, indeed of all higher education, should be to change society and to make it more inclusive. The abrogation of this task has only galvanised progressive social forces towards identity politics and identity-based organisations and activities. Hence, in the new millennium the higher education system faces the ever more complex task of having to use the very specific concerns expressed by such organisations, as well as the issues of race and gender specific politics, as building blocks for reconstructing a more inclusive basis of knowledge.

To take a frightening African-American example – how to reconcile the genderised positions of radical feminists such as bell hooks with that of Cornel West or Henry Louis Gates who joined the Million Man March on Washington, 'which was so conservative politically in its critique of welfare and its support of militarism and imperialism' (hooks 1998: 45). Here we see positions initially built on common concerns about racialised exclusions now so firmly fragmented that possibilities of dialogue, or of constructing more coherent frameworks of struggle outside the academe, are made impossible inside the academe.

Moreover, these black–white, male–female, racialised and genderised versions are further complicated by class constructions imbricated into different moulds. Manning Marable, for instance, blames what he sees as betrayal by the socially mobile middle-class African-Americans, and would turn the struggle into establishing a mass-based formation which would advocate progressive public policy agenda. These differing trajectories seem irreconcilable. Yet, as Peter Kwong recalls:

> The objective of defining identity should not be an abstract theoretical exercise. In fact, the original mission of ethnic studies and Asian American studies was to end racism in the spirit of the larger struggle for equality and social justice.
>
> (South End Press collective (ed) 1998: 65–6)

Once again, as with the lesson of affirmative action, we have a warning from across the Atlantic which those active in the British universities should heed.

Deepening democracy means strengthening the institutions of civil society, especially the so-called non-government sector. Here we confront another problem, that civil society is stronger in the more democratic societies, and weaker in the more autocratic. What recourse, for instance, is there for democratisation in Russia which, under the Czars and under communist government, never experienced a civil society while, in the present post-communist period, civil society is represented by the criminal fraternity, and a proliferating culture of violence.

When a culture of violence becomes manifest among groups with ethnicised identities, the problems for deep democracy are further compounded. As Immanuel Wallerstein writes:

> If one has an inegalitarian historical system, and the capitalist world system is an inegalitarian system, then it follows by definition that there must be an understratum.
>
> (1991: 86)

It was the ethnic dimension of these understrata that Myrdal found long ago as the source of the American 'moral dilemma' and presented as a challenge – a challenge that has still not been met today.

At the international level in relation to the third world, Wallerstein goes on:

> The remedy is said to be education. The Third World must learn the skills, and even more, absorb the underlying values, of the industrialised world, and they will then 'catch up'. The industrialised must learn to shelve their prejudices, and aid their brethren to catch up. But tomorrow, for the dilemma of development, as for the dilemma of racism, is a long time away.
>
> (ibid.: 90)

If it appears that racism and underdevelopment are primary conditions, essential for the unequal distribution of surplus value, there is no use social scientists construing them as secondary symptoms. Wallerstein calls for a historically aware social science to unpick the complexity of that 'hydra-headed monster' capitalism and develop active intelligence and active organising energy that is simultaneously reflexive and moral, in the class struggle of the majority against the minority, of those who are exploited against the exploiter, of those who are deprived of the surplus value they create against those who seize the surplus value and live off it.

(ibid.: 166, 169)

This demands a broad and complex strategy at the level of higher education and, in particular, the development of historical social sciences, in the tradition set by Braudel and the *Annales* school. Here is the one vital contribution that academics and the institutions of higher education they work in can make. And here the role of multidisciplinarity, transcending limited visions of complex social realities, has immense implications, not just for organising the structures of higher education, but in the reconceptualisation of knowledge and scholarship.

The Way Forward

Identity-based movements need not be balkanised. Forging overlapping interests would allow the development of a movement with a broader base of popular support and political power which could establish frameworks and influence the state institutions to become more just, inclusive and democratic. Here the issue of human rights is particularly important in demanding the emergence of greater justice for socially excluded groups. Class-based groups with their own specificities and exclusions can still converge. The mobilisation of grassroots has, for instance, led to major United Nations Summit Conferences based round single issues. Those who have worked around these issues are also able to see the connections between them and develop agendas on a broader front, based on these interconnections. Yet, The United Nations system has failed to develop an inclusive broadly based international initiative which deals with not just the totality but also the specificity of issues.

Over the years we have seen how the Commonwealth, which started as a political institution based on colonisation and historical accident, has developed increasingly as a norm-based organisation which has involved itself not only in conflict resolution and asserting issues of human rights within democratic contexts, but also in establishing Commonwealth Youth Centres to develop values of democracy, diversity and human rights among young people. Obviously the Commonwealth can be criticised as a neo-colonial British-oriented network. Yet the joining of it by Mozambique, and potentially Palestine, Yemen and Ireland, and the reversal in nine countries from military regimes to democratic governments are partly attributable to the deep commitment of institutionalised Commonwealth principles to human rights and democracy.

The Commonwealth ideals formulated in 1949 are by no means forgotten. There is also growing evidence of its institutionalising its intentions in an effective manner. The temporary suspensions of Nigeria and Sierra Leone are examples. There is also the exclusion of Parkistan with the assumption of power by the military. Moreover, the multicultured, multilingual Commonwealth is a powerful counterweight to the necessarily Eurocentred European Union and to such (in practice, whatever the Québequois and Mexicans may be told) anglophone institutions as the North American Free Trade Alliance.

To turn from the supranational to the national and local we find growing numbers of community-based can-doers who have helped change the agendas of divided neighbourhoods. In London, local can-doers in the impoverished Broadwater estate have been able to bring together different constituencies within a divided housing estate which in the past had been a scene of resistance, racism and crime. The catalyst provided by the Scarman Trust, a civil society organisation, to be an enabler of this can-do mentality has borne fruit in small but meaningful initiatives in Birmingham, Bristol, Brighton and other regions of Britain.

'Asymmetries of power' have made it difficult for groups to move beyond reified differences, except when they acquire 'structural understanding and engagement in change' (Sohat and Stein 1994: 355–6). Establishing new communities and coalitions based on shared interests requires the development of new strategies, including media-based pedagogies. And here the role of education must always be to establish a critical, rather than an ideological arsenal.

Above all we need civil society institutions which bring into play a multitude of diverse voices – and the start of new 'ethico-political variety which brings with it the commencement of politics' (Clarke 1996: 116). It would also bring the end of hegemonic history (not of history, as hegemonists would have it) and the commencement of a variety of histories.

Deep democracy demands deep citizenship. The activation of civic values in public and private domains to activate civic virtues puts into place a new, nontraditional understanding of citizenship. Here, deep democracy can be assisted by eliminating the previous private/public divide.

> The fundamental change in the way in which the particular and the universal are related to the public and the private is to admit the civic virtues to wide areas of life: most generally wherever one can act towards the universal, therein lie the civic virtues and therein lies deep citizenship.
>
> (Clarke 1996: 118)

Part of the solution to resolving the contradictions, dilemmas and complexities lies in the recognition of multiple citizenship, multi-level citizenship and a variety of political loyalties. In the contemporary British context being an active member of a local street association, being Scottish or Welsh, British and European are all consistent with the notion of deep citizenship.

FURTHER READING

J. Habermas (1998) *The Inclusion of the Other: Studies in Political Theory*, Cambridge, Mass: The MIT Press.

G. Millett (1998) *Theorising Multiculturalism: A Guide to the Current Debate*, Oxford: Blackwell Publishers.

C. Taylor (1992) *Multiculturalism and 'The Politics of Recognition'*, Princeton: Princeton University Press.

I. Wallerstein (1999) *The End of the World, As We Know It: Social Science for the Twenty-First Century*, Minneapolis: University of Minnesota.

References

Aikman, S. (1997) Intercultural Education in Latin America, in Coulby, D., Gundara, J. and Jones, C. *World Yearbook of Education: Intercultural Education*, London: Kegan Paul.

Akhtar, S. (1997, 1998) in *Times Higher Educational Supplement*, 22 August 1997, 13 February 1998.

Amin, S. (1974) *Accumulation on a World Scale*, New York: Monthly Review Press.

Amin, S. (1989) *Eurocentrism*, London: Zed Books.

Amin, S. (1997) *Capitalism in the Age of Globalization*, London: Zed Press.

Anderson, B. (1983) *Imagined Communities: Reflections on the Origins and Spread of Nationalism*, London: Verso.

Anderson B. (1998) *The Spectre of Comparisons: Nationalism, Southeast Asia and the World*, London: Verso.

Archbishop of Canterbury's Commission on Urban Priority Areas (1985) *Faith in the City: a Call for action by Church and Nation*, London: Church House Publishing.

Axtman, R. (1998) *Globalization and Europe*, London: Pinter.

Balibar, E. and Wallerstein, I. (1991) *Race, Nation and Class: Ambiguous Identities*, London: Virago.

Bard, S. (1993) *Traders of Hong Kong: Some Merchant Houses, 1841–1899*, Hong Kong: Urban Council.

Bartlett, R. (1993) *The Making of Europe: Conquest, Colonization and Cultural Change 950–1350*, London: Allen Lane.

Batelaan, P. (1983) *The Practice of Intercultural Education*, London: Commission for Racial Equality.

Batelaan, P. and Gundara, J. (1993) Cultural Diversity and the Promotion of Human Values through Education, in *European Journal of Intercultural Studies*, 3 (2/3).

Berger M. J. and Borrer, D. A. (1997) *The Rise of East Asia: Critical Visions of the Pacific Century*, New York: Routledge.

Berger, J. and Moore, J. (1975) *A Seventh Man*, London: Penguin.

Bernal, M. (1987) *Black Athena*, London: Free Assoiation Press.

Best, F. (1993) *Education, Culture and Human Rights and International Understanding: The Promotion of Humanistic, Ethical and Cultural Values in Education*, UNESCO paper, no. 4.

Billig, M. (1979) *Psychology, Racism and Fascism*, Birmingham: Searchlight Press.

Bloom, A. (1987) *The Closing of the American Mind*, New York: Norton.

Bloom, H. (1995) *The Western Canon*, London: Macmillan.

Blum, L. (1998) Recognition, Value and Equality: a critique of Charles Taylor's and Nancy Fraser's account of multiculturalism, in Willett, C. (ed) *Theorizing Multiculturalism: A Guide to Current Debate*, Oxford: Blackwell.

Bookchin, M. (1992) *Urbanization without Cities: The Rise and Decline of Citizenship*, Montreal: Black Rose Books.

Bourne, R. and Gundara, J. (1997) School-based Understanding of Human Rights in Four Countries, in ICIS, Department for International Development (unpublished).

Bourner, T. and Barlow, J. (1991) *Part-time Students and their Experience of Higher Education*, Buckingham: Open University Press.

Brah, A. (1996) *Cartographies of Diaspora: Contesting Identities*, London: Routledge.

Brah, A. and Shaw S. (1992) *Working Choices: South Asian Young Men and Women and the Labour Market*, London: Department of Education and Employment.

206

Carby, H. (1980) Multiculture, in *Screen Education*, 34.
Castells, M. (1989) *The Informational City*, Oxford: Blackwell.
Castles, S. and Kosack, G. (1973) *Immigrant Workers and Class Structure in Western Europe*, London: Oxford University Press.
Castles, S., Booth, H. and Wallace, T. (1984) *Here for Good: Western Europe's New Ethnic Minorities*, London: Pluto.
Chambers, I. (1994) *Migrancy, Culture, Identity*, London: Routledge.
Clifford, J. (1988) *The Predicament of Culture*, Cambridge: Harvard University Press.
Clarke, P. B. (1996) *Deep Citizenship*, London: Pluto Press.
Claydon, L., Knight, T. and Rado, M. (1978) *Curriculum and Culture*, London: Allen and Unwin.
Coard, B. (1971) *How the West Indian Child is Made Educationally Sub-normal in the British School System*, London: New Beacon Books.
Cohen P.(1991) Monstrous Images, Perverse Reasons, London: Institute of Education, International Centre for Intercultural Studies, Working Paper no. 11.
Cohen, P. (1997) Forbidden Games, Working Paper 5, London: CNER.
Cohen, R. (1994) *Frontiers of Identity: The British and the Others*, Harlow: Longman.
Cohen, S. (1992) *Moral Panics and Folk Devils*, London: MacGibbon & Kee.
Coles, B. (1995) *Youth and Social Policy: Youth Citizenship and Young Careers*, London: UCL Press.
Colley, L. (1992) *Britons: Forging the Nation 1707–1837*, New Haven: Yale University Press.
D'Souza, D. (1992) *Illiberal Education: The Politics of Race and Sex on Campus*, New York: Vintage.
Dahl, R. A. (1998) *On Democracy*, New Haven: Yale University Press.
de Bary, W. T. and Chaffee, J. W. (eds) (1989) *Neo-Confucian Education: The Formative Stage*, Berkeley: University of California Press.
Delamont, S. (1995) *Appetites and Identities*, London: Routledge
Department of Education and Science (1973) *Adult Education: A Plan for Development*. Report by a Committee of Inquiry appointed by the Secretary of State for Education and Science under the chairmanship of Sir Lionel Russell, London: HMSO.
Department of Education and Science (1977) *Education in Schools*, London: HMSO.
Department of Education and Science (1981) *The School Curriculum*, London: HMSO.
Department of Education and Science (1992) *Choice and Diversity: A New Framework for Schools*, Cmnd 2021.
De Waal, A. (1999) in *Times Literary Supplement*, 2 July 1999.
Driver, G. (1980) *Beyond Underachievement: Case Studies of English, West Indian and Asian School-leavers at Sixteen Plus*, London: Commission for Racial Equality.
Driver, G. (1988) *Education for Citizenship and the Teaching of Democracy in Schools*. Final Report of the Advisory Group on Citizenship, London: QCA.
Eggleston, J. and Delamont, S. (1983) *Supervision of Students for Research Degrees*, London: BERA.
Ehrenreich, B. (1997) *Blood Rites: Origins and History of the Passions of War*, New York: Metropolitan Books.
Enzensberger, H. N. (1994) *Civil War*, London: Granta.
Evans, R. (1997) *In Defence of History*, London: Granta.
Eysenck, H. J. (1971) *Race, Intelligence and Education*, London: Temple Smith.
Fijalkowski, J. (1996) Aggressive Nationalism and Immigration in Germany, in Caplan, R. and Feffer, J. (eds) *Europe's New Nationalism: States and Minorities in Conflict*, Oxford: Oxford University Press.
Fisher, J. (1993) *The Road from Rio: Sustainable Development and the Nongovernmental Movement in the Third World*, Westport, Conn.: Praeger.
Freedland, J. (1997) in *The Guardian*, 3 September 1997.
Fry, H., Mawe, J. and Simmons, H. (1991) *Dealing with Difference: Handling Ethnocentrism in History Classrooms*, London: Institute of Education, University of London.
Fryer, P. (1984) *Staying Power: The History of Black People in Britain*, London: Pluto Press.
Fukuyama, F. (1995) *Trust*, London: Penguin.
Fyfe, C. (1994) Using Race as an Instrument of Policy: A Historical View, *Race and Class*, 36 (2).
Gibbs, J. T. (1991) Black Adolescents at Risk, in *Encyclopedia of Adolescence*, 1, New York: Garland,
Giddens, A. (1998) *The Third Way: The Renewal of Social Democracy*, Cambridge: Polity.
Giddens, A. (1990) *The Consequences of Modernity*, Cambridge: Polity.
Gillborn, D. (1995) *Racism and Antiracism in Real Schools*, Oxford: Oxford University Press.
Gillborn, D. and Gipps, C. (1996) Recent Research on the Achievements of Ethnic Minority Pupils,

in *Ofsted Reviews of Research*, London: Office for Standards in Education.

Gilroy, P. (1987) *Ain't No Black in the Union Jack: Cultural Politics of Race and Nation*, London: Hutchinson.

Glazer, N. (1997) *We are all Multiculturalists Now*, Cambridge: Harvard University Press.

Glennerster, H. and Hills, J. (eds) (1998) *The State of Welfare*, Oxford: Oxford University Press.

Goddard, V., Llobera, J. and Shere, C. (1994) *The Anthropology of Europe*, Oxford: Berg.

Goldberg, D. T. (1993) *Racist Culture*, Cambridge MA: Harvard University Press.

Goontilake, S. (1999) *Towards a Global Science*, Bloomington: Indiana University Press.

Gordon, M. (1964) *Assimilation in American Life*, New York: OUP.

Gould, S. (1981) *The Mismeasurement of Man*, New York: Norton.

Gourley, B. (1998) in *Times Higher Educational Supplement*, 27 February 1998.

Gray, J. (1998) *False Dawn: The Delusion of Globalization*, London: Granta Books.

Green, J. (1998a) Educational Multiculturalism: Critical Pluralism and Deep Democracy, in Willett, C. (ed) *Theorizing Multiculturalism: A Guide to Current Debate*, Oxford: Blackwell.

Green, J. (1998b) *Black Edwardians: Black People in Britain 1901–1914*, London: Frank Cass.

Grew, R. (1983) On the Prospect of Global Hisory, in Mazlish, R. and Buultjens, R. (eds) *Conceptualising Global History*, Boulder: Westview Press.

Guha, R. and Spivak, G. C. (1988) *Selected Subaltern Studies*, New York: Oxford University Press.

Gulbenkian Commission *Report on the Restructuring of the Social Sciences* (1996) Stanford: Stanford University Press.

Gundara J. (1982) Lessons from History for Black Resistance in Britain, in Tierney, J. (ed) *Race, Migration and Schooling*, Eastbourne: Holt & Rinehart.

Gundara J. (1983) Political Education for Adults in a Multicultural Society, in *Advisory Council for Adult and Continuing Education Report*, Lancaster: ACACE.

Gundara, J. (1988) Adult Continuing Education in a Multicultural Society: the British context, in Knoll, J. M. (ed) *Internationales Jahrbuch der Erwachsenen-Bildung*, 16.

Gundara, J. (1990) Societal Diversity and the Issue of The Other, *Oxford Review of Education*, 16 (1).

Gundara, J. (1991) Western Europe: Multicultural or Xenophobic, *Berlin Interkulturell*, 20.

Gundara J. (1993) Values, National Curriculum and Diversity in British Society, in OHear, P., and White, J. (eds) *Assessing the National Curriculum*, London: Paul Chapman.

Gundara J. (1996a) Socially Diverse Polis: Social and School Exclusion, *European Journal of Intercultural Studies*, vol 7 No 1 pp 20–8

Gundara, J. (1996b) Political Consideration: Equity and Interculturalism, *Education Review*, 10 (2).

Gundara J. (1997) Intercultural Issues and Doctoral Studies, in Graves, N. and Varna, V. *Working for a Doctorate: a Guide for the Humanities and the Social Sciences*, London: Routledge.

Gundara, J., Jones, C. and Kimberley, K. (eds) (1986) Racism, Diversity and Education, London: Hodder and Stoughton.

Guppy, D. and Gipps, C. (1996) *Recent Research on the Achievements of Ethnic Minority Pupils*, London: OFSTED.

Habermas, J. (1991) Citizenship and National Identity: Some Reflections on the Future of Europe, paper presented at the Colloquium: European Cultural Identity, Brussels.

Hall, P. (ed) (1990) *Cities of Tomorrow*, Oxford: Blackwell.

Hall, S. (ed) (1978) *Policing and Crisis: Mugging, the State and Law and Order*, London: Macmillan.

Hampton, W. (1987) Continuing Education in a Plural Society, *Multicultural Teaching*, 6 (1).

Harris, C. (1990) *The Dark Side of Europe: The Extreme Right Today*, Edinburgh: Edinburgh University Press.

Hartmann, G. H. (1997) *The Fateful Question of Culture*, New York: Columbia University Press.

Hassan, M. (1997) *Legacy of a Divided Nation*, London: Hurst.

Hashim, R. (1996) *Educational Dualism in Malaysia; Implications for Theory and Practice*, Kuala Lumpur: Oxford University Press.

Haynes, J. (1995) *Religion, Fundamentalism and Ethnicity: A Global Perspective*, Geneva: UNRISD.

Hazell, R. (ed) (1999) *Constitutional Futures: A History for the Next Ten Years*, Oxford: Clarendon Press.

Hefner, R. and Horvatich, P. (1997) *Islam in the Era of Nation States*, Hawaii: University of Hawaii.

Herrenstein, R. and Murray, C. (1994) *The Bell Curve: Intelligence and Class Structure in American Life*, New York: New York Press.

Hewitt, R. (1986) *White Talk, Black Talk: Friendship and Communication among Adolescents*, Cambridge: Cambridge University Press.

Higher Education Funding Council (1996) *Widening Access to Higher Education*, Bristol: HEFC.

Hillgate Group (1986) *Whose School? A Radical Manifesto*, London: The Hillgate Group.

Himmelfarb, G. (1995) *On Looking into the Abyss*, New York: Vintage Books.

Hogan, R. and Emler, N. (1978) The Biases in Contemporary Social Psychology, in *Social Research*, 45 (3).

hooks, b. (1998) *Talking about a Revolution*, Cambridge: South End Press.

Hughes, R. (1993) *Culture of Complaint: The Fraying of America*, New York: Oxford University Press.

Hurst, P. and Thompson, G. (1996) *Globalization in Question*, Cambridge: Polity.

Inayatullah, S. (1998) Imagining an Alternative Politics of Knowledge: Subverting the Hegemony of International Relations Theory in Pakistan, *Contemporary South Asia*, 7(1)

James, S. (1999) *The Atlantic Celtic: Ancient Peoples or Modern Invention*, London: British Museum.

Jensen, F. N. (1969) in *Harvard Education Review*, 39 (1).

Kamin, L. J. (1977) *The Science and Politics of IQ*, London: Penguin.

Katz, W. (1986) *Black Indians: A Hidden Heritage*, New York: Athenaeum.

Katz, W. (1993) *A History of Multicultural America*, Austen: Raintre Steck-Vaughn.

Kazamias, A. M. (1997) Lauwerys Comparative Education Lecture, Institute of Education, University of London.

Kelly, D. and Reid, A. (1998) *Asian Freedoms: The Idea of Freedom in East and South East Asia*, Cambridge: Cambridge University Press.

Kepel, G. (1994) *The Revenge of God: The Resurgence of Islam, Christianity and Judaism*, Cambridge: Polity.

Khuri, R. (1998) *Freedom, Modernity and Islam: Towards a Creative Synthesis*, London: Athlone Press.

King, A. (n.d.) (ed) *Culture, Globalization and the World System*, London: Macmillan.

Knox, Bernard (1993) *The Oldest Dream which Europe Makes*, New York: Norton.

Kohin, M. (1995) *The Race Gallery: The Return of Race Science*, London: Jonathan Friedland.

Kothari, R. (1993) *Poverty*, London: Zed Press.

Kristeva, J. (1991) *Strangers to Ourselves*, New York: Columbia University Press.

Kruger, P. E. (1990) *Community Education in the Western World*, London: Routledge.

Krupat, A. (1992) *Ethnocentrism: Ethnography, History, Literature*, Berkeley: University of California Press.

Kumar, K (1993) Hindu Revivalism in North-Central India, in Marty, M. E. and Appleby, R.S. (eds) *Fundamentalism and Society*, Chicago: University of Chicago.

Küng, H. (1991) *Global Responsibility: In Search of a New World Ethic*, London: SCM Press.

Kymlicka, W. (1995) *Multicultural Citizenship: A Liberal Theory of Minority Rights*, Oxford: Clarendon Press.

Lawton D. (1989) *The Education Reform Act: Choice and Control*, London: Hodder & Stoughton.

Learning in Terror (1988) London: Commission for Racial Equality.

Lester, A. (n.d.) *Citizens without Status*, London: Runnymede Trust.

Levine, L. (1996) *The Opening of the American Mind*, Boston: Beacon Press.

Lowe, K. (1991) Hong Kong's Missing History, *History Today*, 41 (12).

Lynch, J. (1987) Cultural Diversity in Post-School Education, *Multicultural Teaching*, 6 (1).

Mander, J. and Goldsmith, E. (1996) *The Case against the Global Economy*, San Francisco: Surva Book Club.

Marable, M. (1998) Black Fundamentalism: Farrakhan and Conservative Black Nationalism, *Race and Class*, 39 (4).

March, J. G. and Olsen, J. P., (1995) *Democratic Governance*, New York: Free Press.

Marty, M. D. and Appleby, R. S. (eds) *Fundamentalism and Society*, Chicago: Chicago University Press.

Mayer, A. E. (1995) *Islam and Human Rights*, Boulder: Westview Press.

McCarthy, C. and Critchlow, O. W. (1993) *Race Identity and Representation in Education*, London: Routledge.

Mirza, H. S. (1992) *Young, Female and Black*, London: Routledge.

Monee Project (1998) Education for All?, *Regional Monitoring Report*, 5, Florence: UNICEF/ICDC.

Munslow, A. (1997) *Deconstructing History*, London: Routledge

Myers, N. (1996) *Reconstructing the Black Past*, London: Frank Cass.

Naipaul, V. S. (1998) *Beyond Belief: Islamic Excursions among the Converted Peoples*, London: Little Brown.

Nussbaum, M. (1997) *Cultivating Humanity: A Classical Defence of Reform in Liberal Education*, Cambridge, MA: Harvard University Press.

O'Brien, J. (n.d.) *Brown Britons: The Crisis of Ugandan Asians*, London: Runnymede Trust.

OECD/CERI (1989) *One School, Many Cultures*, Paris: OECD.

Ogbu, J. and Mature-Branchi, E. M. (1986) *Understanding Sociocultural Factors; Knowledge, Identity and School Adjustment*, California State Department of Education: Bilingual Education Office.

Outlaw, L., Jr. (1998) Multiculturalism, Citizenship, Education and American Liberal Democracy, in Willett, C. (ed) *Theorizing Multiculturalism: A Guide to Current Debate*, Oxford: Blackwell.

Parker, A. and Raybould, S. O. (1972) *University Schools for Adults*, London: Michael Joseph.

Paxman, J. (1998) *A Portrait of a People*, London: Michael Joseph.

Phillips, F. M. and Pugh, D. S. (1994) *How to get a PhD*, Buckingham: Open University Press.

Plunkett, D. (1990) *Secular and Spiritual Values: Ground for Hope in Education*, London: Routledge.

Potts, A. (1989) Constable Country between the Wars, in Samuel, R. (ed) *Patriotism: The Making and Unmaking of British National Identity*, 3, London: Routledge.

Preiswerk, R. and Perrot, D. (1978) *Ethnocentrism and History*, New York and Lagos: Nok Publishers.

Puolmatka, T. (1990) *Pluralism and Education in Values*, Helsinki: University of Helsinki Research Bulletin, no. 74.

Puxon, G. (1980) *Roma: European Gypsies*, London: Minority Rights Group.

Rampton, A. (1981) *West Indian Children in our Schools*, London: HMSO.

Rampton, B. (1995) *Crossing: Language and Ethnicity among Adolescents*, Harlow: Longman.

Rattansi, A. (2000) On Being and Not Being Brown/Black British: Racism, Class, Sexuality and Ethnicity in Post-imperial Britain, *Interventions*, Vol. 2, no. 1, February.

Rifkind, J. (1996) *Technology, Jobs and your Future: The End of Work, the Decline of the Global Workforce and the Dawn of the Post Market Era*, New York: Putnam and Sons.

Rist, R. (1978) *The Invisible Children; School Integration in American Society*, Cambridge, MA: Harvard University Press.

Robertson, R. (1992) *Globalization: Social Theory and Global Culture*, London: Sage.

Robinson, F. (ed) (1996) *Cambridge Illustrated History: Islamic World*, Cambridge: Cambridge University Press.

Rushdie, S. (1982) in *New Society*, 9 December 1982.

Rutter, M. and Smith, D. (1995) *Psychological Disorders in Young People*, Chichester: Academic Europea.

Said, E. (1978) *Orientalism*, Harmondsworth: Penguin.

Said, E. (1983) *The World, the Text and the Critic*, Cambridge, MA: Harvard University Press.

Said, E. (1993) *Culture and Imperialism*, London: Chatto and Windus.

Salmon, P. (1992) *Achieving a PhD: On Student Experience*, Stoke-on-Trent: Trentham.

Sayyid, B. A. (1997) *A Fundamental Fear: Eurocentrism and the Emergence of Islamization*, London: Zed Press.

Sen, A. (1993) The Threats to Secular India, in *The New York Review*, 11 March 1993.

Singh, C. (1971) The Problems of Citizenship, in Gupta, A. (ed) *Indians Abroad: Asia and Africa*, New Delhi.

Singh, G. N. (1971) *Landmarks in Indian Constitutional and National Development*, Benares.

Sivanandan, A. (1982) *A Different Hunger: Writings on Black Resistance*, London: Pluto.

Skuttnab-Kangas and Cummins, J. (1988) *Minority Education: from Shame to Struggle*, Multilingual Matters.

Smith, A. (1990) Towards a Global Culture, in Featherstone, M. (ed) *Global Culture and Modernity*, London: Sage.

Smith, V. A. (1901) *Asoka*, Oxford: Clarendon Press.

Sohat, E. and Stein, R. (1994) *Unthinking Eurocentrism: Multiculturalism and the Media*, London: Routledge.

South End Press Collective (ed) (1998) Talking About a Revolution, Cambridge: South End Press.

Stevenhagen, R. (1990) *The Ethnic Question, Conflict Development and Human Rights*, Tokyo: United Nations University.

Stevenhagen, R. (1994) *Double Jeopardy: The Children of Ethnic Minorities*, Florence: ICDC, Innocenti Occasional papers.

Street-Porter, R. (1978) *Race, Children and Cities*, Milton Keynes: Open University Press.

Swann, Lord (1985) *Report of the Committee of Inquiry into the Education of Children from Ethnic*

Minority Groups: Education for All, London: HMSO.
Tate N. (1997) in *Times Educational Supplement*, 19 September 1997.
Taylor, C. (1992) *Multiculturalism and 'The Politics of Recognition'*, Princeton: Princeton University Press.
Taylor, W. H. (1991) Preparing Teachers for the Universalising of Education in India in the 1990s, *Journal of Education for Teaching*, 17 (2).
Tehranian, K. (1995) *Modernity, Space and Power*, Cresskill, NJ: Hampton Press.
Tizard, B. and Phoenix, A. (1993) *Black, White or Mixed Race*, London: Routledge.
Trade Union Congress (1996) *United against Racism in Europe*, London: Trade Union Congress.
Tsai, C. and Bridges, D. (1997) Moral Piety, Nationalism and Democratic Education: Curriculum Innovation in Taiwan, in Bridges, D. (ed) *Education, Autonomy and Democratic Citizenship*, London: Routledge.
Verma, S. L. (1986) *Towards a Theory of Positive Secularism*, Jaipur: Rawat Publications.
Visram, R. (forthcoming) *A Long Presence: Asians in Britain's History, 1600–1947*, London: Pluto Press.
Vogler, D. and Hutchins, D. (1988) *Parents as Tutors*, Alexandra, VA: National Community Education Association.
Walford G. (1995) *Educational Politics: Pressure Groups and Faith-Based Schools*, Aldershot: Avebury.
Walker, D. (1998) Analysis: Welfare Reform, in *The Guardian*, 29 September 1998.
Wallerstein I. (1974, 1980) *The Modern World System*, New York: Academic Press.
Wallerstein, I. (1991) *Unthinking Social Science: The Limits of Nineteenth Century Paradigms*, Cambridge: Polity Press.
Warriors (1994) *A Global Journey through the Centuries*, 14 (2) Calgary: Glenbow Museum.
Waters, M. (1995) *Globalization*, London: Routledge.
Wei Miy Tu (1996) *Confucian Traditions in East Asian Modernity*, Cambridge, MA: Harvard University Press.
West, C. (1992) *Race Matters*, New York: Vintage.
Whitty, G., Power, S. and Halpin, D. (1998) *Devolution and Choice in Education*, Buckingham: Open University Press.
Widlake, P. and McLeod (1984) *Raising Standards*, Coventry: Community Education Development Centre.
Williams, R. (1958) *Culture and Society 1780–1950*, Harmondsworth: Penguin.
Willis, P. (1990) *Common Culture*, Milton Keynes: Open University Press
Wilson, E. O. (1998) *Consilience*, New York: Little Brown.
Wittek, F., Nijda, M. and Kroeger, P. (1993) in *The Journal of Ethno-Development* 2 (3).
Wolf, E. (1982) *Europe and People without History*, Berkeley: University of California Press.
Wulff, H. (1995) *Youth Cultures: A Cross-cultural Perspective*, London: Routledge.

Index